Women of the Bible Speak to Women of Today

Women of the Bible Speak to Women of Today

Dorothy Elder

DeVorss & Company, Publisher
Box 550
Marina del Rey, California 90294-0550

SECOND PRINTING, 1989

ISBN: 0-87516-574-5
Library of Congress Card Catalog Number:86-70873

Printed in the United States of America

Lovingly Dedicated
to
My Mother
(1878–1970)

Contents

Preface   xv

Part One: Old Testament Women

1. EVE   3
    Eve, the Divine Feminine   3

2. SARAH   10
    Impatience Blocks Progress   10
    Esoteric: Faith the Foundation   14

3. LOT'S WIFE   17
    Living in the Past   17
    Esoteric: Lifting Up the Fallen Feminine   20

4. REBEKAH   22
    Her Favoritism Brought Sorrow   22
    Esoteric: Intellect Supplants the Physical   24

5. RACHEL AND LEAH   27
    The Opposites Within: Human and Divine   27
    Esoteric: Our Goal: Cosmic Knowing   31

6. POTIPHAR'S WIFE   32
    Woman as Temptress   32
    Esoteric: Anima and Animus   34

7. JOCHEBED   37
    A Mother's God-given Task   37
    Esoteric: Birth of the Divine Inner   39

8. MIRIAM   41
    Ego versus Meekness   41
    Esoteric: Humility a Necessary Ingredient   43

9. DAUGHTERS OF ZELOPHEHAD 45
   Women's Rights 45
   Esoteric: Steps on Our Path 47

10. RAHAB 50
    From Harlotry to Faith and Good Works 50
    Esoteric: Sense Thoughts to Spiritual Thoughts 52

11. DEBORAH 55
    Overcoming Addictions: "The Lord Goes Out
       before Thee" 55

12. DELILAH 59
    "Wherein Does His Strength Lie?": Losing Spiritual
       Strength through Sensual Living 59
    Esoteric: Feminine and Masculine Out of
       Balance 61

13. RUTH AND NAOMI 65
    Mother-in-law and Daughter-in-law Relationships 65
    Esoteric: The Path to the Mystical Marriage 69

14. HANNAH 72
    The Praying Mother 72
    Esoteric: From the Cross to the Ladder of
       Ascension 76

15. MICHAL... 79
    She Worshipped Gods 79
    Esoteric: Intuition Misused by Personal Will 81

16. ABIGAIL.. 84
    A Wife's Decision 84
    Esoteric: Joy and Love Bring Freedom 87

17. BATHSHEBA..................................... 90
    Overcoming Karmic Suffering 90
    Esoteric: Beauty and Love Bring Forth Wisdom 93

18. TWO MOTHERS OF SOLOMON'S TIME   95
    "Give Her the Living Child": Abortion   95
    Esoteric: Double-Mindedness to Oneness   98

19. THE QUEEN OF SHEBA   101
    Relationships between Men and Women   101
    Esoteric: The Mystical Path   104

20. JEZEBEL   109
    The Religious Fanatic   109
    Esoteric: The Negative Animus   113

21. ESTHER   117
    Truth and Divine Love Defeat Evil   117

Part Two: New Testament Women

22. MARY, MOTHER OF JESUS   129
    The Great Mother Freed Her Son   129
    Esoteric: Birth of Our Christ   136

23. ELIZABETH   142
    Birthing an Advanced Soul   142
    Esoteric: The Bridge from Law to Love   145

24. ANNA   148
    The Path   148
    Esoteric: Graciously Turning toward God   150

25. MARY AND MARTHA   151
    Activity or Meditation?   151
    Esoteric: The Mystical and Occult Paths   153
    The Raising from the Dead: Forever Young   154
    Esoteric: Eternal Life, Not Death   157
    The Anointing: Blocks on Our Path   159
    Esoteric: Love—the Mystic's Devotion   161

26. THREE WOMEN WHO WERE HEALED 163
     Spiritual Healing   163
     Esoteric: Trial by Fire, Earth, Water, and Air   168

27. HERODIAS 172
     A Wife's Influence   172
     Esoteric: Ego versus the Christ   174

28. THE SYRO-PHOENICIAN WOMAN 177
     Humility Brings Healing   177
     Esoteric: Seek Your Path   178

29. THE MOTHER OF JAMES AND JOHN 180
     An Ambitious Mother   180
     Esoteric: Ego Is Lost in Service   182

30. THE SAMARITAN WOMAN AT THE WELL 185
     Choosing a Marriage Partner   185
     Esoteric: Lifting the Feminine   189

31. THE WOMAN TAKEN IN ADULTERY 193
     The Battered Woman   193
     Esoteric: Balancing the Feminine   195

32. MARY MAGDALENE 197
     Healing of Thoughts and Emotions:
         Psychotherapy   197
     Esoteric: The Physical Becomes Spiritual   201

33. WOMEN OF THE EARLY CHURCH 203
     Introduction: Essenes and Gnostics   203
     Paul's Teaching on Women   206

34. MARY, MOTHER OF JOHN MARK 209
     A Mother's Spiritual Influence   209
     Esoteric: Love, Faith, and Service   211

35. SAPPHIRA 213
     Sacrifice on the Path   213
     Esoteric: Truth Is God   215

36. TABITHA 217
Too Much Good Works? 217
Esoteric: Dark Night of the Soul 219

37. LYDIA 222
The Career Woman 222
Esoteric: The Path to Redemption 224

38. PRISCILLA AND AQUILLA 226
Unequally Yoked Couples 226
Esoteric: Building the Spiritual Body 228

39. EUNICE AND LOIS 231
The Influence of Mothers and Grandmothers 231
Esoteric: Freedom through God 234

40. THE WOMAN OF PROVERBS AND THE SUN WOMAN OF
REVELATION 236
1. The Woman of Proverbs 31: Caring for Physical
Needs 236
Esoteric: Wisdom: She Carries the Light 238
2. The Sun Woman of Revelation 12: Divinity
Achieved: Generation to Regeneration 241

Glossary 245

Bibliography 249

Preface

It would seem that the women of the Bible are far removed from modern woman, but, not surprisingly, I found many parallels. Enough so that I have been able to glean from their lives direction for modern woman in her ascent to equality and opportunity to express her full personhood in all avenues of living, not only on earth, but in the higher dimension of spirituality.

This is a book written by a woman, to women, about the women of the Bible who have passed their mantle of wisdom and experience down to this generation. It is written to women, but also to men, for it describes the need for each man to lift up his feminine pole in order to be in complete harmony.

Its major theme is: "Christ in you, your hope of Glory." Time after time we are brought back to the "Golden Chord" of all religions: that man and woman are expressions of God through their Spirit, the Christ, that dwells within each of them. This theme is demonstrated as the solution for the problems of earth-living as well as a guide to consciousness development. Practical problems of women as wives, mothers, and career women in our modern age are addressed with suggestions for solutions, always based on the awareness of their inner Divinity.

And, in a broader concept, we are taught the necessity for the upliftment of the feminine pole in man and the masculine pole in women to reach harmony and peace individually and as a species on planet earth. Our spiritual consciousness is returning, which was lost eons ago. This consciousness is moving earth people faster and faster toward a higher evolutionary state, and equality of men and women is rising at the same time.

The spiritual guidance given here is not according to the pattern of the traditional Christian Church. It contains suggestions for those who are trying to solve earth problems without the benefit of spiritual guidance directly from the Father of all. It is for the one who is drawn to a metaphysical path, beyond the literal or physical, to high mysticism. It is for those who are at any level of awareness of God. It is for all.

For centuries womankind has been captured by the fear of want for herself and her children. She is throwing off those shackles through the development of her intelligence and the realization of her place in the divine evolution of all of mankind. The Spirit of Evolution is moving her inexorably toward full expression of her genius (the Christ), and she is helping mankind evolve back to this pure spiritual Being. We are that pure Being, and the encrustation of the ages is being removed so that all may realize that fact. Woman is in the forefront of this movement. The feminine pole is being lifted up to an upright position, to stand erect with the masculine pole—both equally needed for the healing of the nations.

I have used the teachings of many others, as well as being guided by my intuition, to write about these wonderful women. They have so much to teach us. They are familiar to us, for they remind us of ourselves as well as of other women in our life. They are not ancient but contemporary, as the teachings from them lift us up to a freer, more joyful expression of who we really are: Christ, our hope of glory. So be it. May your journey be touched by something written about these women who are immortal as we are also.

I give special thanks to many friends who have encouraged me in writing this account.

I also want to express special appreciation to two women whose writings were of inestimable assistance in the writing of this book. They are Edith Deen, who wrote *All the Women of the Bible,* and Corinne Heline, whose *New Age Bible Interpretation* gave me much understanding of the esoteric interpretation ideas. Each has given to womankind outstanding help in their progress on the ladder of evolution. The *Metaphysical Bible Dictionary,* compiled from the writings of Charles Fillmore, was the source of many a metaphysical interpretation.

And lastly, I want to thank Arthur Vergara for his enthusiasm and commitment to the editing of this work.

Part One

OLD TESTAMENT
WOMEN

1

Eve

(Genesis 1–3)

EVE, THE DIVINE FEMININE

The story of Adam and Eve is an archetype in mankind's history. It is told with various names and distinctions through mythology and accounts from many religions and cultures. It is the story of Creation, a theme that has intrigued our humanness forever.

Taken in a literal sense, it brings to us the answer to our question "When did it all begin and how?" But this answer must be taken on faith. When we read it from a symbolic stance it takes on a different hue, tinting the answer with a metaphysical color. This is how I shall approach it.

God, so it is written in Genesis 1, "created the heavens and the earth." He created Light, the firmament Heaven, the earth and seas, the sun and moon and stars, fish and birds, and creatures of earth, which included man; then God rested on the seventh day (Gen. 1: 1–31).

In Genesis 2 we have the account of God's deciding that man was lonely and therefore creating woman from the man's rib.

They lived in the Garden of Eden, and the man had been instructed to eat of every tree except the tree of the knowledge of good and evil. (Good and Evil exist in our minds, in the knowledge area of our being.) Through the serpent's convincing suggestion, Eve did eat of this tree, Adam followed suit due to her suggestion, and they were both evicted from the Garden.

It is the knowledge of duality that God tried to protect them from and which has been mankind's burden ever since.

Because Adam and Eve (first named in Gen. 3) were disobedient, they had to be punished. Eve was to have pain in child-bearing, and her husband was to rule over her. Adam had to work by the "sweat of his face" and finally returned "to the ground." "You are dust and to dust you shall return." Adam and Eve brought death to mankind.

This is the setting for humankind's struggle through the ages. And Eve has been greatly maligned as the reason for mankind's fall from grace.

This legend has affected humankind's history. Let us now see how it affects you and me as we listen to the inner Voice and learn what we can about our own Divinity. Eve is the example of our fall. We all seem to go through this age-old story in our lives. But Eve, the feminine pole, is being lifted up, and Eve is within the psyche of each of us.

For ages upon ages we have had students of the Bible interpreting the story of Adam and Eve and the Garden of Eden. I felt this was too large an assignment for my intellectual understanding, and so I turned within, listened to my inner Voice, and recorded what I heard. I hope this interpretation will be meaningful to you, for it really tells the story of each of us. We, humankind, are Adam and Eve. Our lives follow pretty much their pattern until we return to the second Garden of Eden, the kingdom of Heaven, which Jesus taught about.

You might like to read the story of Adam and Eve in the scripture cited above. Then read this which came to me:

To name Eve without Adam is unusual but she can stand alone when she has balanced the masculine within herself. (Until then she needs Adam, the outer man, to provide the masculine counterpart.) She it is who creates, who brings forth, not only mankind but the ideas to fit the will of the Most High.

Eve is of the elect who came to earth. She is the Virgin Mary and Mary Magdalene. She is the most spiritual of womankind. She is what sews together the ragged edges of the world and brings peace and good will. Without Eve there would be no world!

On the night of her "birth" the angels sang and brought peace and light and love to earth. There was great rejoicing throughout the planes of existence as all realized a new way was being introduced. She came, aware of her divinity but not fully conscious of it. She was mature and knew more about God's way than the man Adam. But she was not perfected yet, else she would not have been born on earth.

At the time of her "birth" there was great loneliness on the planet felt by all the living. Adam was lonely. It is the woman who brings the sense of well-being to man. It would appear that woman can live alone more comfortably than can man. But each needs the other to have a balanced life.

The relationship between Adam and Eve was at first pure. As friends they enjoyed each other. They were in their spirit bodies and there was no passion, no sensual pleasure was experienced or anticipated. Many men and women are thus today even with physical bodies, and their thoughts are pure.

The animals were multiplying, and Eve was aware of the birth of the babies and the love and caring their mothers gave them. She observed the coupling of the animals and wondered if that was related to the birth of the young. Sometimes she was lonely and yearned for young of her own. She loved the baby animals but did not find satisfaction for her emotional needs in them. She and Adam knew pure love but she felt a lack.

One day she was aware of a snake following her. She was not afraid, for there was no fear on the face of the earth at that time. She was able to converse with the animals in love, and they talked to her. Finally she paused and asked the snake if he needed something.

The snake rose up on its tail and spoke: "I feel you are not happy at times and would like more than the peace of this beautiful garden and the company of Adam. I am sent from God to give you another option. You can remain in this state of bliss forever, but there is another bliss available out there. This bliss is not all. If you want to know the secret you must do as I say."

Now Eve, as we have seen, loved all the animals. She was not as aware of God-out-there or His direction as was Adam. She was discontent in a measure. So she asked for the snake's advice. The snake was male, by the way, which is not brought out in the biblical account.

So the snake told her that she could have the other bliss if she would eat fruit from the tree of the knowledge of good and evil. He explained that within her was a divine energy that could be used to enhance her spiritual beauty or to have pleasure and perhaps babies. If she would eat of the fruit she could have both.

Now the fruit, as you have suspected, was the fig; and the fig has many seeds, as does the semen of man. So the fruit was not actual fruit but symbolized the phallus and semen from Adam. However, for the physical relationship to develop they both had to partake of the knowledge of good and evil. (The apple as the fruit was inferred by many because love apples or mandrakes were eaten as an aphrodisiac by the Jews for generations—so the story of Leah and Rachel tells us.)

She ate and had a great longing to be with Adam. When he came, he observed a change in her. She told him that she was in ecstasy, for she had eaten of the fruit and felt so good. She explained that the snake had said that she would be so happy to have little ones, and he had said that this was the first step. She convinced him, for he wanted her to be happy—and so he also ate.

Then they "knew" each other like the animals. They dropped to animal level. But no baby appeared. She wondered why; but the snake did not return to explain.

One day they were walking in the garden covered by their fig leaves, the need for which had come to them after their first sexual experience. Adam heard the voice of God through his intuition. He and Eve hid from God (fear had entered the earth plane); then Adam talked to God and blamed Eve for having enticed him to eat of the fruit of the tree of the knowledge of good and evil. She told God what she had done but blamed the snake. But neither denied having eaten of good and evil. (Thus projection of responsibility for our actions came to earth.)

The literalists have interpreted this story to mean that sex and Eve are evil. The true meaning lies much deeper.

The story goes that God in his mercy wanted to save Adam and Eve from forever being divided between good and evil, for if they remained in the Garden, they could not be trusted and might eat of the Tree of Life, which, by the way, was the abode of the snake. The fruit of this Tree of Life would give them eternal life, and they would never be able to evolve from the concept of the opposites, or good and evil. God is eternal, and "being like gods" meant being eternally in duality, good and evil, rather than being at One with God.

So they were given animal skins to wear, which symbolized putting on the flesh and animal nature. Eve was given the babies she yearned for and Adam was given work and the opportunity to satisfy the physical needs of his family all the days of his life. Eve was made subject to Adam, losing her freedom, because she had led Adam away from this divine portion of life, oneness with the Creator in the Garden, and they both lost the life they had been given, through death.

Jews and Christians have interpreted this legend negatively and have groaned their way through life believing that the curse of Adam and Eve was the cause of their ills. (Projection again.) However, it is not Adam and Eve who are responsible, but what they symbolize within each man or woman.

Eve is love, compassion, caring, the soul of each human being. Her temptation came from human loneliness and the desire to have something to love. Adam symbolizes the natural mind without the balance of Eve, the feeling nature, the divine feminine. He is lonely without his feeling nature as he lost it when he was separated into two, having lost part of himself when Eve was created. Thus he followed Eve's advice, her feeling nature, without thought of the consequences. How often this is true of man even today!

Most of humankind's misery is based on loneliness and the lack of the feeling of love or being loved. Each repeats the story of Adam and Eve until they turn to their Creator to fulfill their needs.

Woman, being more of the feeling nature, will turn more quickly to the Creator. The creation of the tree of good and evil was pronounced good by the Creator at the time of Creation. Why, then, was it the "downfall" of man, this belief in two powers? Because it has been misinterpreted. Good and evil exist, but the power of Good is real and the power of evil a delusion. Yet the power of evil is equally real when man thinks it is real. Evil is in the eye of the beholder. Adam and Eve believed in both powers.

Each of my children is subject to this. The woman has a great responsibility to lead the man out of delusion into the realities of the spiritual need that he is searching for. Woman needs to develop her reasoning power, weigh the effects of her feeling nature on her choices, and balance her life. Man needs to allow those natural feelings of love, compassion, and intuition to develop and follow their lead in order to find an answer for his loneliness. This comes, of course, when each of us is aware of the Divinity within and consciously lives his or her life by God's Will.

But womankind through the ages has remained subservient to the male because she married and had children and could not support them, as she had not developed her intellect, had not been courageous enough to reach out for something besides mother-hood, which came as a result of her needing someone to love and take care of and to assuage her loneliness.

Man, being bereft of natural female feelings, reaches out to woman and expects her to fulfill this longing within. It does not work, of course, but he continues to labor by the "sweat of his brow" to support the consequences of this misconception, which brings responsibility.

And they both find death. For life lived on a purely physical base does reach death. Eternal life is hidden until you become aware of your Spirit and know that the Spirit never dies. Then you can reach the point of transforming the physical into the spiritual, and all desires of the body are lost, as in the Garden. Then there is no need to reincarnate in a physical dimension.

But you must go back to the beginning to understand this. For in the beginning, all was Spirit and in the end all will again be Spirit. This is the Secret of the Ages that all religions teach, for it is Truth directly from the Creator.

This equality of men and women, reason and feeling, is difficult to achieve in Western culture and religion. Westerners need a mixture of the Eastern religious thought that was taught by Jesus. The Old Testament and the New Testament when mixed and followed will result in a new concept of equality on all levels of living.

The male prejudice against women (their own feeling nature) will pass as women lead men toward the New Life that is available. This New Life will come as each becomes aware of Me as their inner Guide and individually follows his or her star. The Eastern concept of meditation will bring this about. Thus their loneliness will cease when they reach a higher awareness of God. Women will not need babies and men will not need women to satisfy their longing for fulfillment. Celibacy will be practiced when they lose their physical desires. Abhorrent as this seems to modern man, it will be welcomed at some stage in man's development and enjoyed as a greater ecstasy than any physical one. Man is having one last fling before this becomes a serious option for him.

And the snake and the fruit? The snake is that divine energy that flows through our physical and ethereal bodies and that can be used to change the physical to the spiritual and improve the thinking and feeling processes; or it can be used for sexual pleasure and generation of new bodies. Those who use it for creative purposes will lift up the human race to a higher dimension and make it possible for all men and women to realize the truth of their own being. God has given us the option of what we do with our soul's energy. We are free to choose.

The "fruit"—sexual activity—will finally fade away, and the beings on this planet will not be physical but spiritual and unavailable to physical sight. There are many planets with living beings. Physically, they have no bodies, but when they visit earth they take on a physical form and can be seen. Physical eyes and instruments do not see them when they are "at home" on their own planet.

It is all evolving and cannot be stopped. Adam and Eve show you where you came from and how you lost your way. Eve, love, will lead humankind to the apotheosis of the New Jerusalem.

The divine feminine fell with Eve, and we have been under that fallen state for many years. We have not lifted it up in our inner and outer lives. But we have a Way to go. The accounts of the other women of the Bible teach us of our course. Let us pursue our way in the name and consciousness of Jesus Christ. Love leads us on.

2

Sarah

(Genesis 11, 12, 16–18, 20–25, 49)

IMPATIENCE BLOCKS PROGRESS

It is very difficult to write of the women of the Old Testament without giving a detailed history of the man or men who were so important to their story. This is certainly true of Abraham, the husband of Sarah. In the interest of brevity, I suggest that you read the full story of Abraham and Sarah in the chapters of Genesis cited above. Abraham is a strong character and is considered the father of the monotheistic religions—Judaism, Islam, and Christianity.

One of the main teachings we have from Sarah is her devotion as a wife. She was loved deeply by Abraham, and not until she suggested it did he take a concubine. He had deep faith in the one God, and she tried to follow, but she wavered once in a while. She made decisions that later brought her pain and anguish, but she grew in faith and loyalty to God's guidance through it all. Her greatest blessing was to become the mother of Isaac when she was ninety years old.

Now of course one can deny this possibility, and perhaps this is an allegory and not a factual account; but we shall find that other women had what was considered a miraculous pregnancy and gave birth to a child through the Holy Spirit in other accounts in the Bible. And so let us assume that the teaching is for us no matter what our doubts may be.

Abraham was told to leave his family and take his wife and entourage and go into a new land. He was seventy-five years old and Sarah was sixty-five years old. They began to travel and finally, because of a drought, went to Egypt. There he passed her off as his sister and she entered the Pharaoh's harem. The Pharaoh found out that she was Abraham's wife and sent her back with many gifts. (Josephus, the ancient historian, says that she told the Pharaoh that she was Abraham's wife.) Then they left and went to Bethel.

Some years later Sarah, who had always grieved that she had not given Abraham a son, decided to offer him her slave, Hagar, to see if she could bring forth the child that God had promised to him who would be the father of many nations. Hagar conceived and turned against her mistress. Sarah dealt harshly with Hagar after Abraham gave her permission to do whatever she pleased. Hagar then fled to the wilderness, where God came to her and advised her to go back. He also told her to name her son Ishmael. She returned, bore Ishmael, and lived in the household until she and her son were again sent into the wilderness, where they stayed.

Sarah was a loyal and devoted wife. Her husband's life was her life. She shared his dangers, heartaches, prosperity, poverty, and dreams. Abraham was blessed with much material wealth and had a large tribe. Sarah seemed to be considered equal with her husband in authority, as demonstrated by Abraham's telling her to do what she would with Hagar. Ishmael was born of the flesh and brought sorrow to many (Gal. 4:22f.). In giving Hagar to Abraham, Sarah showed impatience and disbelief in God's promise. She never thought she would bear a child.

God came to Abraham and told him that Sarah was to bear a child. He laughed, knowing that he was past the age of being able to impregnate her. He was 100 years old and she was certainly past child-bearing age. Later three messengers came from God and told him the same. Sarah heard them and laughed too, thinking it was a great joke. But confidence in God's word soon prevailed, occasioning a change in name for each. Up to this point Abraham's name had been Abram; Sarah's, Sarai. Corinne Heline says that the adding of the *h* to each of their names showed a change in consciousness and that the external was conformed to the internal, which is a sign of wholeness and pure Divinity. They had both grown in consciousness through the years and now they were to be rewarded.

The account does not say that Abraham "went in" to Sarah or "knew" Sarah, which is the Bible language for having sexual intercourse, but that "The Lord visited Sarah as he had said and the Lord did to Sarah as he promised. And Sarah conceived" (Gen. 21:1,2).

Isaac was born and there was great rejoicing. Isaac means laughter and joy. Later, discord arose between Hagar and Sarah; and Ishmael, who was fourteen years old at the time of Isaac's birth, often teased and taunted Isaac. Finally Sarah demanded that Hagar be excluded, and Abraham sent her into the wilderness, where God cared for her and gave her water, and where her son grew up and learned to hunt.

Isaac grew, and God tested Abraham. He told him to take Isaac, go to the land of Moriah, and there offer him as a burnt offering, a sacrifice to the Lord. Abraham took his son and did as he was told. When Abraham was ready to slay Isaac, God stopped him; instead, he was allowed to offer a ram caught in the thicket. God said that now He knew that Abraham "feared" Him. This must have been a great trial for Sarah also, but there is no account of it.

Isaac became one of the great patriarchs of the Hebrews. It was meant to be as God told Abraham—he was father of great nations. Isaac had two sons, Esau and Jacob. Jacob became the father of twelve sons who were blessed by him as heads of the twelve tribes of Israel.

These wonderful Old Testament stories can be taken as meaningful allegories and with decided symbolic meaning. We shall look at this one, as it pertains to us as women today, and also to see what meaning it has for us esoterically, or what spiritual meaning it has.

Again we must see Sarah as a loving and loyal wife. She and Abraham loved each other and had much to be grateful for. But she failed at that which society expected of women—the bearing of many sons. This was a love marriage, and as Abraham learned to listen to the inner Voice and follow it, their life became better.

Here we have exemplified impatience versus faith. For the faith of Abraham brought much patience to the household, but the lack of faith on Sarah's part brought impatience. Sarah believed in God and had waited many years to have the child He had promised Abraham. But when she didn't have the child, she took things into her own hands and sent Hagar in to Abraham. (In those days the slave's child belonged to the mistress, in this case Sarah.) Out of this impatience came much sorrow for Sarah, Abraham, and Hagar. Ishmael founded a different nation.

Jealousy motivated Sarah when she saw that Hagar's child was favored by Abraham. Her impatience brought on another problem when Hagar conceived the first to be born, an important position. So the two were sent into the wilderness. But God sent Hagar back and she lived there another fourteen years until Sarah, through jealousy, impatience, and lack of faith, insisted that Abraham send them into the wilderness forever. All of this yielded hard feelings.

We should learn to rest in the Lord and wait patiently for Him. Whenever we attempt to force our good, the result is unsatisfactory. Our patience sometimes runs short if we do not receive that for which we pray. God knows what we need; and when we wait for it, the time will be right, and what is best for us will be given us.

Another lesson is to learn from Abraham's listening to the inner Voice and following it. Sometimes we read these stories in the Old Testament and do not believe they apply to us. But this inner Voice is within you, and through quiet and attention you also can be guided. This Voice is our guide, our protector, our comforter, our love, our wisdom, our health and prosperity. Through meditation we learn to listen.

In the early days of my consciousness development, I thought that I would surely be able to follow the Will of God and would learn of that Will through meditation. It took me several years to learn how to discriminate between the voice of God and my own desires. Eventually I knew that when an idea came to me that I had never thought of or that seemed to come from another level of knowing, I could follow with confidence. But this took much practice. Sometimes I received direction when I did not think I was ready. And if I did not follow, I had a negative experience, and then it registered with me why I had been given the direction in the first place. So it is with us as we seriously, with faith, follow the inner Voice.

Abraham showed in his preparing Isaac for the sacrifice that he had lost his small self and was following his great Self. This was the measure of his faith. Sometimes we are required to give up that which is most precious to us. We need to learn to put God first.

Sarah developed this kind of faith also before she conceived Isaac. It was out of that change of consciousness that he was born and her name changed to Sarah. Sarai means bitter, quarrelsome. Sarah means princess, noble woman, noble lady. But the old Sarai was not completely eradicated.

So patience and faith are to be developed by us. And from Abraham we learn that we are to follow in pure faith the guidance of our Higher Self. Each of us is important in God's plan. You too can be a wonderful example as you follow His Will. And Sarah, who was often mentioned as filled with faith, is an example of moving from lack of faith in God's word (giving Hagar to Abraham) to allowing Abraham to follow God's direction for the sacrifice of Isaac.

Sarah died at age 127 and was buried in the cave of Machpelah by Abraham.

Sarah gave birth to Isaac by the Spirit. Isaac was a great soul. When the birthing of our offspring, either physically, intellectually, or emotionally, is by the Spirit, then we are on the right path. We need patience and faith to allow this to happen.

Esoteric: FAITH THE FOUNDATION

In the divine plan of our spiritual development it would seem that we start with no awareness of our Divinity and build level on level to the highest dimension of faith. So this account of Sarah and Abraham teaches us. It is not a teaching only for women; mankind in general goes through this ascension back to the Father. It is our task, and we will do it in this life or another.

Abram represents the initial stages in the development of faith. We all have some faith—if not in God, then in someone or in our own strength. Abram illustrated faith in the invisible forces. He became obedient to his inner Guide. Although he did not understand it, he knew there was something special about him and his Path. He acted on faith and waited, and finally he became Abraham. The inner force of the Spirit ever works within us and in the silence.

Sarai enters into our story in her treatment of her barrenness. Here she was about seventy-seven years old and had not brought forth the son that Abraham had been promised. I think we can learn from this account that it is never too late for us to bring to our awareness the Christ of our being, for to birth a son is symbolic of having a "new birth" or bringing to awareness the inner Christ, which is our Guide. She was impatient, though, and gave her self-will (Abram) over to sensual attachment (Hagar), and from this came forth physical attachment (Ishmael). This is our task on earth —to overcome the sensual—and the only way we can do this is to believe in our God and follow His Will. Jesus taught to love God first, and this we must do if we are to come closer to the goal of transformation.

But God is always with us and attempting to help us in our weaknesses and mistakes. He came to Abram and Sarai and promised them a son. The feminine then gave birth to the Christ, and it was through their faith that it happened. Her name was then changed to Sarah.

You see, with faith we start with a little. Perhaps it will be someone else's faith, as was the case when Jesus healed the child of the centurion. Maybe for us it is the faith of our spouse, our mother, our father, our friend. In any case, we can start with the faith of another and then build on that. Sometimes the way looks dark (Sarah did not think she would have the experience), and we may be more attached to our senses during this time, but eventually with God's grace we will succeed.

Sarah means gracious lady. That is the name of the inner feminine principle that so enhances our ability to come into this new awareness of our Divinity. And when Isaac was born, she was full of joy and laughter, the meaning of his name. When we have this inner Knowing, our joy reaches great bounds of awareness. True joy is ours. Happiness is a tiny fraction of what our joy can and will be.

Abraham means father of peace based on faith. It is through our faith that we have peace, and it was through Sarai (bitterness) who became Sarah (gentle lady) that together they brought forth that which the world needed—joy and laughter and the awareness of divine sonship. This divine sonship is our inheritance; and as we realize our great Divinity, we shall also be a father of many nations, or bring forth many thoughts that will uplift us as well as many around us.

After Isaac was born, Ishmael, fruit of natural sense thoughts, had to diminish. As the Divine comes into our life, we will let go of the negative, the sensual, the satisfying of sense thoughts rather than the divine ones. However, the mother of these thoughts, Hagar, is not abandoned by God. For God is present in every experience of our life, and the sense thoughts are important to the survival of our physical body. Our task is to find a balance between the sensual and the Divine.

Sarah and Abraham were of a high spiritual consciousness, and in love and faith they brought forth joy. That is our path also as we sift out from our experience that which is less important for the sake of that which is all-important. When we give birth to this divine awareness, we will remember Jesus' words, ''And I will pray the Father, and he will give you another Counselor, to be with you for ever, even the Spirit of truth, whom the world cannot receive because it neither sees him nor knows him . . . for he dwells with you, and will be in you'' (John 14: 16–17). And this Spirit of Truth will guide us into all Truth. And that is what we need and want. It is this Spirit of Truth that we all long for, although usually unconsciously.

When Abraham (faith in the Will of God) was asked to sacrifice Isaac (joy), he followed the guidance from within his own soul and would have sacrificed even his son (joy) that he loved so much. For this is our path also. It seems a great price to pay, to sacrifice that which we love the most. But it would seem that if we are to go all the way in faith, we must give up all to God. And God will reward us, for it is a law that our reward will be based on our love of Truth. It is not an easy path, but the result is to be ''father of many nations.'' And our influence may spread to untold millions if we are willing to follow God in faith to this limit. We are tested, and we can come through shining when our faith is strong enough.

3

Lot's Wife

(Genesis 18: 16f., 19: 1–38; Luke 17:29–33)

LIVING IN THE PAST

In Luke 17:32, Jesus is speaking. He commands, "Remember Lot's wife." And so must we. Through hundreds of generations, the story of Lot's wife has come down to us for our benefit, and so we should learn from her.

When Abraham and Sarah came out of Egypt, they went to live at Bethel. He took his nephew Lot with him. When some dissension arose among the herdsmen, they separated, and Abraham gave Lot his choice of the land. Selfishly, Lot chose the best, the valley of the River Jordan. Eventually Lot went to live in Sodom, where there was great wickedness. God decided to destroy the city and all in it. But through Abraham's intercession, Lot, his wife, and two daughters were warned by angels to leave the city before it was destroyed by fire.

Lot and family were hurried out of the city early in the morning. The angels told them: "Flee for your life; do not look back or stop anywhere in the valley; flee to the hills lest you be consumed."

Lot's wife disobeyed. She stopped; she looked back; and "she became a pillar of salt."

And Jesus said, "Remember Lot's wife." I wonder why.

This story has been the subject of art and literature and sermons again and again. It has caught the imagination of mankind. But it is seldom understood at the deepest level.

Lot and Abraham represent different levels of consciousness, Abraham represents faith. Lot, being associated with Abraham, had some of this, but he was too swept up in worldly things. His was the negative side of faith. His faith was veiled. (Lot symbolizes the veiled, the hidden, the concealed.) Lot was wealthy; he was one of the leaders of Sodom, and his wife and daughters probably had everything they desired. Lot still was a righteous man, however, for God did not destroy him. He was saved. He was given a chance to escape. But his wife, his feminine pole, died.

When we are swept into a new way of living, a new belief, a change from one level of consciousness to another, we may think that we can continue to live the way we have lived and merely add this new religious belief to what else we have. But we will soon learn that something has to be given up to make room for the new spiritual belief. We may have to let go of certain pleasures, sensual appetites, things of the world, a good job that does not fit our new belief. We may have to sacrifice positions of power, ease, comfort, for what is at first a path of loneliness and hardship. We must seriously consider this before we make our commitment, for it is a commitment "to the Lord."

Also, be aware that you may go through times, maybe years, when nothing seems to go right. This will usually happen at the beginning of your journey. Often the cleansing of your life comes rapidly, with the negative surfacing and needing to be dealt with. Your whole life may be changed.

Now these are warnings, but if the angel's advice is followed (angel is the inner Voice), then you will be ready for a wonderful faith-full life. But don't vacillate, don't look back, or you may be atrophied.

Lot's wife was evidently very much attached to the past, as so many of us are. The Sodomites practiced sexual deviation, among other things, which was not acceptable to the Lord. (The word *sodomy* comes from this historical account.) The people of Sodom were completely captured by sensual pleasure, it would seem. As we follow Lot and his daughters after they left Sodom and went to Zoar, then to a cave in the hills, we find the daughters committing incest with their father. Both had sons from that sexual contact. The daughters, touched by the licentiousness of race consciousness* all around them, did not look back but chose their new life out of fear: "There is not a man on earth to come into us" and "We may preserve offspring through our father."

It was through Lot that his wife was taken out of Sodom. But she yearned for the past, was afraid of the future, had no faith in the good that awaited her, and so became a pillar of salt.

Race consciousness is a term used to denote the totality of beliefs, thoughts, memories, feelings, and experiences of the human race; more specifically, the beliefs and actions of that society in which we live that affect our own choices.

Perhaps this is too extreme for you to take seriously, but it is a symbol of what can happen to us. We can become rigid in our beliefs, we can develop stiffness in our body, we can become blind to the realities of our life, we can become unchanging and very unhappy. When change occurs in our life, in the life of our family, in our world, we may resist. And we may appear as dead. Life requires change. Life is ever pulsating. Life moves on. Will you be left behind, stiff and encrusted with a preservative? Yes, your ways can be preserved, but you may be lifeless, a mere monument to "looking back" to the way things used to be.

In the religious area, we have many old encrusted attitudes and interpretations of the scriptures that have turned many well-meaning people to pillars of salt. They have never moved out of their old ways. Jesus spoke often of these people, who were controlled by the Law instead of by Love.

But I am most concerned about those who are entrapped in the materialism of this world and who cannot escape; or who, if they do, turn back and long for the old life. If you decide to turn toward the metaphysical philosophy, the New Age, know that you can never go back; for if you do, your last state will be worse than your first. If you become a metaphysician, you will eschew the ways of the majority and find your own individual way. Jesus said, as reported in Luke 17:22-36, that one will be destroyed, another saved, on the day "when the Son of man is revealed." The Son of man is the Christ within. We cannot go back to the old life based on physical pleasure alone. Once the commitment is made to follow the Will of God, it will be difficult for anyone to return to the past.

I have seen many well-meaning folk who believed they were "born again" but who were not strong in that experience. They looked back, tried to live the same old life, and went under into deep pain and agony. "God will not be mocked."

This lesson from Lot's wife can apply to many areas of your life. Trying to live as you did last year may cause you all kinds of grief. No matter what your age—the retiree who lives in the past or the young person coasting on the glory of high-school days—you cannot look back without losing something, perhaps your life.

Lot's wife, commanded by God's angels (the inner Voice) to go ahead into the future, is our example. Let us learn from her mistake.

Esoteric: LIFTING UP THE FALLEN FEMININE

Lot's wife is another example of the fallen feminine principle that has through the ages dragged down womankind, for as women they were imprisoned in their femininity in a male-dominated society, and they raised sons who grew up affected by this frozen position of women.

The fallen feminine needs regeneration. Bringing the feminine to an upright position in both men and women is the keynote of the New Age teaching. Jesus showed us how. We need only follow his teaching—not the Church's interpretation of his teaching. For Jesus continually lifted up the feminine. To his apostles and his disciples he taught the need for love. He exemplified that Love in his life and teachings. And Love is the feminine pole.

He taught us to listen to our inner Voice, to be guided by the Father's Will. That is intuition, the feminine pole.

He taught forgiveness of sins and looking to our own selves first before we judge another. That is compassion, a feminine trait.

He healed the sinful, he broke the masculine Law, he left the past and pointed us toward the future. He showed creativity as a part of our birthright—and all this is feminine.

So Lot's wife demonstrated the fallen feminine, and womankind is still touched by this. As women, we often sell our souls for sexual pleasure, for financial security, for the approbation of society. We give up too much for friends and family. And we become stiff and unchangeable.

Salt is a symbol of the lower feminine. It is that which tempts men and women to be less holy than they are. It is that which springs from emotion without regard for thought. It is heart without head. It is imbalance.

Again and again we will speak of the balance of feminine and masculine, balance between head and heart. Men and women both need to work on this.

Lot did not look back, because he had more faith. But he did regret leaving Sodom, which he should have been glad to escape. Out of his thinking and the lower feminine active in his daughters came their sons Moab, representing carnal mind and lust, and Ben-Ammi, father of the Ammonites, symbolic of a thought in the darkened phase of consciousness. Lot also has a lesson to teach us.

The potential for high spiritual achievement was in him with the help of Abraham (faith), and he was saved from destruction because God considered him a righteous man. His feminine principle (his wife) was frozen.

Look ahead, do not look back! Lift up the feminine in the society of humankind. Follow the guidance of intuition. Love and be loved. Do not regret the past or feel guilty about it. Make restitution and forgive—then look ahead. Turn your small will to God's Will. Find your place in the world in honor and Truth. And look to the future. Thus you will lift woman to an upright position—parallel with the upright masculine pole, which will stand straighter as the feminine is lifted up in all of humankind.

4

Rebekah

(Genesis 24, 25, 26)

Her Favoritism Brought Sorrow

This special child born to Sarah and Abraham—Isaac—was forty years old before Abraham found him a wife. Abraham was advanced in years, Sarah was dead, and he directed his servant to go to his father's family in Mesopotamia and find a wife for Isaac. The servant, a prayerful type, prayed to God for direction in finding the right wife.

He stopped at the well in Nahor, the home of Abraham's family, and watched the young women come to the well with their jugs. When Rebekah responded to his needs, as he had prayed the right maiden would, and it was established that she was of the house of Abraham, he knew that he had found the right wife. Her brother was Laban. After her family learned about Abraham and Isaac, Rebekah agreed to go immediately with the servant to the land of Canaan to be married to Isaac, her second cousin. Isaac was meditating in the fields, saw her coming, went to her, and married her.

Rebekah waited twenty years to become pregnant. How often in Bible accounts a woman is barren many years before she gives birth to a son who becomes famous! Rebekah and Isaac had the first monogamous marriage recorded in the Bible.

Rebekah bore twins—Esau and Jacob. Esau, being the older of the two, was the inheritor of his father's wealth and his blessing as head of the family. Esau was a hunter and more attached to earthly things, and he was Isaac's favorite. Jacob was quiet and meditative and was far more spiritual. He was Rebekah's favorite.

You have read the story of how Esau sold his birthright to Jacob one day when he came in from the fields and was very hungry. Jacob bought it for a "mess of pottage" (food). Now all Jacob needed was Isaac's blessing to be head of the family and he would be over Esau, the elder.

When Rebekah overheard Isaac ask Esau to bring him a bowl of savory food so that he could bless him before he died, she told Jacob to bring two kids. She prepared the special dish before Esau returned from his hunting trip. She insisted that Jacob go in to his father and pretend that he was Esau so as to get his blessing. Jacob protested, but she insisted and helped him appear to be Esau. The ruse was successful. Jacob got the blessing and Esau was left out.

When Esau learned of the duplicity, he swore to kill Jacob. Rebekah heard about Esau's threat and again practiced deceit, getting Isaac's permission to let Jacob go to Haran to take a wife from the daughters of Laban, his uncle. They were fearful that Jacob would marry a Canaanite as Esau had done. His wives had caused trouble. So Jacob left. Rebekah bade him goodbye. She was separated from her favorite son by her dishonesty and would never see him again, for she died before he returned.

We have here a deep lesson for us as mothers. To love and pamper one child over another as Rebekah did, to use dishonesty to fool her blind and ill husband, to then lose her favorite son and have to live near the son who would remember her part in deceiving him and with a husband who had lost confidence in her all remind us of our own very human side. The law of cause and effect cannot be circumvented.

When Rebekah was carrying the twins, the "children struggled together within her," and she was in pain. She inquired of the Lord why it was thus. The reply was that they would be divided and be two nations, and one would be stronger than the other. (The nation of Edom descended from Esau, that of Israel from Jacob, and in this form the struggle for supremacy would continue.) The elder, the Lord said, would serve the younger. Perhaps she pondered this in her heart and believed that she was to fulfill this prophecy and that Jacob (the younger) was to have the blessing over the elder, Esau. She believed she was doing the right thing.

Perhaps she was. Perhaps she was the instrument that separated the two, for perhaps Jacob had to leave in order to live and to find his own way. If she had not acted the way she did and helped Jacob get his father's blessing, the outcome—Jacob's becoming Israel and having twelve sons who became the twelve tribes of Israel—would have been very different.

However, for us as mothers, the example of loving one son

more than another, of having favorites among our children, of treating one better than the other will eventually bring pain to us and the favored child as well as to the other children of the family. Each child has a right to our full love, for we brought him or her into the world. We are responsible, and although they may disappoint us, we still will love them and care for them no matter what choices they make.

This is often difficult, but we must remember that each child has a unique soul with its own needs to grow in consciousness of the Divine. A child's path may be very different from ours, but we must know that it is all right for that soul. We release that child and love him or her whatever the differences.

When we mistreat our child we may be sure that sometime, later perhaps, we will suffer too. And when we use dishonesty to influence our husband, this too will rebound on us in pain and sorrow. Sometimes this mistreated child will be the very one that we must live with in our advanced years, and if forgiveness has not been asked and given, we will suffer as do they.

It is a delicate balance, this rearing of children to maturity. Whatever our good intentions, they may be misunderstood, and division may occur between us and them.

This might not have happened if Rebekah had believed and trusted in God. She thought she had to take things into her own hands. Since the Lord had edicted it, she should have allowed the events to take their course. But her personal love for Jacob and her dislike of Esau got in the way, and she acted. Thus she brought on herself the pain of separation.

Let us realize that centeredness in the will of God is our task. To love and care for our offspring, to be a spiritual example, and to let God do the rest is our direction. Prayer, faith, and love heal many separations.

Jacob and Esau later forgave each other and were friends. Rebekah's need, then, was to wait on the will of God.

Esoteric: INTELLECT SUPPLANTS THE PHYSICAL

For our own spiritual growth we shall interpret this story differently, for it depicts what must happen to us as we pursue our spiritual goal.

Isaac symbolizes "born of the spirit." Rebekah symbolizes "beauty that ensnares." She did not seem to be as far advanced spiritually as Isaac.

Esau was more physical of the two brothers and represents the physical body. Jacob represents the intellectual, with leanings toward the spiritual. He was quieter, stayed in the tents, meditated.

Now, in our own life's path, the soul reincarnates many times in different bodies, and we live each life, learn our lessons, and hopefully advance on the spiritual path. Sometimes, however, we seem to make more strides in one life than another. Sometimes we are centered on taking care of the physical. Sometimes to develop our intellect through education and experience seems our lot, and other times the spiritual growth and development takes priority. Each is right at the time. In one life we may go through all three phases. And the goal is pure Divinity.

Esau, the physical, will be supplanted by the intellectual. As we go up the ladder of evolution, our physical needs will be taken care of, and then we will have the desire for something more in our life. We may turn to developing our mind to have a richer life. We study many books—history, philosophy, psychology, theology, science—and all are efforts to answer the nagging questions that give us discomfort and dis-ease. Finally we "wrestle" with God as Jacob did (Gen. 32:22f.), and we accept that the spiritual has the answer for us. Then we become the "father of many nations," head of the twelve tribes or the twelve powers that lie within our conscious awareness. (See *The Twelve Powers of Man,* by Charles Fillmore.)

Now, if our love for beauty that ensnares has the effect of interfering with this step-by-step process, we may experience pain and sorrow.

Esau (the physical) needs to decrease while Jacob (the mental) increases. Finally, the intellect changes to the inheritance of Isaac (born of the Spirit), and we become single in purpose, and our destiny, foreordained, comes to pass. When we are born of the Spirit we are favoring neither the physical nor the intellectual; rather, we are one-pointed.

This is a natural process, and no human being need interfere with it. It is in God's plan for each of us, and it will be carried out in some life or another.

My own life is a reflection of this process. I married young, had three children—two daughters and a son—and was engrossed in raising them, accumulating financial security, taking care of my husband, and doing community work—but I was unhappy. Through a vision and necessity, I was given guidance to develop my mind. I went to school for years, loved every moment of it, thought I could find the answers to my question of what happiness is through the intellect. When I was full of "book learning," I realized that I did not have the answers. And so as a result of separation from my son by his death, I started my spiritual quest. Study of spiritual books, meditation and prayer, and focusing on the Will of God in my life has brought the answers. It is the only way.

So we are right in supplanting the physical with the intellectual, which eventually becomes the spiritual. Rebekah's pain was the result of how she did it. We must make our choices prayerfully and allow God to do His Will.

5

Rachel and Leah

(Genesis 29, 30, 31, 32, 35)

The Opposites Within: Human and Divine

In the last chapter we had Jacob going alone to Haran where his mother's brother, Laban, lived in order to take a wife. We remember the deceit that Jacob and Rebekah practiced in order that he might have his father Isaac's blessing as head of the family. But he could not claim the birthright or the blessing, for his brother, Esau, was bent on killing him. So he was sent away, with no inheritance, to make his own way. His karma came to him immediately. He had given up his integrity to be rich and powerful. Now he had nothing.

Rachel, a daughter of Laban, met him at the well, and they were both smitten with love. He was told by her father that he must work seven years in order to marry her since he brought no riches with him. "Jacob served seven years for Rachel and they seemed to him but a few days because of the love he had for her" (Gen. 29:20).

At the marriage feast Laban sent Leah, the older sister, in to Jacob, and he took her. The next morning he discovered the duplicity and protested. Laban told him that Leah, being the elder, must marry first, and that he could have Rachel in exchange for seven more years of labor. Two sisters married to the same man was bound to bring trouble! Again Jacob was paying off the karma of his deception of his father. In seven years he had Rachel also.

Leah had six sons, and her maid Zilpah two sons, by Jacob. Rachel was barren for many years. She was very jealous of Leah and her prolific production of sons, which of course was a woman's reason for being in those days. Rachel gave her maid Bilbah to Jacob and had two sons by her. Finally "God remembered Rachel, and God harkened to her and opened her womb." She named the son Joseph, for she said "God has taken away my reproach." He was greatly loved by Jacob. Later she had Benjamin as they were traveling back to Canaan. She died in childbirth. Benjamin was Jacob's favorite after Joseph was sold into slavery by his brothers, who were jealous of him.

When Jacob and his wives and children and his company of men and animals left Haran to return to Canaan, Laban pursued them. He accused Jacob of many things, among which was that he had stolen his household gods. Jacob denied this and told Laban to search everything and if he found them, the thief would be killed. Rachel had taken them and was hiding them under a camel's saddle as she sat upon it. She did not allow her father to search there because, she said, "the way of woman is upon me." Then Jacob and Laban made a covenant of peace and Laban uttered the famous blessing, "The Lord watch between you and me when we are absent one from the other" (Gen. 31:49). And Laban left in peace.

From the Bible account we can see Leah as quiet, docile, accepting of what came to her. She was spiritual and accepted Jacob's God. But she was still human enough to want human love from her husband. She thought that with each son he would surely love her, but he never did. She was not as beautiful as Rachel, and she never felt equal to her.

Rachel was beautiful and highly spirited; she envied her sister, and was jealous of her ability to give Jacob sons. When her maid's second son was born, she said, "I have wrestled with my sister and have prevailed." She it was who hid her father's household gods and pretended she could not stand up to greet him because of her female condition. She deceived her father. She had the potential for high spiritual awareness but showed her humanness and possibly her lack of acceptance of Jacob's one God. In spite of this, she bore Joseph, who became the bright and shining example and saved his father and brothers from starvation in Egypt.

These twelve sons of Jacob (Gen. 36) became heads of the twelve tribes of Israel. Jacob's name was changed to Israel by God as he went to meet his brother, Esau, to ask for forgiveness. Jacob represents the intellect. Israel represents power with God and man —power of the Spirit. He became one with the I AM.

The boys grew up, and the other sons were jealous of Joseph because he was arrogant and the favorite of his father. He was sold by them and taken to Egypt, became powerful, and eventually brought his father and brothers there to live.

Now what do we have here that can be valuable to us who live monogamous marriages and do not have to strive with another wife for our husband's attention?

All of us have within us the opposites. We have the negative and the positive; we have love and hate; we have the good which we turn to evil. We remember God and then forget God. All the time we are loved by God and are producing in the outer that which he sends to us. We make choices that bring us unhappiness. We have a degree of happiness; but we are discontented. We do not have the perfection that our soul longs for. Our husband may not understand us and say, "You are two persons. Who are you?" And we may be asking ourselves the same question.

When we are so divided, we are not at peace. We look for ways to assuage our unrest. We blame ourselves, we blame others. We blame our husband. We seem to be lost in a wasteland of desire, of wanting what we cannot have. We may try deception to find our peace. We dislike ourselves when the negative arises in our thoughts and actions. We feel guilty and continue to make a larger separation within ourselves.

Rachel had the love of her husband but was dissatisfied. She wanted something else, something that Leah had—sons. Leah *had* sons—but always longed to be loved by Jacob. How like them are we!

Leah could represent the human soul, that human part of each of us. Rachel could represent the more spiritual aspect, but not fully developed; it was in a transitory state and became very human at times.

In our marriages we are ever learning the lessons that we came to this life to learn. One of the greatest values of marriage is to teach us what love means and how we can best express it. Marriage on the earth plane is preparing us for marriage on the spiritual. As we love and are loved we learn something of the characteristics of God. We learn to lean on faith in the difficult times. We learn to rejoice with God when all is well. Through our sexual union we experience the ecstasy of divine marriage. But all of this may not be enough. We may still be discontented and long for something more. It is at this time that we should realize that love of man and woman is not the ultimate. We should recognize that household gods will not fill our great longing. For fulfillment of our desires comes only from God the Father. He is All and in All. No human can fulfill this deep longing for completion. And so we appeal to God for direction.

God sends Joseph (imagination) and Benjamin (an acting, accomplishing faith). These two together will lift us to a higher place as we center in God.

Our imagination is very important, and as we activate it for the positive, we bring good into our lives. And of course faith is important for all our achievements in the Spirit. When we have faith in ourselves and our God—indeed, when faith is born—the opposites, jealousy and envy, die. Rachel died at Benjamin's birth.

These two women taken together and married to Jacob (intellect, which became spiritual understanding) produced the twelve sons who represent in us various levels of achievement on our spiritual journey. Within each of us these two vie for attention, and until we realize the birth of imagination and faith, they—human consciousness and spiritual consciousness—will not be one. The love that we long for will come as we imagine that love in our life and have faith that God will bring it about.

Leah and Rachel found their reason for being in producing sons. We must find our reason for being in producing the high spiritual qualities exemplified by Jesus. His twelve disciples represent various components of our personality. These characteristics, from Charles Fillmore, are: faith, will, understanding, imagination, zeal, power, love, wisdom, order, strength, elimination, regeneration/life. We are on the beginner's level in many of them but through believing in, and following, the teachings of Jesus, we can rise higher. The human quality of our soul (Leah) will be displaced by the more spiritual quality of Rachel. For in the end, Rachel produced the most outstanding sons, who affected the lives of so many. Leah's son Judah was in the lineage of Jesus, so her human side was blessed and filled with the Spirit of the most high. They are both important in our own life.

Esoteric: OUR GOAL: COSMIC KNOWING

Corinne Heline has written a New Age interpretation of the Bible, and I should like to give her ideas on what each son represents in our own consciousness.

These qualities are ones we may want to think about and assess in our own personality. It was Jacob's path to higher spirituality that produced these sons.

Reuben, altruism; Simeon, duality; Levi, division; Judah, power of love; Dan, judgment; Naphtali, mastery; Gad, upsurge of new life; Asher, joy of spiritual knowing; Issachar, material possessions and karma; Zebulun, mystic wedding; Joseph, light brought out of darkness; Benjamin, Cosmic Knowing.*

The final son is Benjamin, who represents that high ecstasy of Knowing, without question, that we are one with God. Rachel's death symbolized the end of this phase of consciousness development. So our goal is Cosmic Knowing, and when that happens to us, all division will be unified.

After God appeared to Jacob a second time and told him that his name was changed from Jacob to Israel, Benjamin was born.

Israel indicates high spiritual consciousness. Benjamin, Cosmic Knowing, was conceived and born. Our intellect will give way to Spirit as we pass these mileposts and reach Cosmic Knowing. And the element of forgiveness is a part of the Path also. As Jacob was going to ask his brother's forgiveness, his name was changed. All karma is lost when we are redeemed and centered in God.

Rachel and Leah: how could we forget them? How much they depict to us the qualities in ourselves that we want to transform into higher consciousness! In our changing, we bring to birth Cosmic Knowing and find our joy.

*New Age Bible Interpretation, 5th rev. ed., vol. 1 (Los Angeles: New Age Press, 1985), ch. 10.

6

Potiphar's Wife

(Genesis 39)

WOMAN AS TEMPTRESS

She is nameless, having her identity in her wifehood, which is true of most of the women of the Old Testament. She is nameless, but her kind are legion.

We must review the story of Joseph in order to gain any understanding from this incident, as the story of Potiphar's wife would not exist without Joseph.

Joseph, the son of Jacob and Rachel—greatly loved by his father, handsome, a dreamer and in favor with God: his name means Light in the darkness (or, some say, imagination). His brothers grew to hate him and so they sold him to some Ishmaelites. He was taken to Egypt and sold into slavery. He was purchased by Potiphar, who was captain of the Pharaoh's guard, and eventually rose to a position of being over all Egypt. Through the years Joseph had grown in faith, possibly through his "dark sea journey" to Egypt, and had learned to trust God. "The Lord was with Joseph" (Gen. 39:2).

The wife of Potiphar was lonely and attracted to this handsome young man. She approached him many times and asked him to sleep with her. She was persistent, and no doubt Joseph felt a little pang of pride that this powerful man's wife found him attractive. But his loyalty to his friend, Potiphar, kept him from allowing his imagination to roam in that direction. When she tried to make him come to her bed, he fled, leaving behind his coat. She used this as evidence against him and told her husband that he had tried to rape her. "Hell hath no fury like a woman scorned." Joseph was put in prison, where he remained three years until the Pharaoh needed him to interpret two dreams. Joseph so impressed the Pharaoh that he was put in charge of all Egypt and married a priest's daughter. That was a high honor and went only to those of high consciousness. Later he and his brothers became reconciled, and his father and brothers came to Egypt to live. Years later their descendants and other Hebrews under the leadership of Moses would escape Egyptian slavery.

This myth, legend, story, history has been very applicable throughout the ages as man and woman have danced their way through life balancing their sensual desires with their spiritual or moral beliefs. In a nutshell, these fifteen verses give us a view of temptations we might face. Some, who are enamored of the sensual life, will see Joseph as a fool. What rewards and delights he could have had as the plaything of Potiphar's wife! Others, more serious about their psychological and spiritual growth, will see Joseph's imprisonment as a necessary result of declining to bow to sensual desire.

Many of us are open to this type of temptation and often are unable to overcome our passion and desire. Our reason, which says our loyalty to others is more important, is ignored. And frequently this happens when we think we are far advanced on our spiritual path. Perhaps Joseph was plagued by pride. After all, he had risen very quickly to this high position, although he was a slave. He needed another challenge—prison, perhaps—to teach him.

So it is with us occasionally. We may fall for a time, but inevitably we realize that we cannot continue to have an affair, be dishonest to our spouse, friends, or family. In such dishonesty we separate ourselves from God.

Our guidance is from Joseph's actions. This need to express sexual desires in an illegitimate way must be denied. It is better to be imprisoned for a few years than to bow to the demands of this desire and risk hurting ourselves as well as many others. When we believe we are in love with the other party, we have a more difficult problem; but adultery has never brought happiness for very long to most people. Adultery, greatly condemned by both Jews and Christians, is a short-gap solution to our problems. It cannot bring joy.

Denying the impulse toward sexual promiscuity with a friend's (or a stranger's) wife or husband will bring its reward eventually. One must have a higher calling to successfully deny this temptation, and that calling should be in God's Will for our life. Joseph said, "How then can I do this great wickedness, and sin against God?" So as we turn away from our sensual desire and toward God, we may still suffer, but through that suffering we will reach a higher dimension of consciousness of our Divinity if that is our goal.

When woman takes the aggressive action, as did Potiphar's wife, we can know that she is suffering from a deep lack of fulfillment in her marriage. Woman often reaches out to another man in hopes of finding the love she does not have from her husband. Many times she excuses herself because she loves the other man. The action seldom brings happiness to all concerned. For the dishonesty that such action implies will cause a greater division between her and her husband; and thus happiness is further removed. The ecstasy of the affair may satisfy for a short while, but again something more will be desired. There are far better solutions to her predicament.

Potiphar's wife lost the possibility of a friendship with a fine man and took on the guilt of knowing what she had done to Joseph as well as the guilt of lying to her husband. Nothing was made better for her, but worse.

We know nothing more about her, but she has left her mark on the history of mankind, and the story is as fresh today as it was then—and ever will be.

Esoteric: ANIMA AND ANIMUS

From a deeper psychological level as relating to our own consciousness development, we are back to the theme of the struggle between the human choices versus the spiritual; between sensual pleasure versus desire for God; reason versus feeling.

Our feeling nature often overwhelms us and we make demands on others and on ourselves that cannot be fulfilled. When our feeling nature runs away from our reason, we are bound for trouble. The feelings must be an important part of our personality; we cannot deny them. But feelings based on desire for sensual pleasure and not based on love and concern for others will lead us astray.

Carl Jung teaches a great deal on the need to change the inner characteristic called the *anima* in men, and the *animus* in women, from the negative to the positive. Through our many experiences in growing up, through race consciousness, through the relationship we have had with the opposite sex, we learn to admire or be revolted by this inner contrasexual element within our psyche. This is masculine in the female and feminine in the male. He calls them potential guides to our unconscious that can lead to higher dimensions or to lower. These are revealed to us through our relationships with the opposite sex. Sometimes the wrong people are drawn to us because our feelings are based on the negative anima or animus. In dream analysis we can learn about these guides, and it is a valuable lesson.

Joseph was tempted by his negative anima. He later married a priest's daughter, which designates one of high spiritual understanding, a positive anima. In order to find this positive loving guide, however, he had to confront the negative aspect, he had to suffer, be imprisoned in the unconscious reaches of his mind, do some dream interpretation, and finally be able to achieve a successful position with the higher forces. When we finally confront this negative element in our psyche, we start our journey to health and balance of the masculine and feminine in our nature. The negative anima was confronted when Joseph refused to "sleep" with Potiphar's wife. And he was on the road to healing.

The same is true of the negative animus, or negative masculine characteristic within woman. She can be tempted by her desire to find a response to her need for love from a man, and her reason goes to sleep. If she allows herself to fall prey to the temptation, then she has not overcome this negative element in her psyche. She must depart from the scene of temptation saying no and confront the tempter. Then she can find the positive guide to the unconscious, which will satisfy her longing and bring her peace. This is her Spirit within. Then real Love will be hers with the right man. The positive invites good relationships into her life (see ch. 20).

(If this subject interests you, you can read more about it in *Boundaries of the Soul,* by June Singer.*)

*New York: Anchor Books, 1973.

Our imagination leads us into many of the negative as well as positive experiences of our life. When our imagination dwells on a high spiritual plane, we are led that way. "The Lord was with Joseph" and is with us. Our temptations are more subtle the higher we go on the Path; but our Christ, our Divinity within, our positive anima or animus, is always waiting to rescue us.

Let us not allow ourselves to be Potiphar's wife. We gain nothing and lose much. We, as women, should not be the temptress but the leader of mankind to higher awareness of who we really are—children of God.

7

Jochebed

(Exodus 2:1-11, 6:20; Numbers 26:59;
Acts 7:20-22; Hebrews 11:23)

A MOTHER'S GOD-GIVEN TASK

For many centuries after Joseph brought his father and brothers to Egypt, the Hebrews were enslaved by the Egyptians. They multiplied very rapidly, and the Pharaoh, alarmed over the large population of Hebrews, was afraid that they might take over the country. So he ordered all the boy babies killed who were two years old or younger. This is where the story of Jochebed begins.

This woman, mother of Aaron, Miriam, and Moses, figures so greatly in Hebrew history, and ultimately in Christian history, that we must give her due acclaim. She was one of the great mothers of the Bible, parent of two renowned men and of a woman who was named a prophetess. Her influence is never-ending.

Miriam was her oldest child, with Aaron the second. Moses was born at the time the Pharaoh had edicted the killing of babies. Jochebed hid Moses in an ark (basket) in the bullrushes of the Nile River. He was three months old. She hid him near the bathing place of the Pharaoh's daughter and her maids. They found the baby, and the princess named him Moses ("drawn out of the water"). His sister, Miriam, waited nearby and suggested that she find a Hebrew nurse for him. The princess said "Go," and Miriam brought Jochebed to nurse him. Some accounts say she gave him up to the Pharaoh's daughter when she weaned him. Another esoteric source has it that she had him with her for seven years. Then Moses grew up in the royal household, fleeing to the wilderness when about forty years old. At the end of the wilderness period of forty years, he was commissioned by God to lead the Hebrews out of Egypt. He was God's chosen Savior of His people.

Aaron, Moses' brother, helped him and became the first high priest. Miriam led the women in song and dance and was an advisor and seer. What a wonderful mother Jochebed had to be!

We, as mothers, cannot take all the claim to fame for our children, of course. They have their own way—their own path to follow. But the example of a mother's faith in God is never lost by the child as it grows to maturity. Consciously or unconsciously, it leans upon the memory of the mother's faith.

When Jochebed hid Moses for three months, she was taking a great chance of being killed by the authorities. But she must have realized that he was special. A highly attuned consciousness recognizes the spiritual essence in another person. Also, she had no way of knowing whether the princess would accept the small baby. She might have sought out the mother by forcing Miriam to reveal the secret and thus baby and mother would have died. But Jochebed had the requisite courage, based on faith that this child would be saved.

Moses was aware that he was Hebrew. Perhaps Jochebed did influence him for seven years, taught him the history of his people, instilled loyalty, and taught him of the One God. Remember, also, that he grew up in Egypt, where the common people had many gods. He was trained in the Mysteries, however, which taught the concept of one God. The Hebrews were tinged by the "many gods" concept as is shown by their history in the wilderness. But Moses followed the One God. Jochebed may have influenced him in this also.

She had to be a very holy woman to have raised a son like Aaron, who dropped everything to help Moses in his difficult task, and he it was who led the people in their religious evolution, being the first high priest. He was worthy to enter the Holy of Holies.

And what of Miriam, the little ten-year-old girl who helped save the baby? Her mother had set her the task, and the girl had carried it out. She had courage. Later, when Miriam became the leader of the women in the song and dance of worship, she was highly respected. But Aaron and Miriam showed their humanness and never reached the level of Moses. They were his faithful helpers most of the time.

Most importantly, Jochebed had reared these two with a high admiration and respect for their brother, Moses, for they followed him immediately when he started his great task. They were a united family.

Yes, we must see that Jochebed had great influence. Her husband, Amram, was there also, but he is not given much attention in the story as told in the Bible.

It is for us as mothers to realize our great responsibility in this God-given task. And only through faith in God can we really fulfill it. For the exigencies of rearing a family in these times make a spiritual commitment imperative. How else can we remain wise and calm in the face of many happenings in our world and in the lives of our children?

Jochebed was no doubt of a high spiritual bent, else she would not have attracted these beautiful souls. She was of the tribe of Levi (love). Again love is our base. Either what she had achieved in former lifetimes and/or the grace of God brought her these children. But she, like the potter, had to be aware of the quality of the material she was working with. She exemplifies for us the high feminine principle that brings only good into the world.

Esoteric: BIRTH OF THE DIVINE INNER

Jochebed (Jehovah is her glory) and Amram (kindred of God) brought forth Moses (drawn out of the water or subconscious). His story is the story of our own birth of Christ awareness and its growth.

The feminine principle centered on Jehovah gives birth to the awareness of our spiritual journey. It comes out of the depths of our subconscious. After its birth, it may be protected for some time by the feminine (love, intuition, compassion) within our soul, but the outer powers of darkness (Pharaoh) want to kill it. Then it is that we need to hide this small child. For in secrecy it can be saved and be allowed to grow and mature. If it is exposed, it may be killed by fear, by the power of darkness that lurks in our conscious mind and the minds of others. So we hide it in an ark, our inner awareness of the depth of Spirit.

When this deep awareness of our divine Inner comes to us, is birthed in our awareness, we know that it is important and we want to protect it and experience it. We know that it has a great work ahead of it.

When the good—the love of the feminine—adopts it, we then nourish it but are still secretive about where it came from.

It is recognition that Jehovah is our glory, that we are children of God (kindred of Jehovah), that gives birth to this Christ Child, this Moses. And it is faith in that God that saves it.

This idea, this realization of our inner Spirit, will grow and mature in the household of royalty. We surround it with beauty, with prosperity, with health. It knows all the Mysteries. It may go through a wilderness experience, but out of this isolation and, possibly, pain comes the great realization, I Am That I Am, and our task is assigned to us by that great I AM. And we perform it and are rewarded.

Moses (out of the subconscious) and Aaron (intellectual to spiritual) and Miriam (feminine love quality) are leaders in our exodus from darkness (Egypt) to an illumined state. We will make great progress. We may not reach Canaan (enlightenment) in this lifetime, but we are well on our way.

It is the realization of the glory of Jehovah and our connection with God that brings it about. We recognize this idea immediately as very special. We protect it and nurse it until it is old enough to function separately from our original awareness. (Seven years symbolizes the time of completion.) And it grows to maturity, a blessing to so many through our leadership and service.

We cannot do without Jochebed. Knowing the glory of God is our compass.

8

Miriam

(Exodus 2:4–10, 15:20, 21;
Numbers 12, 20:1)

EGO VERSUS MEEKNESS

We find this woman mentioned several times in the Old Testament. Since she was the sister of Moses and Aaron and helped lead the Israelites out of Egypt, we know she is important.

In Exodus 2:4–10 we have the story of Miriam watching over the basket of rushes that contained the baby Moses, her brother. When the Pharaoh's daughter found him, Miriam brought her mother to the princess to nurse Moses.

In Exodus 15:20, 21 we are told that she was prophetess and a musician. A prophetess is one inspired to teach the will of God. She was not married to a prophet, so she was a prophetess because she was at a high level of illumination. After the people of Israel were saved from the Egyptians by the parting of the Red Sea, Moses sang to the Lord and later Miriam led the women in song and dance, repeating "Sing ye to the Lord, for he hath triumphed gloriously; the horse and his rider hath he thrown into the sea." A joyous occasion—and Miriam led them. She sang in praise of, and thanksgiving to, God.

Now we come to the third episode that we will dwell on for our enlightenment (Num. 12).

Moses, many years previous to this account, had married Zipporah, the daughter of Jethro, with whom he studied and worked for years before God called him to the great task of freeing the Israelites. We do not know much about her or when she died.

According to our account, he married a Cushite woman, a dark-skinned woman from Ethiopia. In this scripture we read of the judgment and criticism both Aaron and Miriam thought and spoke against Moses because he had married a Cushite woman. They said, "Has not the Lord spoken through us also?" Just who does he think he is? they were implying. They were also implying that Moses was not any closer to God than they, and that he had done the wrong thing.

Moses was meek and followed the Lord's directions to the letter of the Law—with one exception, which kept him from entering the Promised Land. God heard the two and told all three to go to the tent of the Tabernacle to be spoken to. There He chastised Aaron and Miriam for their arrogance and spiritual egotism. He pointed out that to beginners on the Path and to prophets he spoke in visions and dreams; but with his servant Moses he spoke "mouth to mouth," and "he beholds the form of the Lord." Why then, He said, do you speak against my servant? Mouth to mouth means that what Moses spoke was God speaking through him.

Then Miriam became leprous; Aaron begged Moses' forgiveness (he repented) and asked him to intercede for the healing of Miriam, which he did, and after seven days she was healed and the people could move on. Repentance is very necessary if we are to be permanently healed. A healer who appeals to God, as Moses did, is often needed.

The fourth account is of Miriam's dying in the wilderness of Zin in Kadesh. She was buried there.

Moses had a tremendous task bringing the Israelites out of Egypt. He needed all the help he could get. Aaron had stood by him but was not strong in leading them toward the one God sometimes (Exod. 32:1-6). However, he was chosen by God for the task. Miriam showed her high spiritual awareness in being a prophetess, but she did not stay at that high level. She let spiritual pride go to her head and probably influenced Aaron to speak against Moses. The feminine, our feeling nature, often leads our intellect. Moses did not need this problem among all the others he had. Miriam and Aaron could have influenced the people against him.

Jealousy, especially among members of the same family, is very common. Many times we are not big enough to rejoice in the achievements of our brothers or sisters, and because we are so close to them we can hurt them deeply by our attitude.

Many of us get caught in spiritual pride. It is very subtle. It catches us unawares. We so much want to believe we have reached a high place of awareness and begin looking at others from this exalted position, and judge. We are bound to fall when this happens. Judging others is an intellectual exercise, not a spiritual one. Jesus said, "He who is the greatest among you is the servant of all." God called Moses his servant. Miriam and Aaron had forgotten that true spirituality is true meekness. Moses was meek. Those who have arrived at a high consciousness are often unaware of it. But they do not judge, for they release others to choose their own path.

Judgment, envy, jealousy, and pride will often bring challenges in the physical body. Our thoughts block the flow of energy in our body, and illness develops. Miriam became leprous, a most dreaded disease of the time, which isolated the victim from human contact.

This is what a judgmental attitude will do for us. When we become the chief critics of our associates, they turn from us. This criticism need not be spoken—just to think it is reflected in our attitude, and the other one knows.

Miriam had a spiritual healing—seven days was a short time for a healing of leprosy. But God heeded the healer Moses, and she was made whole. Her pride was demolished, for all the people knew what she had done and what had happened to her. They had to wait for her to heal before they could move on. She was humbled.

Her story is so typical of many of us. We do not always learn from another's experience but need to have our own. Then we realize our mistake and turn again to a meek position, asking forgiveness for our offense. We follow the way of Aaron. He asked forgiveness immediately and was forgiven. Miriam was punished and through the grace of God was healed.

Humility, love, forgiveness are all marks of one who is spiritually advanced. This is what we strive to express.

Esoteric: HUMILITY A NECESSARY INGREDIENT

These three—Miriam, Moses, Aaron—came from the tribe of Levi, and their parents were no doubt of a high consciousness.

From our center of love (Levi) comes our own spiritual consciousness, which leads us higher and higher. Moses symbolizes the evolutionary law that is forever moving us onward and upward to the Promised Land. Aaron is that illumined, enlightened consciousness that is our goal. He was the first priest of the Israelites. Miriam is the contradiction that lies within our conscious and unconscious mind. She is bitterness and sweetness; perversion, exaltation. She is the high prophetess and the carping, complaining feminine aspect of our personality.

These three came out of Egypt, or sense consciousness, darkness, the subconscious, and are on an evolutionary journey led by the law of evolution, Moses. He married a Cushite woman. This marriage is necessary for our enlightenment, for *Cushite* is the idea of the body being dirty, evil, dark, corrupt. These are dark thoughts that need to be filled with the light of understanding that the body is divine also. We need to bring this low thought up if we are to evolve. Moses did so in the marriage.

Miriam, the contradiction in our thoughts, fights this idea. She believes the Cushite woman to be wrong for our evolutionary law or path. This we often do, not realizing that God is all. This contradiction was at rest for a long time, and the sweetness of our consciousness was a leader of the feminine aspect. But we vacillate. When we do, we resist the evolutionary law—and often our body shows the results. Leprosy is an impure condition in the organism.

Now Aaron, an enlightened being who was affected by the contradiction of his feminine consciousness, also was dimmed. The potential of illumination that lies within each of us is often dimmed by the contradiction in our thinking, and we are brought down for a moment. But higher awareness of God brings about our repentance over such negative thoughts, and we are healed.

The body shows forth what we think and act upon. We are one—body, mind, emotions, spirit. When one is out of balance, the other follows. Illness of the physical is the easiest to detect and the most difficult to hide. So it is a blessing when our body shows forth some impure condition. Our direction then is to believe that God can heal, to search out what has caused the condition, to cleanse or repent, and to let go and let God do the healing. The services of a doctor and medicine may also be needed. Our need to evolve will be the instrument of our healing.

Thus all three—Miriam, Moses, and Aaron—are needed. Seven days to be healed, as with Miriam, is symbolic of whatever time it takes to reach physical perfection. Then we can move on to the Promised Land.

Miriam, contradiction, died in Kadesh, which symbolizes a pure, sinless, perfect, ideal state that exists in the depths of our consciousness. The contradiction within our nature will finally find that inner peaceful Center, the perfection of God.

We "Sing unto the Lord" as we are healed in body, mind, and emotions; and our spirit rejoices.

9

Daughters of Zelophehad

(Numbers 26:33, 27:1-11, 36:1-13; Joshua 17:3-6)

WOMEN'S RIGHTS

You will find throughout these chapters of *Women of the Bible* that I shall be trying to help women lift themselves, to free themselves from the shackles of archaic law, archaic religious beliefs, archaic rules about their reason for existing. This chapter is one of many that will point out the necessity for each of us to make some progress in this lifetime in freeing the feminine in our world and making it an equal partner with the masculine. And men likewise need to free their feminine.

This legend is important to us as women because it is the first recorded account of daughters inheriting their father's estate. It was a precedent, a law, that was followed thereafter and is sometimes referred to by lawyers. It is one of the few places in the Old Testament that indicate woman's equality with man.

It is also important for it will teach us the qualities that develop in our evolutionary spiritual journey as we come from denial of the negative in our lives. Each daughter symbolizes a step up the ladder.

The story is that five daughters of a deceased man, Zelophehad, came to Moses and the high priest Eleazar and asked that, since their father had no sons, they be given his possessions. They used a wise argument: "Why should the name of our father be taken away from his family because he has no son?" That was a telling argument, for in order that the name of a father be remembered the sons were identified by their father's name. So Moses asked the Lord and was told that they were right: they should be considered first. So they set the precedent. Later the elders got worried that the inheritance would pass out of the tribe of Manasseh—their tribe—if the girls were allowed to marry just anyone. God, through Moses, edicted that they must marry in their own tribe. They married their cousins.

We as women are showing this kind of courage now. Laws have been changed in favor of women's rights because groups of women and individuals have gone to the highest legal authority and pleaded their case. But there is much yet to be done. And it *will* come to pass, because women have the courage to be told "no" yet continue on in the face of defeat.

The evolutionary journey of mankind needs the strength, wisdom, and emotion of both men and women. Many men are beginning to join the ranks of women who are working for equality in the home, the marketplace, the government, the church. Like any minority that insists on their rights, it seems to be a slow process. But every step counts.

One of the major steps that are quietly being taken is to secure the right of woman to decide how her own body is to be used. For too long men have exerted their conjugal rights in the marriage bed and women have been taught to obey, to be submissive to their husbands—probably a holdover from the traditional concept of Eve. Now there is action and talk about "rape in the marriage bed." Woman's right to deny sex to her husband if she does not want it is being upheld in court. This is another source of marital discord as well as divorce.

Woman's property rights still need some changing and will inevitably come as women become freer to own property and not only to inherit property from their husbands but to get an equal share of what the couple has accumulated when there is a divorce. There is still inequity here, for many judges are still thinking in Old Testament law. But it will change.

Always there is the need to evolve in all ways. The body, mind, emotions, and spiritual awareness evolve. At this particular time in history the change is coming very fast. So let us get in "sync" with the times and help men and women share equally in responsibilities as well as in monetary gain.

These girls went to Moses, the Lawgiver and close companion of God, and to the high priest, Eleazar. Not only must the courts change the law but the Church too much change. The old is making way for the new.

The string attached to the inheritance—that the girls had to marry within the tribe—may be considered a negative. But as we women make strides in our seeking equality, we may need to realize that things do not change completely in a few months or even years. We will need to practice patience in some cases and wait to get the next change. It will come.

Women need not antagonize men in order to gain equality. In fact as man becomes more aware of his feminine side he will be able to help women in their crusade. We should be aware that we need men as they need us. Our femininity may appear to make us less equal, but a balance of reason with our natural feelings will bring us more success. Men can help us with this balance.

And so these daughters changed the course of history for many women. We are doing so as well, and we are building on the past successes of many other women who have gone before us. We owe them a debt of gratitude.

Esoteric: STEPS ON OUR PATH

Now let us look at this account from a spiritual, metaphysical view. As we do this we shall be aware of the teaching for ourselves personally.

Each name has a symbolic meaning. Moses, the Lawgiver to lead to higher consciousness. Eleazar, the priest, symbolizes spiritual strength through individual recognition of God.

In the beginning of our journey in this lifetime we already have certain religious beliefs that are carried in our unconscious from a former life. Perhaps we were born into a family that has these same beliefs, and we may be comfortable in this religion all of our life. However, there are those whose time has come to move to another religious understanding. Perhaps they feel the law of the past does not fit and they are dissatisfied with their religious life. They may long for more spiritual strength through inner recognition of their Christ spirit. When these thoughts come to them, they will eventually be affected. And when they start reaching out for a new concept, help will be at hand.

We need the Law for a time. Jesus taught the Kingdom of Heaven, which may change the Law for us. One of the first steps to this new concept is denial and affirmation.

Our personal unconscious is filled with all kinds of misconcepts if we have been in a Law-type religion that does not see the need to change. In order to let new Light in, the old must be forgotten or transformed by the Light. When we use denial—a statement that something is not true—and affirm the truth, we cleanse out these old memories and ideas, and we take on the new. The tribe of Manasseh symbolizes [he] who makes to forget or changes understanding through denial. Zelophehad, the father, means letting go of error in order to bring forth fruit in the inner. From this seed come forth five daughters who represent various levels of perfection, or steps to inheriting the qualities of God. New positive qualities express as error is denied, and then affirmations of the Good must follow.

The following interpretation of the five daughters' names will give us some ideas for our own growth.

Mahlah, the first daughter, represents harmony and inharmony and is pulled both ways. We have negative experiences after we start on our Path and may become discouraged until we realize that errors, conflicts, and challenges are part of our spiritual growth. As we work through these experiences, we grow in consciousness. Then we are delivered from inharmony and find harmony.

Haglah represents progress in understanding, although the progress may be restricted. Progress in understanding ourselves as well as our spiritual Self leads us further. Sometimes it is our ego that gets in the way and causes disharmony. The ego is that I of us, the small self that thinks it does all. To understand this—that the ego is leading us astray—means progress.

Noah, which is poise, peace, and equilibrium in the individual consciousness, is another daughter. These moments of peace and poise will never be forgotten. They are times when we feel whole. We may drop down to our earthly consciousness, but we will never forget that we can have this experience of peace.

Tirzah, the next daughter, represents pleasant, delightful thoughts and experiences in our soul. This is our reward. The positive becomes real. We have cleansed the negative shadows from our thinking. There may be moments when we return to negativity, but if we continue to meditate and find this place of pleasant delight, we shall go on.

It is through meditation that we reach this state of being. Quiet the mind, listen to the inner Voice, and follow It. Peace and poise follow.

I have chosen Milcah, the last daughter, as representing the soul's expression of dominion, wisdom, and good judgment. This is from our intuitive knowing, and when we center here, we will have the peace, poise, harmony, equilibrium, understanding, wisdom, and good judgment we need for a good life.

Wisdom is the balance between head and heart. Our transformation continues as we follow its guidance. And eventually our inheritance—the kingdom of Heaven—is surely ours, for we are all, men and women, children of God.

10

Rahab

(Joshua 2, 6; Hebrews 11:31; James 2:25; Matthew 1:5)

From Harlotry to Faith and Good Works

Moses led the people of Israel to the edge of the Promised Land and then turned the leadership over to Joshua. He died in Moab and was buried there. Joshua, blessed by Moses, took on his mantle.

To set the stage for this chapter we need to know the history as recorded. Joshua sent two spies to Jericho, a city in Canaan. He wanted to take control of it. The two spies went to Jericho and to the house of Rahab, the harlot, for lodging. The king of Jericho heard about them and sent his agents to Rahab to get her to reveal the spies to him. She hid them and said that they had left and directed the searchers out of the city to look for them. The spies were grateful. She told them that she knew the Lord meant for them to have the land, that she had heard of the people crossing the Red Sea, what they had done to Sihor and Og, two kings. She declared her faith in their God, who was in heaven above and earth below. She asked that when they took Jericho they protect her and her household. Then she let them down outside the wall (her house was built between the double walls) by a rope and told them to hide for three days. They told her to display a scarlet cord in her window when they took Jericho and that she and her family would be protected. She and her household were saved and joined the Israelites; later, she married one of them.

It is suggested by some that the women who demonstrated the greatest faith in God as recorded in the Old Testament were Abigail, Sarah, Rahab, and Esther. Rahab is also mentioned in Hebrews and James as having great faith.

This woman Rahab was not perfect by Jewish or Christian standards. She lied to the king. She hid spies who were planning to destroy the city and the people. She acted against the best interests of her people—and she was a harlot. Her story is for me a great demonstration of one who turned from dishonesty, disloyalty, and use of her body for sensual pleasure and monetary purposes to one who declared, "For the Lord your God is he who is God in heaven above and on earth beneath." We would interpret this statement to mean that God is in our higher consciousness and also in our lower earth consciousness. What Truth!

So often we have believed we were not worthy of the love of God. Many criminals, mentally disturbed people, those who are considered sinners by the Church—Paul lists them in Galatians 5:19-21, among whom are found idolators, fornicators, sorcerers, and such characteristics as jealousy, anger, selfishness, envy, drunkenness—feel that they are lost forever to the love of God. Our Christian Church teaching has been that all may be forgiven if the person turns to Jesus Christ to be saved. And it is certainly true that we have seen people turn their lives completely around 180 degrees and follow the One God. We must be careful that we do not condemn such of our brothers and sisters as well as ourselves.

It is more important that we realize that what we have done in the past that is considered immoral by some can be forgiven and our karma wiped out when we fully and gloriously give ourselves over to God's Will. It may take a change of environment, some counseling or therapy, a change of work, a letting go of friends and relatives to make this happen. But it can be done through the love of God and the teaching of Jesus Christ, which is our Spirit within.

Rahab turned her loyalty to the Israelites, which symbolize high spiritual thoughts and belief in one God. Her work was also changed. She showed her love and caring for those people who depended upon her in her household. But she was ready for a change of environment to support her consciousness change.

Many have been very judgmental of a harlot and her life. Consider, however, many wives who seem to be living a very circumspect Christian life, who are staying in relationships, selling their body for protection, security, and a position in society. When we use our feminine wiles to achieve security for our physical needs, we might ask how close we are to harlotry. Many times when women awaken to what they are doing, the despair and guilt they feel leads them to the One God. "Man's extremity becomes God's opportunity." Then they understand and are less judgmental of the harlot. Jesus taught us this great lesson (see John 8:3-11).

The faith and the courage of Rahab were outstanding. It takes both to change our way of life. If our faith is deep enough, we shall have the courage and strength to do what we must.

And we must never forget how our actions may affect the lives of many, many others. Starting with our children and the members of our own household, our example is observed and often followed. We can help save them as did Rahab. She helped the spies so that they could make their report, and the Israelites were successful in entering the Promised Land.

The account of the demolition of the people, the walls, and the city of Jericho may make us wonder if Rahab's sacrifice was for a good cause. So many of these stories in the Old Testament have made people question the holiness of the Israelites' cause or the holiness of the Bible. But we must remember that the times were different then and that they were living under a different covenant. Besides, how much have we really advanced when we have the potential to destroy our planet with our nuclear stockpile? Can we really be judgmental of them?

I feel that women have a grave responsibility to lead men from masculine aggressive, intellectual choices to choices based on compassion, love, and their feelings of goodness. We, like Rahab, can help; and it is through faith that we have the courage and determination.

Never believe that your life is lost and seek out death. Know that life is our heritage, is our very Being—and no matter what depths we have sunk into, we can turn our life around to success, happiness, and joy through faith in our One God.

Esoteric: SENSE THOUGHTS TO SPIRITUAL THOUGHTS

Rahab and her faith is a wonderful topic for us to consider for our personal spiritual growth. So many of our Bible characters demonstrated faith that we may grow weary of reading about it, but faith is basic to the good life. Don't you agree?

The Israelites represent high spiritual thoughts, belief in one God. They were returning to the land of their origin, Canaan (the redeemed, spiritualized body). Remember, that is where we started in the Garden of Eden—with a spiritual body. Jericho (intellect) was the first attribute to be conquered with spiritual thoughts.

This changing from thoughts based on the intellect to intuition begins the process of changing the physical body into the spiritual one through transforming and destroying the cells of darkness.

Rahab represents the depths of sense that the natural love has fallen into. Her climb out of that is the same as ours.

The two spies (thoughts) were sent to Jericho by Joshua to see what needed to be done to overcome it. Joshua means "Jehovah is deliverer." Joshua is the Hebrew name for Jesus. Jehovah is the I AM within each of us. So what do we have?

For us, in this dispensation, the Jesus teachings send thoughts into our intellect to find out what would be needed to spiritualize it or replace it with redeemed spiritual thoughts. These thoughts are lodged with Rahab (sense thoughts). But the I AM had sent them. They had the power to transform her into a follower of the I AM. Also, by her testimony of the knowledge that the Lord had dried up the Red Sea (race thoughts) and that the Israelites had destroyed the two kings (sex sensation ruling man), she had been changed and was now centered in Jehovah. She hid these thoughts (spies) under flax (chastity and purity). Thus she was allowed to have life in Canaan (the spiritualized body).

The scarlet cord that she displayed in the window and that saved her from destruction has been interpreted as the spinal cord in the body, which is used to raise the Life Essence in order to purify the body. For one centered in sensual desire, this requires a change in order to conserve the divine energy for spiritual rather than sensual purposes. Perhaps this displaying of the scarlet cord indicated the start of her change. It is necessary for us also, if we are to follow the teaching of Jesus, to become as he was and to do what he did.

Our thoughts, our intellect need to be cleansed, and thoughts from God taught by Jesus Christ is the start. When these thoughts (the spies) are lifted up (hid on a high mountain) for three days, the transformation occurs. (Mountains are high spiritual places.) A challenge often follows our trnasformation, and to be in a high state of awareness of God brings the resurrection. The number three symbolizes self-control, conservation, and transmutation. The two spies (thoughts) had to go through this process before they were ready to report to Joshua (the deliverer). Then the spiritualized consciousness was able to overcome the intellect (Israelites overcome Jericho), and Rahab, who had changed from physical to spiritual thinking, was accepted in the company of high spiritualized awareness.

Rahab helped a "new" religious concept to take over her life. We, in our changeover from the teachings of Paul through the traditional Church to the teachings of Jesus through his example, are pioneers of a New Age. When we understand that our goal is to be pure Spirit, we will be protected and grow toward that goal.

It takes great faith to chance a new way. Ours can be as Rahab, knowing that God is omnipresent in heaven and earth.

Some scholars suggest that Rahab was in the genealogy of Jesus. She is said to have been the mother of Boaz, who married Ruth, whose son, Obed, was David's father, an ancestor of Joseph. From the darkness to pure light—Jesus. It took many generations. It may take us many lives.

11

Deborah

(Judges 4, 5)

This legend of Deborah is to teach us how we can overcome habits of the body, sense habits, by the combination of personal will (Barak) and intuition, God's Will (Deborah). Many of us are caught up in these sense habits and do not know how to overcome. Let us learn from the overcoming of Sisera (inner unrest based on carnal thoughts).

Deborah was a prophetess and judge in Israel. The Israelites were under the domination of King Jabin of Canaan and had been for twenty years (numerologically, 20 reduces to 2, which is duality, our physical condition). They were afraid to rebel, for King Jabin (physical habits and needs) had 900 chariots of iron (rationalizations for keeping the physical habit). Even so, they cried unto the Lord for help.

Deborah (intuition from God) sat under a palm tree between Rama and Bethel, symbolizing high consciousness. She was judge as well as prophetess. The palm tree is considered the Tree of Life in the Orient. Her words, her judgments, came from the Tree of Life, the eternal source of Life, God. She was married to Lappidoth, which means wisdom.

Deborah sent for the commander of Israel's army, Barak. She told him that the Lord commanded him to gather his men at Mount Tabor. Ten thousand from the tribe of Naphtali (strength) and the tribe of Zebulun (order) were to be gathered. Sisera, commander of King Jabin's army, would come out to meet him by the river Kishon (emotions swayed by natural desires). Barak would defeat Sisera and his men.

Barak remonstrated and did not quite believe her. He said if she would go with him, he would go. She agreed to go but told him that he would not have any glory, for Sisera would be sold into the hand of a woman.

They led the army to Mount Tabor (a high place in consciousness). Then Barak brought the army down from the mountain and defeated the armies of Sisera. Before the battle, Deborah said to Barak, "Up! For this is the day in which the Lord has given Sisera into your hand. Does not the Lord go out before you?" And He did.

Sisera, the commander of the defeated army, fled to the tent of Heber, whose wife, Jael (rising higher), greeted him, gave him milk to drink, and hid him. Sisera went to sleep. She took a tent peg, and with a mallet drove it through his temple "as he lay fast asleep from weariness." She killed the carnal thoughts that needed destroying. It is the feminine within us that lifts our consciousness to Spirit and defeats the negative, earth-attached thoughts. She was later eulogized in song by Deborah and Barak.

Our consciousness of God may be imprisoned by the intellect, by physical habits we have acquired through experiences in the physical world. Israel symbolizes "striving for God." We, like the Israelites, may be imprisoned in our belief in the might of science, education, wealth, government, the gods of nature. And we may be successful in that realm—but in our personal life we are in chaos.

Some of us are captives to the habit of drug usage, or to alcoholism, or to smoking tobacco, or to overeating. Some of these habits are more defeating than others to our success as human beings and to a happy, productive life. But they all attack the physical, emotional, intellectual, and spiritual realms of our being. And they seem like the chariots of iron, invincible. In order to overcome them, we need to use our personal will to make the effort, the initial attack on the habits, and then we need intuition, which comes from the marriage of our awareness of the Spirit to wisdom. We also need another person, sometimes, to give us the message from God that will direct us in overcoming the habit. Many people have gone down in defeat when attempting to overcome, by use of the will alone—the egotistic will—a physical or emotional attachment. When the body and feelings become accustomed to a substance that seems to quiet them, it is difficult to do without it. No matter how much we repeat our affirmations, no matter how strong-minded we are, it takes something more to defeat these habits.

When we are imprisoned by the circumstances of our life, we may believe that there is no way out. We seem to be overwhelmed by our physical needs, which get in the way of our following what we know is best for us. Our will seems to be weak and incapable of functioning.

When we pray to the Lord with deep conviction, an answer will come. Perhaps we are still afraid to try; but if we will take our positive thoughts, our armies, to Mount Tabor (a high place in consciousness) and stay there for a time with Deborah, the mouthpiece of God, then we will defeat the habits of the physical and the emotional. Will—personal will—is not enough to defeat the iron chariots (habits of the body), for only with the grace and help of the Spirit can we overcome.

You see, our personal will is ego-centered, and we must be warned, as Deborah warned Barak, that our ego will not be rewarded, for it will be the feminine within us that will finally defeat the inner unrest that causes our misery. When we come to the river Kishon (emotions swayed by natural desires) where the battle must be fought, Deborah—being at one with God—will give us the direction, the strength, the confidence to move ahead and defeat the negative situation in our life.

Deborah warned Barak that he would not get the glory, but that another woman, not herself, would. She said that the captain of the enemy forces, Sisera, would be defeated by the Lord through a woman. We must lose our pride and our ego if we are to be successful in this battle. In the Alcoholics Anonymous organization the ability to say "I am an alcoholic" is paramount to the healing, for when an alcoholic says this with meaning, he is truly humble. For years his pride has kept him or her from admitting the facts.

Sisera, inner unrest from carnal thoughts, was killed by Jael, the desire for something higher in one's life. This desire for a better life and the guidance of God will defeat the huge, seemingly impregnable, army of our physical desires and fears. The Lord through our intuition, good judgment, and Wisdom helps us free our spirit from the physical entanglement. It soars, and we begin our trek back to the realization of who we really are—children of God. And there are many of our brothers and sisters who have gone before us who can lend us a helping hand.

Deborah is our own personal prophetess and judge. She combines the feminine characteristics of strength, spiritual discrimination, and guidance from our inner Knowing. She joins our personal will, and our forces are strong enough to overcome any condition in our life that seems to be defeating us. But we must "pray to the Lord" first for Deborah to be able to pick up the message and strengthen us in our climb out of the valley of despair to the Mount Tabor of higher consciousness. Our unconscious desire to rise to higher experiences will slay our attachments to the physical, to the intellectual ego, and to negative emotions. And then we will sing unto the Lord.

The Song of Deborah as recorded in Judges 5 is a great triumphal song of the overcoming of the imprisonment of each of us. For we are all imprisoned to one degree or another as long as we do not rise up and overcome the habitual thoughts that are our fears, our resentment, our judgmental attitude, our greed, our dependence on something in the outer to bring our happiness. She begins the song: "Praise ye the Lord for the avenging of Israel." She took no credit to herself but gave all the credit to God, for she knew that only He could overcome. Deborah also pays tribute to Jael for putting Sisera to death. God needs us as his instruments for the redemption of others and to help them find their salvation. Jael, our desire for higher knowledge, can be in the form of another one who helps us see that this is our real desire.

The last verse of the chapter is "And the land had rest for forty years." So it is with us as we match our intuition with our personal will and climb Mount Tabor to do His Will. "Does not the Lord go out before thee?" Deborah asked the frightened Barak (Judg. 4:14). Indeed He does!

12

Delilah

(Judges 16)

"WHEREIN DOES HIS STRENGTH LIE?":
LOSING SPIRITUAL STRENGTH THROUGH SENSUAL LIVING

The story of Delilah must include the story of Samson. Delilah would not have been so famous had Samson not come to her.

The Israelites were under subjection to the Philistines. Samson was born to a barren woman after an angel of the Lord announced to her that she would bear a son who would be a Nazarite from birth and who would begin to deliver Israel from the hands of the Philistines. A Nazarite, as long as he was under the vow of the Nazarite, would not cut his hair or drink anything from the grape vine, and could not touch a dead body.

As a youth, Samson fell in love with a Philistine woman whom he eventually left because she caused him to lose a wager with some of her relatives. In revenge against him, her father gave his daughter to the best man at the wedding. Samson burned Philistine orchards and fields with foxes which were set loose into the fields after he had tied their tails together* and set fire to them. The Philistines wanted revenge.

Through various experiences Samson proved himself to the Israelites and was judge for twenty years. He showed his super-human strength many times. He killed 1000 Philistines with the jawbone of an ass.

Then he went to the valley of Sorek (material aspect of life) and there he loved Delilah. This was his seeming downfall. The five kings of the Philistines came to Delilah and each offered her 1100 pieces of silver if she would find out Samson's secret of great strength. For Delilah that was too great a temptation, and so she

*Good News Bible.

asked him three times where he acquired this great strength. He gave her various untrue answers, so that she and the Philistines were fooled. Finally, at her accusation that he did not love her, he revealed that he was a Nazarite and that if he never cut his hair, he would keep this great strength. She told this to the leaders; they cut off his hair while he slept, gouged out his eyes, and condemned him to grinding at the mill in the prison. As time passed, his hair grew out.

One day, at a great gathering of the leaders of the Philistines, he was brought in to be laughed at. By a trick, he was allowed to touch the two pillars that supported the roof. He prayed to God for strength; the pillars came crashing down, and with them the roof. All the Philistine leaders were killed, as was Samson also.

All of us have the potential of being a Samson, for we are all chosen for a task in life, and our strength comes from God. However, because we are not totally committed to God, we may have weaknesses that separate us from our strength, and one of our greatest weaknesses is the misuse of our vital force for pleasures of the flesh. This may be due to the fact that we are all searching for love, searching for wholeness, and believe we can find it in another person of the opposite sex. Sometimes people carry this search to an extreme, running from one relationship to another in a frenzied effort to find the treasure on earth.

The Hindu religion has taught for centuries that the saving of the divine energy through abstaining from sexual activity, conserving the fluid generated by the sex organs, would make the body strong as well as build a higher physical body that eventually would be pure Light. This was all dependent on the individual's decision to be at one with God in body, mind, emotions, and spirit. When Samson gave in to his strong desire for Delilah in the guise of love (the Bible says he loved Delilah), he was taking the step that eventually brought his loss of strength, of vitality from the Lord. Hair symbolizes the vital essence of the body. It is taught by some Eastern religions that it is through the hair that much divine energy enters the body and consciousness. The Sufis do not cut their hair from birth onward if devoted to the Path.

So from the outer view we are being taught that misuse of the vital essence of energy may bring our separation from divine strength. This often happens through our choice of sexual behavior. Prostitution, promiscuity in unrestrained sexual activity, and centeredness on sensual desire may cause this. In our time this is a "hard" teaching, for pleasure through sex is uppermost in the minds of many.

The loss of the vital energy can be overcome when we withdraw from our lustful practices, allow our vital energy to accumulate (symbolically, let the hair grow), center on God, and pray and meditate. We can overcome the enemy of our spiritual consciousness, the Philistines or error thoughts and activities based on sense gratification. But we may have to go through a time, in our life, of imprisonment and being tied to the wheel of life before we fulfill our destiny.

And what of Delilah? She seems to represent that which is reprehensible in womankind. For financial gain she took advantage of a man who loved her. Many women through the ages have followed this path due to their unequal position in society.

Now Delilah and Samson were obviously not man and wife. Neither was she a prostitute, according to the biblical account. Samson was ever attracted to Philistine women. We wonder why. *Philistine* symbolizes forces foreign to the Spirit. Was he attracted to them because he longed for that which piqued his masculine pride? And they brought many tests to him. He was a judge, and Delilah was probably a courtesan, for the leaders of the Philistines were acquainted with her. She was using her womanly wiles to support herself, which is acceptable even in modern society.

Delilah was loyal to her people. She was probably more loyal to the 5500 pieces of silver. How often our loyalties are changed over a few pieces of money!

We women often prostitute the best that is within us. Men also prostitute the best within them, as did Samson. We must watch what we do to the men in our life. How we use our femininity is a great responsibility.

Esoteric: FEMININE AND MASCULINE OUT OF BALANCE

Let us now turn to the esoteric meaning of this story of Delilah. We shall seek the symbolic meaning of her influence on Samson.

Each of us is feminine and masculine. We need a balance of both in our thoughts, words, and activities. When we are out of balance either way, our life will be disturbed, and the way to purity of Being will be blocked. When we are totally at one with God, we will be androgynous, *andro* ("male") and *gyne* ("female") in balance. The further apart these two opposites, the further are we from being in that state of pure bliss and joy called *Cosmic Consciousness.* Samson and Delilah demonstrate separation within the personality of the average man or woman.

Samson means strength from the Spirit. Delilah means lustful pining. The two represent a split in the personality. This split will bring our downfall. Samson, the masculine, is taking the place of the feminine in woman. Delilah, lustful desire, is leading the masculine in man on to his loss of strength and direction. When we become serious about our reason for living, we will bring together the opposites in our personality as well as in our outer activity.

Woman has a grave responsibility in the upliftment of man. She can symbolize for a man at least three different personalities: the siren or enchantress; the mother; or the unknown damsel (mythologically)—the beloved, the perfect feminine that his soul searches for. We as women can choose to be any one of these for the man, but until we choose to be the perfect feminine based on spiritual understanding, we shall cause him many problems.

When the feminine becomes prostituted in the man, his physical and emotional strength will be lost. And when the feminine symbolizes the mother, he will be too dependent on the females in his world. Both lead to unhappiness.

Delilah, female wiles, decreased Samson's strength, but he regained it. He lost his vision and was imprisoned. He worked hard at a meaningless job. But his strength returned as his hair grew, and he planned how he could overcome the Philistines, or sense gratification. Blind, he could not enjoy the beauty of women. His reason for being—to cleanse out the Philistines (forces foreign to the Spirit)—came to him again. If he had not been imprisoned, he probably would not have "come to himself." It was not a defeat for him but the beginning of giving his life for the lives of others, for all are affected when we carry out our mission.

Delilah—that within us which seems to drain off all our strength —is sometimes our greatest blessing. We should treat our defeats with the energy and strength of God. We can return to our own path and fulfill our destiny. Sometimes it takes a seeming defeat to awaken us.

Samson was a special child. He was dedicated to the Lord. He lost his way for awhile, but he rose above defeat and fulfilled his mission. And Delilah, his feminine siren that led him astray, played a most important part in his spiritual journey. He delivered the Israelites (high spiritual thoughts) from the Philistines (sense realm of man) as his mother was told he would. We too may be diverted, but we shall eventually succeed.

Samson himself caused his loss of power. It was he who went to Delilah, who played games with her about his source of strength, who depleted his divine energy to the extent that he was so unconscious that the Philistines were able to cut his hair without awakening him. It was Samson who invoked the anger of the Philistines when he killed so many of them with the jawbone of the ass. It is we ourselves that cause our downfall. And the law of karma requires payment.

Delilah, you see, was not the reason for Samson's downfall. The reason was his search for love from a woman rather than from his inner Center. Delilah was a positive in his life, for through her, the attachment to the sensual was lost and he came to his Source and fulfilled his destiny. Delilah, often derided, was an instrument of Good. Good is in all. God is all.

In traditional Bible interpretation, the woman is usually presented as the temptress of the man. As we women of today look at these women in the light of Truth, we realize that they were not the reason for the man's downfall. Man then, as now, chose his actions. Men and women must take responsibility for their own actions, their own karma. When the masculine and the feminine are in balance within each of us, we will choose the harmonious way and blame no one else—for it all lies within our own consciousness, our own thinking.

13

Ruth and Naomi

(The Book of Ruth; Matthew 1:5)

MOTHER-IN-LAW AND DAUGHTER-IN-LAW RELATIONSHIPS

This very short book has all the elements of a love story that will be eternal. It is about Love. Ruth was beloved by all because she gave love. She proves that love can lift one from poverty and obscurity; can bring forth a wonderful child; can take care of and uplift an old, weary mother-in-law; and can overcome the barriers of race prejudice. It is about Ruth; but Naomi, her mother-in-law, plays an important part.

Naomi, her husband, and two sons left Bethlehem of Judah when times were hard and went to Moab, where there was a better livelihood. Both sons married Moabite women, Orpah and Ruth. Naomi's husband died, and ten years later the two sons died. She then decided to return to Judah, since food was plentiful there. Both girls started to return with her, but Orpah turned back when Naomi urged them to stay with their own people and blessed them. Ruth, showing her loyalty and her love for her mother-in-law, said, "Entreat me not to leave you or to return from following you; for where you go I will go, and where you lodge I will lodge; your people shall be my people, and your God my God; where you die I will die, and there will I be buried. May the Lord do so to me and more also if even death parts me from you" (Ruth 1:16, 17). How this stirs the love in our own feeling nature as Ruth declares her love and devotion to Naomi!

They returned to Bethlehem. Naomi was very bitter over her losses, but Ruth never complained. It was harvest time, and Ruth supported Naomi and herself by gleaning in the barley fields.

The owner of the field, Boaz, noticed her, told her to glean only in his field, and told his servants to help her. She showed her humility by falling at his feet and asking why he should be so kind to her, a foreigner. Love is always humble. He replied that it was because she had left her father and mother, and her country, to take care of her mother-in-law. He assured her that she was "under the wings of the God of Israel."

Later, through directions from Naomi, Ruth came to Boaz and asked him to take care of her since she was related to him through Naomi. He treated her kindly, and they were eventually married. From that marriage Obed was born. Naomi claimed him as her grandson and was his nurse. She was restored to her position of importance with her neighbors and lost her bitterness. The last of the book traces the genealogy of David from Obed. From Obed, the Moabitess and the Israelite brought forth eventually the Living Light, Jesus Christ, whose father, Joseph, was of this line. And Obed was born in Bethlehem, the birthplace of our Lord.

Ruth represents our ideal of love. She shows us how human love can be raised to divine Love by its willingness to leave one state of consciousness to go to another, higher state.

There are many lessons here, but I am called to talk about the relationship of mother-in-law and daughter-in-law. This relationship can be such a blessing to many, or it can be the source of much friction. As a mother-in-law, I have experienced both. And as a daughter-in-law, I doubt if I lived up to the best.

Sons and mothers have a special relationship—not any more special than with some daughters, but a mother seems to find it more difficult to let another woman take over her son's life and be more important to him than his own mother. This is not a new problem. It is depicted in many places in the Bible and in mythology. In Bizet's opera *Carmen,* José has to choose between his mother and his beloved Carmen. We have literary examples of the conflict that can develop and also of the great love that there can be between them.

My son was married for such a short time before his death in Vietnam that I did not know his wife very well, nor did she know me. In spite of that, we were drawn together by our grief, by the birth of their son, and by our need to share. She became another Ruth and through the years has shown me much love and caring although she remarried. She often said, "You will be my mother-in-law no matter whom I marry."

My experience with my mother-in-law was not like that, possibly because I did not know how to love. She and my husband were always close because of their common religious belief, which was not mine. She was unable to accept me as the best wife for her son, and I did not understand her. Fear, jealousy, loneliness entered in.

What is the answer? It would seem in the case of Ruth and Naomi that Ruth had to take the lead at first to convince Naomi of her love. Let us see what she said in the famous quote from her:

> Do not ask me to leave you for I want to be only with you.
> I will live with you. I will leave my parents and my people.
> Your God shall be my God. I will die and be buried with you.

Now what had Naomi done to call forth such loyalty? We do not know much about her life before the sons died, but notice what Naomi said when she tried to get Ruth and Orpah to return to their own people. She was very unselfish. She was an old woman alone and did not cling to the girls or expect them to take care of her needs. She did not imply that they owed her anything. She freed them and encouraged them to marry, to go on with their lives, with their people. She blessed them and prayed for them. She thanked them for their care of her sons and of her.

After this the girls showed their affection for her, and then Orpah turned back. Naomi again unselfishly told Ruth to turn back, but she declined.

We have here the recipe for a happy relationship between two women who were connected by one man, and each helped the other.

Ruth supported Naomi. Ruth followed the wise counsel of her mother-in-law. Naomi had Ruth's good and her future happiness uppermost in her mind. She did not say to Ruth that out of loyalty to her son she should not marry. No, she helped her get Boaz to ask her to marry him. And their child was precious to Naomi as her own.

Are you beginning to get the picture? It seems to me that both women are teaching us how we can handle such a delicate relationship. And it is, of course, through the expression of divine Love. There is no other way.

We as daughters-in-law often have greater understanding for our husband's mother after we raise our own sons. But a division may have occurred much earlier, and we may not have forgiven, talked out, or tried to solve our differences in love. It takes both committed to a loving relationship, as well as love expressed in thought, word, and deed, to heal the break if we are to have the close relationship here written about.

Sometimes this all has to be worked out without the help of the son and husband. Two women can make a man's life miserable if they are pulling him in opposite directions. He cannot solve the division, but he can help as he works to satisfy the mother's need for attention and the wife's need to be first in his life. Both women need to understand his position and each other's needs.

And how beautiful can be the relationship! Both wanting the best for the other. Both helping the other as needed. Both expressing their admiration and love for each other. And how blessed are the children, for a peaceful feeling between grandmother and mother enriches their lives also.

Boaz, a rich landowner, no doubt cared for Naomi in her old age. And this sensitive problem can be so much easier for modern people who need to care for the older relatives, provided that love is practiced for years previous.

Ruth is also a romance based on perfect love. Boaz showed his kindness, consideration, protection, and desire to help his kinswoman. He went through the legal process necessary before claiming her. Ruth was bold and at the same time humble. She did not rush Boaz and demand his care of her as a relative. She was willing to work and wait. Boaz showed himself a man of high morals and recognized in Ruth a special woman. He, too, demonstrated love at a high level. He never mentioned her difference of race except when he complimented her on caring for Naomi and leaving her own people.

In-law jokes are rampant in our society. We are not supposed to love our in-laws. Or perhaps the only way to deal with them is with a sense of humor. But so often we are led to believe that they will be a bone of contention. There were great differences between the backgrounds of Naomi and Ruth, but through love they were able to overcome them. It is a personal task, and society's view of what we should feel about our in-laws should be ignored.

Naomi and Ruth have gone down in history as a great example to us. Can we do any less for our children and their children?

Esoteric: THE PATH TO THE MYSTICAL MARRIAGE

This story, it seems to me, is a fine illustration of the Eternal All in our consciousness and the goal of the Mystical Marriage. Over and over we are taught this Way in the Bible. The Book of Revelation gives us directions on how to achieve this, the final state of perfection.

This teaching of the Mystical Marriage is difficult for Westerners to understand, for the Christian teaching has been quite different from the Eastern. I believe that we are to spiritualize the body and the mind and become pure spirit, as did Jesus before his Ascension. Let us see if this account cannot be interpreted that way.

Naomi and her family left Judah (prayer and praise) and went to Moab, where physical sense consciousness is satisfied. Naomi is representative of our soul, or some say mind, in passage from the higher to the lower. Sometimes when we do not get sense satisfaction, we leave our spiritual place and go elsewhere. Prayer and praise do not seem to bring what we want. But there is no lack in the Spirit. It takes us some period of time to recognize this. At first, when we make this change, all seems to be better. Many people start consciousness growth in order to have more prosperity. Prosperity may lead us to the Presence, but it may not. If our reason for seeking the Presence is in order to have prosperity in material things, we may gain them only to lose them. Seeking the Presence should be for consciousness expansion. Then prosperity will follow. Leaving prayer and praise will inevitably bring loss. When Naomi lost all, she returned to Judah (prayer and praise).

When Naomi, the soul, decides to return to Bethlehem, the house of bread or Spirit, she tries to leave Ruth, divine Love, behind. But Ruth says to the soul (Naomi): I shall always be with you, your needs will be my needs. Your God shall be my God. Where you die I shall die. (Or where you cease to grow and live, divine Love will also cease to grow and live.)

When the soul or mind decides to go back to the spiritual center, it often feels bereft and discourages any help from anyone else. It feels that the soul in love with the outer man (Orpah) and divine Love (Ruth) have no place in its search or return. When we have lost all that is dear to our spiritual life, we are depressed and do not believe that anything good lies ahead for us. But divine Love will not leave us, for it is a part of our Being. Personal love must leave at some point in our evolution.

Naomi returned to the land of prayer and praise, Judah, in a depressed and bitter mood. She even told her old friends that she should change her name to Mara, or bitterness. When we are bitter over the loss and failure of our choices, we may try to separate ourselves from love. Instead, we should realize that all our experiences are lessons on our way and not allow ourselves to get lost in a quagmire of self-pity.

Ruth and Naomi, divine Love and soul, lived together. Each helped the other. Soul and Love together.

From a metaphysical point of view, divine Love is always within our mind or our thoughts. Divine Love, when in control, taking care of the soul or mind, is always directed by the Supreme Being, which we are. We only need to allow that Light to shine forth and care for us. At some point our thinking cooperates with divine Love (Ruth) and allows it to shine, to function, to serve, to provide for our needs. Our personal thoughts based on the small self-will are necessary at first, but later we allow the Will of God to direct our thoughts. When we reach the place of turning within to receive our guidance, we are being directed by divine Mind or divine Love. Ruth started out by being directed by Naomi, mind, and later took over the direction of the mind when she gave Naomi her child to nurse.

As time goes on, it is apparent that our divine feminine Love must find a mate in order to be balanced. Our soul knows this and arranges for the coming together. Boaz, strength of character, is needed with divine Love. When they are married, they bring forth Obed, meaning service and worship. Then we worship God as our only source and serve Him through service to our fellowman.

To some, Obed may mean mystical adoration. When the divine Love and strength of character become one, we may experience a great high of mystical adoration, as do the mystics. This indicates that all sense of division has been lost and that the consciousness is one with the All. These times of ecstasy bring forth other spiritual experiences until we become the Christ, which has led us all the way.

The soul or mind, divine Love, and strength and purity of character work together, and we reach the height of Reality and leave forever the land of unreality, or Moab. Our home is in Bethlehem, substance of the Spirit, the Christ within. There it is that our Christ is born and ascends on high.

This is what is called the Mystical Marriage. It is the mystic's goal. It is our goal. Divine Love leads us on.

14

Hannah

(I Samuel 1, 2)

THE PRAYING MOTHER

One of our most important responsibilities as mothers is to pray. Some mothers do not feel this is necessary. Usually, however, if things become desperate enough, we turn automatically to prayer. A case of emergency certainly brings out "O God"—a very simple prayer.

Hannah shows many of the human characteristics that we are familiar with. And so let us see how she used prayer effectively.

Hannah lived with her husband, Elkanah, in the hill-country of Ramah. There were two wives—Peninnah, who had children, and Hannah, who was barren. Peninnah would taunt Hannah to annoy her, because she had sons and daughters and Hannah had none. She taunted her more when they went to the Festival of Tabernacles each year and Elkanah offered up sacrifice and gave a portion to each wife to eat; Hannah got one portion and Peninnah several, because she had children. Hannah wept and would not eat even though her husband reassured her of his love (she was his favorite) and asked if he wasn't enough for her, better than ten sons.

One year they went to Shiloh for the festival, which was held in the fall as a feast of thanksgiving. After the banquet, Hannah arose and went near where the priest Eli was sitting. She was depressed and deeply moved because of her barrenness. She made a vow to the Lord that if He would give her a son, she would dedicate him to the Lord all the days of his life, and his hair would never be cut. (Those dedicated to God's service did not cut their hair.)

As she prayed, she was silent—although her lips moved. Eli saw her and berated her for being drunk. She told him that she had drunk no strong drink or wine but that she was pouring out her soul to the Lord. She said, "I have been speaking out of my anxiety and vexation." Eli prayed that God would grant her petition and gave her his blessing to go in peace. Then she left, much relieved, and ate her portion, after which they all went home to Ramah. She conceived and bore Samuel, so named for "I have asked him of the Lord." She gave the Lord all the credit.

When Hannah had weaned Samuel, she took him with her gifts and sacrifices to the Tabernacle and to Eli. She reminded him of who she was and that his and her prayers had been effective, and so she was bringing Samuel to "lend unto the Lord, as long as he lives." Now that took lots of faith on her part, for conditions in the Tabernacle were rather degenerate. In spite of that, Samuel grew up and served Eli in this holy place where the Ark of the Covenant resided. She did not forget him but each year brought him a new robe, made by her own hands, and he knew who his mother was. Later she bore three sons and two daughters.

Samuel grew up in the service of the Lord. When Samuel was spoken to directly by the Lord, Eli knew that he was chosen for great work. He eventually became a great prophet to the Israelites. He anointed their first king, Saul, and their second king, David. And Solomon, the son of David, became the great and wise builder of the Temple. Samuel listened to God, then spoke and acted. A great prophet and leader.

Hannah, it seems to me, is one of the greatest examples of the effectiveness of prayer. So let us learn from her.

Of what value is prayer? you may be asking. Why should we pray? Is God really waiting out there somewhere, listening and ready to answer our prayers with "Yeah, Yeah"? Is all of this a figment of our imagination? Is there really a Power that is greater than the sum of all its parts?

Prayer is getting in contact with, becoming aware of, and vibrating with a Concept higher than ourselves. Prayer is based on faith that some Being is listening and will answer. It is based on faith, and the amount of faith makes all the difference in our dependence on it and the answers we get through it. If we pray believing that we will receive, it is most effective.

Years ago we may have said our "Now I lay me down to sleep" and, if our family life was so organized, gathered around the table for our meals and listened to the blessing of the food. We might not have understood either, but somehow we felt right doing it.

Many years may pass after we are grown before we remember prayer and use it again as a means of quieting our fears, asking for something, pleading that we have success. Many of us finally come to prayer as a last resort when all in the outer has failed.

Let us understand why Hannah prayed. In the first place, she was married to a religious man who led his wives and children to worship and sacrifice to the Lord. She was living in a home where prayer and worship were accepted as necessary. Her prayer reflected this.

When Hannah found that she was barren and Peninnah bore children, she acted as most of us would. She reacted to Peninnah's words of derision and criticism in tears, refusing to eat. And her depression upset her husband.

After years of this, she was driven in desperation to a prayer that most of us could not make. She was deeply distressed; she prayed; she wept. Her prayer was humble: she acclaimed God as her provider, she admitted her affliction, and she asked for that for which her heart longed—a son. But she promised to give him to the Lord's service and she dedicated him to the Spirit. She prayed from her heart, in a whisper, privately. She was consumed by her prayer. She told Eli that she was "pouring out her soul before the Lord." When she was finished, she was at ease, with no more anger or anxiety. Prayer cleanses the thoughts.

Often we utter words that have no meaning or feeling behind them. They are an exercise in speaking from the mind without the feeling. They are often futile, although mantras seem to be effective for those who believe in them. But they are not this kind of prayer. Many of us repeat the Lord's Prayer over and over without taking it into our own consciousness and understanding.

Hannah's prayer was from the heart, laden with emotion—and she had results. But we must not forget that she promised to give her son to the Lord's service. Now this is what makes her prayer important to us.

When we pray, it is usually for ourselves or someone else. When we pray for forgiveness, we forget that we must forgive ourselves and others as God forgives us. And often we forget to give thanks.

Hannah's prayer was based on deep faith. She was not going through an exercise; she meant what she said. She would bring her son to the Tabernacle to serve God. What unselfish love she exemplified! Not only for God, but for her son—because she knew that this son, if given to her, would come as a result of her prayer and would be special.

Sometimes we pray without full faith. We are not even certain there is a God to pray to. We live our lives based on human choices and strength, we think, until one day we face a circumstance in our life over which we seem to have no control. Then we *pray;* and we learn that God is there and has been all the time. This prayer is effective. The answer may not come immediately or the way we expect, but it will come. Something in our mind moves something in the Heart of God, and we are answered. Then our faith starts to birth, and from there we pray, believe, worship, and thank God. And our faith grows.

Prayer is most important to our spiritual growth when we first start out. It may be asking, it may be praising, it may be confessing, it may be thanking. Later we will use the prayer of dedication to God's will and wait for our direction from our inner Christ through meditation.

Sometimes we are told that there is no need for prayer. But prayer releases our concern, and we are then free from the negative emotions that may be blocking our thoughts and feelings from expressing in a creative way so as to overcome our problems. Hannah conceived after she prayed and promised her son to the service of the Lord. Her prayer freed her to conceive.

At a certain point on our path, all that we get through prayer should be dedicated to God, else it will not bring us the blessing we need. It is for Him that we live. However, I am not suggesting that we "make a deal" with God when we pray. But I do believe that our prayer should be released and that we should realize that the answer may be no. Prayers that are deep and heartfelt are answered. But the answer may be something other than what we ask for.

As we grow in consciousness, we shall continue to pray, but our prayers will become more of praise and gratitude, for eventually we shall be centered in the Will of God and so shall not need to ask for anything. All will be provided us for our good. And when the crises come, we will turn quietly to our Center and say, "Peace; be still," as did Jesus when he quieted the storm. Then the guidance will come for our need. At-one-ment will prevail, and we shall be healed and so experience the highest and the best.

If we are serious about our path, we shall eventually be guided to more meditation than prayer. We will learn to turn within, quiet our thoughts, relax in full faith, and wait for the experience of knowing our Christ. The further along we go on this path, the more easily will peace, prosperity, love, right relationships, and "effortless success" come to us. We may still have challenges for the growth and development of our consciousness, but we *know* where peace and love are. We do not have to speak. We just know it.

After Hannah dedicated Samuel to God, she sang the Song of Hannah—a beautiful prayer and a model for us. It also has deeper meaning than meets the eye.

Esoteric: FROM THE CROSS TO THE LADDER OF ASCENSION

From the beginning of the Bible to the end, motherhood is treated as a high estate of womanhood. Eve was the great mother of all mankind, so Genesis says. Mary was the mother of the Spirit force that cleansed the earth and continues to lift it up. Jesus was his name. And the Sun Woman of Revelation is the mother in all of us. Men and women have the potential for being mothers, for the feminine principle abides in all.

Hannah, our sacrificing mother, is our model, for she gave to the Lord that which came from her mothering. Peninnah gave to her husband, the earth-plane husband, the results of her motherhood. The feminine principle can be used for generation or *regen*eration.

Mothers should be honored. On them has depended the evolution of the race of mankind, for it is through the feminine of love and wisdom that we have made our progress. Only through these have we been able to lift up our hands to God and give Him the results of our responsibilities as mothers. The masculine is of the physical, of the intellect, of the strength of the body. The feminine is of the feelings, of the intuitive, of the caring and nurturing. It is love.

As a mother, I have experienced the joy and the pain of the greatest vocation on earth. As a mother, I have grieved for the loss of my son in a war the results of which continue to plague us. As a mother, I lacked detached love for my children, the non-possessive love, until I grew spiritually. I would not have missed the joy of motherhood for anything. But there is something greater.

This story has deep, deep meanings, and I will give you a few of these insights.

The feminine principle of creation is just now being lifted up to stand straight and tall with the masculine principle. These two pillars have for years been in the form of a cross, with the crossbeam the feminine and the upright the masculine. The feminine was supported by the masculine. Each of us has been crucified on this cross, for the inequality of the sexes has been abnormal and has made the woman dependent on the man, with the man losing his freedom by having to support the woman. As these pillars are set in parallel position, a ladder is formed, and our experiences, the new crossbeams, will take us higher and higher.

Motherhood is our example, but motherhood in order to have children to give to this world—to slave, to work by the sweat of the brow, to produce still more children—is not our highest responsibility. Our responsibility is to give unto the Lord the results of our love and wisdom. That is true motherhood, and it can be experienced by man also.

Peninnah had many children and received many portions from Elkanah. This means that the feminine nature can be used for mothering many children. Elkanah rewarded her richly. He gave more of his divine energy to her. This is happening to many men and women today. They do not know any other path. They are praised for having a fine family to give to the world. Having children for some is their reason for living and is right for them. These close-knit families are often the envy of many.

However, as woman stood up straight, she realized that she had something else to express besides being a body to produce babies and rear them into adulthood. And so with birth control, man could still express his sexual cravings but would not need to give his life to supporting the result. And woman began expressing her masculine as well as feminine nature in other directions. This has caused great confusion in our society, and we are seeing the results. The problem is that the use of the divine energy for sexual pleasure and for material pursuits is not enough to lift us up in spiritual evolution.

Hannah, whose portion was small, realized that she must give birth to something besides children to help till the fields. The divine energy must produce something for the Lord. And so she went to a high spiritual place, she spoke to God, she was humble.

She vowed to sacrifice her son to the Lord's work. That which she brought forth was for a high spiritual purpose, and Samuel was born. This high spiritual consciousness became the leader of many.

We, too, can follow Hannah. We, too, can be mothers to children devoted to the Lord's work. But these are not children of the body. These are children of the Inner. The feminine principle is the same as the Christ principle, which abides within and can guide our lives if we open to it.

The deep meaning of Hannah's gift is that she gave her most precious possession to the Lord. She continued to give it attention and love as she clothed it with garments made by herself. But the spirit, the divine energy, was freed to do God's work, to be God's instrument.

We need to realize that if we have fewer children, fewer earthly obligations and responsibilities, the energy and time saved should be devoted to our regeneration and being of spiritual service to others. To put this saved energy into sensual pleasure and attachment to the physical will not bring that for which we long—a son to dedicate to the Lord.

It is our choice. Do we choose to use our divine energy to be mothers, to generate? Or do we choose to use it for regeneration of the Inner? Perhaps in this life we must continue on our course of caring for our children in the outer. Perhaps in another life we will concentrate on the Inner. *But we can do both now if we are dedicated to our Lord.*

The "good life" is not living an earth-attached life. The "good life" is described in Hannah's song. It is a life of gratitude to God for strength and love, thanksgiving for our salvation, which comes through devoting our spiritual offspring to God. Realizing that God is all and central to our life will bring rewards for our good deeds and the completion of our destiny.

We are the faith-full ones when we raise the feminine principle of Love and Wisdom to an upright position of service to our Lord. Then pure Light will be our way, and physical might will not prevail—but "He shall exalt the might of his anointed" (I Sam. 2:10).

15

Michal

(I Samuel 18:20–29, 19:11–19, 25:44;
II Samuel 3:14–16, 6:12–23)

She Worshipped Gods

In speaking of Michal, the first wife of David, who became king of the people of Israel, we must necessarily get some background about David. His story fills many chapters of the Old Testament. I will touch on but a few incidents in it.

Samuel, the prophet, anointed David as king when he was a boy, through direction from God. Saul, the king, admired David, but blew hot and cold about him, for he feared him. David played his harp and soothed Saul when he was in an insane frenzy. David was a dear friend to Jonathan, Saul's son. Michal, Saul's daughter and sister to Jonathan, loved David.

Saul promised David that he could have Michal to wife if he would bring him the foreskins of 100 Philistines. He did not think David could do it. But David brought him 200. David felt proud that he would be the king's son-in-law. The people loved him.

However, when Saul was in one of his angry fits, he planned to send his servants to David and kill him. "He was afraid of him because the Lord was with him but had departed from Saul" (I Sam. 18:12). David's wife, Michal, heard about her father's plans and helped David escape. Then, when Saul sent for him, she told him that David was sick. He said to bring him in his bed. She put one of her gods in the bed with goat's hair at its head. Saul was beside himself when he discovered that David had escaped. Later Saul gave Michal to Phalti, who lived in Gallim, as his wife.

Many years passed. David had six wives while he served as king at Hebron for seven and a half years before going to Jerusalem. When David returned to Jerusalem, he demanded that Michal return to him, and he took her away from her husband, Phalti, who wept when she left. She no doubt resented being taken from her husband.

David built a special tabernacle for the Ark of the Covenant in Jerusalem. It had been housed in Kiriath-jearim for some time after the Philistines returned it. He was so ecstatic over its return that he danced in the streets covered only by a linen ephod, a garment worn on holy occasions. When he arrived home, Michal rebuked him for dancing half naked before the maidens. "She despised him in her heart" (II Sam. 6:16). David told her, "It was before the Lord [that I danced] . . . I will make merry before the Lord." The last verse of the chapter states that Michal was barren to the day of her death. She helped raise the sons of her sister, Morab. They were all killed later.

It is possible that Michal never accepted the one God of Israel as her God. Her father vacillated and had gods, figures of gods, that were worshipped. She also had such gods and she used one, called a *teraph,* to place in David's bed and send to her father after David escaped. This lack of belief in one God may have been conducive to many of her woes and griefs.

We who are reaching for a higher knowledge of the Divine, who have faith in God, are able to move through our conflicts, our challenges, our confusion in life and take each as a lesson for our consciousness development. We look to ourselves, determine what we have done to bring this event to us, do the cleansing of our conscious and unconscious mind, make restitution to one whom we may have grieved, ask forgiveness, and accept the blessing of consciousness growth. Consciousness is God, is the Eternal, and our aim is to become fully conscious of That.

But if we believe in idols, in gods of the world, in our own ego, we will not see these events as lessons but as something to resent and hate. Our desire is to hit back, to cry, to vent our anger. Since Michal never understood the great love David had for the Lord, the final blow came as a result of her scorn of his dancing in pure ecstasy before the Lord. She did not understand.

We will find those in our lives who do not understand our desire for consciousness development. Our prayers, our meditation, our study, our devotion to living a spiritual life will not be understood. But we, like David, may have to declare, "I will make merry before the Lord." Those in our life who do not understand will fade away and be barren (bereft of spiritual thoughts). Even within ourselves there can be thoughts that try to move us from our devotion. These, too, shall become less as our faith becomes more.

If we, like Michal, are having many upsets in our life, we can certainly understand her. She started out in love with David; had courage enough to help him escape her father's wrath; was taken from David and given to another by a demented father; had a father who committed suicide, and who for years pursued her first husband to kill him. Then she was snatched by David from a husband who loved her. She had no children, a great tragedy for women of that time, especially the queen. And so we can see why she would have ended up a bitter woman.

This can happen to us if we do not turn to God to worship and praise, to have faith in His goodness, to expect good to come into our life. If our thoughts are caught up in our problems and we do not learn from them, detach from them, we may bring additional challenges into our life. Finally, when we begin to believe in God's love, in our inner Christ, and make our choices after speaking with our Christ, our life becomes happy and joyous. The challenges we have are not so serious, for we are more detached from them. And we become the sweet, loving, happy woman we were meant to be.

It may take years of devotion to God before we reach the peace we seek, but it will come. Only believe!

Michal rejected God in her life—Saul, her father, did also. Both were unsure of themselves and filled with anger and resentment. Neither could possibly have productive, happy lives. God must be accepted by us if we are to benefit from His love.

David became a great king. He was not perfect, but his love was spread over many and he was able to unite the Israelites and make plans for the building of the Temple.

Michal, on the other hand, did not do any great work after she saved David from her murderous father. But her lessons will live on as we learn that centeredness in God is our need and our privilege. Our very life requires it.

Esoteric: INTUITION MISUSED BY PERSONAL WILL

David symbolizes love. Now all love is spiritual, but personal love seems to be based on the needs of our small self, while universal Love is based on love of God and love of neighbor as we love ourself. It comes from the spark of God that is within us, which I call *the Christ*. It is needed for our soul's growth. Most of us, like David, swing from personal love to divine Love. But his potential was to express, to live by, to act from spiritual love.

Michal symbolized intuition that can so easily be displaced by ego. Intuition is based on direction from our inner Center. It is called psychic or clairvoyant by some. It is knowing without knowing how you know. It is absolute. Michal showed this characteristic early in her marriage to David, when she helped him escape Saul, who symbolizes personal will based on unstable emotions.

Intuition and divine Love together can bring all good to us. Basing our choices, our life, on divine Love and being guided by our inner Christ can bring the best of everything to us. The ecstasy and joy of fulfillment of our spiritual needs will follow. But if intuition and love are besieged by our personal will, which is fed by unstable emotions, we may bring tragedy into our lives.

David was beset by many of his own personal desires. His position as king made him less loving. He demanded his rights. He acted on personal need, and not on spiritual *guidance,* when he made Michal come back to him.

Michal did not act from her intuition. Intuition does not function well when we demand it to guide us. Intuition is perfectly free from what we think. Intuition is over and above our thoughts; it comes from the Universal level and cannot come to us on demand. It comes to us when we free our mind of thoughts and wait in the silence. It can come to us freely when we ask a question of our inner Knowing and wait for the answer. It comes when we give our allegiance to the Wisdom that dwells within, and its direction is always right for us.

If, through personal need, we misuse our intuition, use it for personal gain or sensual pleasure, it will be barren. It will not produce the blessings we need. It will become silent. It will die.

Each name symbolizes a potential behind it. Often, the characters of the Bible did not live up to their names. This is for our teaching. Those who are centered on the Wisdom of God either overcome or fulfill the potential that their names indicate. Some names seem to foretell the life of the person. Saul—personal will based on unstable emotions—certainly did. Michal, symbolizing intuition, did not always act from that knowing.

For us there comes the teaching that when love and intuition are working together, they can bring forth many blessings. But personal love and negative thoughts and emotions will bring the opposite. We know our need—to follow the One God of the Universe and dwell in divine Love.

16

Abigail

(I Samuel 25)

A WIFE'S DECISION

Abigail was one of David's wives. She married him after she took food and drink to him and his men, and after her husband, Nabal, died. She gave him one son, Chileab.

For years David was in exile both from his home and from King Saul, who sought to kill him. He gathered some 600 followers and kept sheep, helping other shepherds protect their sheep from thieves and marauding animals. He had done this for Nabal's herds near the town of Carmel. He learned that Nabal, a very wealthy man, was having his sheep sheared. This was a time of festivity, and the custom was that the owner of the flock was particularly generous. Nomads often asked for and received food at this time under the "law of brotherhood."

David sent men to Nabal asking for food and pointing out that his men had helped protect Nabal's flocks. Nabal refused to send food. David was deeply angered. He told 400 of his men to strap on their swords and go kill all of Nabal's household, taking what they wanted.

Nabal was described as a churlish man. His wife, Abigail, is described as a beautiful woman of good understanding.

When Abigail heard that Nabal had refused David's request, she set to work to prepare food for his men. She took the food, without telling her husband, to David. When she met him on the mountain pass, she fell down before him and took responsibility for the affront. She told him that her husband was ill-natured and should not be regarded, and that she had not seen the young men who came with the request. She presented the food and pointed out that the Lord had sent her to restrain him from taking vengeance and thus having guilt. She asked forgiveness and prophesied that the Lord would protect him and help him fight his battles. His life would be preserved, she said, and the "Lord his God" would make him prince of Israel. She asked him to remember her when the Lord "had dealt well" with him.

He blessed her, thanked her, and told her to go in peace. There would be no reprisal.

She went home and, because her husband was drunk, waited until morning, when he was sober, to tell him about David and what she had done. Nabal had a stroke and died ten days later. When David heard about his death, he gave thanks to the Lord for avenging the insult he had received. He sent for and wooed Abigail. She became his wife.

Returning good for evil is a teaching of our Lord, Jesus Christ. He taught "Do not resist one who is evil. But if anyone strikes you on the right cheek, turn to him the other also," and "Love your enemies and pray for those who persecute you" (Matt. 5:39, 44).

Abigail seemed to be far ahead of her time religiously. The way of the Israelites had always been "If any harm follows, then you shall give life for life, eye for eye, tooth for tooth," etc. (Exod. 21:23, 24). She interceded so David would not carry out this law. She was beautiful, possessed of understanding and wisdom.

David was impulsive, afraid, immature. He was running from King Saul, his enemy, who would kill him on sight. He was short-tempered. This wise woman knew that unless she returned good for planned evil, he would attack the entire household, and David would carry the guilt of bloodshed. She was also a believer in the Lord God of Israel and, being of prophetess stature, was following the guidance of God. A prophetess foretells future events, which she did.

We as women can learn two important lessons from Abigail. One is that if our husband has acted in a churlish, selfish way and does not seem responsible for his actions (the servant said, "he is so ill-natured that one cannot speak to him"), we must act from the center of our being and divert the results of his choices if we can. The other is that returning good for evil—preventing the results of negative words and actions by offering their opposite—is our duty.

The first may be very hard for the old-fashioned wife who has been reared in a religion and family where the male is the authority. Despite the Church's insistence that God is our authority, it has imposed the male as the authority on earth. God can keep to His domain in Heaven, they seem to teach—we are not to be guided by Him; woman should see her husband as her authority! Of course, if the husband is centered in his Godward direction, all will be well. But if he is not, it would seem that we as women must go ahead and do what we know is right. Abigail was protecting her household and her husband. She was very courageous, taking the considerable chance that David could not be appeased and would kill her first. But she went because she knew her husband was wrong and she might adjust the wrong. And do not forget, she had wisdom that comes from God.

David, of course, was a very special man. He had been selected by God as the next king of the Israelites. She appealed to his better side, and he heard her with gratitude for keeping him from making a big mistake.

Can you imagine Abigail's feelings when she told Nabal of what she had done? Did he have apoplexy because of his anger at Abigail? Was she saved by the Lord from a life worse than death because she had defied her husband's orders? Or did he have a stroke over fear of what David might have done? There is no record that he was grateful to his wife.

I believe that when we do what is good, when we turn the other cheek, when we practice nonresistance and peace, we will be protected and our way made happy and glorious. As women, when we see what we must do to protect ourselves, our children, or our husband, we should do it and in prayer be guided by our God.

In a sense, Abigail was a forerunner of Jesus' teaching, for she replaced evil with good. To do this may be considered a weak choice by many. But it sometimes takes all the strength and courage one can muster to act. What a wonderful example Gandhi has been to the world! He practiced pacifism to the limit to defeat the great British empire. Sometimes nonresistance is our only, our best, choice.

In our personal relationships we may not reap the results of our negative actions as quickly as did Nabal. Nor do we reap the results of our positive so quickly as did Abigail. But have no doubt, each will receive justice.

Many of our retaliations to those who have affronted us are based on selfishness. When we have done another many good deeds only to receive indifference, active dislike, and negative words and actions in return, should we be oversensitive and resentful, harboring hurt feelings, we are displaying selfishness. It takes a well-advanced person to be selfless at such times. "Be not overcome by evil, but overcome evil with good" will divert our thoughts from selfishness, and we shall grow more selfless. And it takes self-control, love for our enemies, centeredness in God's Will, and courage to carry this out.

The route of unconditional Love and nonresistance brings us closer to our goal of Oneness. It starts on almost a rote basis of practice. With prayer, meditation, and loss of self-will or selfishness, it becomes automatic. And the peace that comes to us and others cannot be measured.

Abigail replaced evil with good. Abigail acted on what she knew was the right way. Abigail took a chance that retaliation from David and/or her husband might harm her. But she followed the Spirit. Her prophecy came true. She was handmaiden of the Lord. David said, "Blessed be the Lord, the God of Israel, who sent you this day to meet me" (I Sam. 25:32). He knew that she was guided. We will know when our inner Christ guides us.

Humility was Abigail's angel and so should it be for us. Unconditional Love and nonresistance come from a humble heart.

Esoteric: JOY AND LOVE BRING FREEDOM

In our step-by-step march to perfection, what are we really seeking? Is it not freedom? Does our soul not cry out to be free of the body, of the physical, of the material world? Does our soul not seek to fly away to a realm where there is no pain, no tears, no death? Do not we long for the kingdom of Heaven and in our searching make our life as close to that as possible? We need to be free, and how to achieve that is what the Bible characters teach us.

Freedom! How was it that Abigail was free? In that day of suppression of women, how could Abigail take it upon herself to

overcome the negative discord that Nabal had developed? How
can we as women of today best express our freedom? How can we
as children of the Most High develop that freedom from within
that so wants to express in our life? What did Abigail represent
that we need?

Many questions and few answers. But there are answers.

Freedom of spirit is the joy of the Lord. To free our spirit to
soar in the highest feeling of joy will bring us the freedom of
thoughts, words, and deeds. Abigail (joy) teaches us this.

When joy is married to unstable emotions which make us foolish,
selfish, vain, there is no freedom. But joy is so strong that it must
act and cannot do otherwise. For joy is of God. And when we
follow this joy, we will overcome our enslavement and be free.

Joy needs to serve Love, the very antithesis of unstable emotions.
When our unstable emotions (Nabal) refuse to do good, then joy
(Abigail) must take over. And joy recognizes that love (David)
must be served.

Sometimes our joy, in its exuberance, allows our negative emotions to control us. When this happens, we reject love. We do not
feed love. And love, when ignored and refused, may reverse
itself—and the opposite emotion of hate expresses. Then it is that
joy must be activated through prayer and meditation, and return
to love.

In the teaching of Thomas Troward we have these suggested
qualities of God: Joy, Beauty, Love, Life, Light, Power, and
Peace. Seven qualities, seven aspects of God. How limited is our
vocabulary to describe God!

Now out of our abundance should come service, giving, loving,
and protecting. But sometimes abundance brings just the opposite
if we are not centered in the Reality of God. Nabal was not centered; the senses and emotional imbalance had control. When this
happens to us, there is only one result: pain, accident, illness,
death. Our abundance comes from God and should go out to serve
others. Joy (Abigail) knew this, for joy can be complete only when
we give in love. Abigail lived at Carmel (abundance). Her joy
was full and running over. She had to share, to transform evil with
good.

We give attention to love (David). (Abigail took food and drink
to him.) We take to love the following: bread (Universal Sub-

stance), wine (vital energy), sheep (Life from the Spirit), raisins (food for the soul), figs (fruitfulness), wheat (the Christ within), barley (wisdom). We ride to meet love on the Path of Wisdom momentarily lost by David. And when joy and potential love (lost in anger and hate for the moment) meet, the joy of the Lord overcomes, and freedom is reached.

True freedom is based on the teaching of Jesus about the Christ. He said, "If therefore the Son makes you free, you shall be free indeed" (John 8:36). And: "You will know the truth, and the truth will make you free" (John 8:32). Paul said in the Galatian letter: "For freedom Christ has set us free; stand fast therefore, and do not submit again to a yoke of slavery" (Gal. 5:1).

Abigail stood free. Her way was open. She helped love regain its essence and do away with hate and anger. And joy is God. Only through God can we have freedom. Joy restored love and also overcame emotional distress. And then joy and Love married, and the ultimate of the Mystical Marriage occurred.

It is natural to want freedom. And if you as woman long for freedom and feel you are enslaved, your freedom will come, true freedom, if you base your choices on inner Guidance. Freedom for the sake of license will keep you enslaved. But freedom based on the Law of Liberty will be true freedom.

Our soul has wings. The Egyptian symbol of the winged disk and the two serpents indicates early realization of this truth. The disk or circle (soul) with wings is a common symbol all over the world. In Nepal, a Buddhist state, I saw it depicted on a hotel desk. It is our path to free it. We, individually, can allow it to fly through our God-given consciousness. It is marriage with Love that finally sets it free.

17

Bathsheba

(II Samuel 11, 12; I Kings 1, 2)

OVERCOMING KARMIC SUFFERING

We have been presenting David as love and have connected love with intuition and joy through his wives, Michal and Abigail. Now, through Bathsheba, he will be connected to physical fulfillment. Together they will bring forth wisdom, their son Solomon.

David is the masculine principle of love that vacillates between impersonal and personal love. And what a difference there is between these two! How well we learn to express Universal Love or impersonal Love is a measure of where we are on the Path. God loves with an impersonal Love. This Love cannot be lost once gained. Personal love goes and comes. Let us explain this better through the story of Bathsheba and David.

Bathsheba, a beautiful young woman, was married to one of David's generals, Uriah. David now had his palace in Jerusalem, the city of peace. He was walking one evening on the roof of his palace when he looked over to a neighboring rooftop and saw Bathsheba bathing. He immediately lusted for her. He sent for her; the king had to be obeyed. He took her to bed. In a few weeks, she sent word that she was pregnant.

After summoning him from the battlefield, David tried to get her husband to go home and sleep with her. He refused to go. So David arranged to have him killed in battle. Then he married Bathsheba.

Nathan, the prophet, came to David and berated him, telling him that the child would die and that he would have much suffering from those of his own household. This came true. David realized the extent of his guilt. When the baby became ill, David fasted, wept, and prayed during the seven-day illness. When the baby died, he rose from his sorrow, washed and anointed himself, and worshiped in the house of the Lord. He had hoped that the child would live and had prayed for it, but when the child died, he accepted that it was gone and could not be brought back.

Bathsheba had four other sons, among whom was Solomon, who followed David as king. Bathsheba is not mentioned again until David is very old and sick, and Adonijah, his fourth son, tries to usurp the throne. Bathsheba was alerted by Nathan, the prophet, who suggested she go and remind David, who was old and ill, that the throne had been promised to Solomon, her son. She told David. Nathan followed her to corroborate her story, and David had Solomon anointed as king, whereupon he assumed his father's throne. Adonijah was deposed.

Later Adonijah came to Bathsheba and asked her to plead with Solomon to allow him to marry a young concubine of King David's. She agreed, and when she went in to King Solomon, he greeted her lovingly and had a chair brought for her to be seated at his right. But the king refused the request, for he remembered an old Semitic custom that the man who inherited the women of the dead king was his successor. For this duplicity, Solomon had Adonijah executed.

Here we have lust, adultery, murder, suffering as a result of personal love, the repentance of David, the birth of a son who became a great king and temple-builder; and Bathsheba, who had not been able to say nay to the king's demand that she come to his bed and thus suffered with him. But she became the respected and beloved queen and helped put Wisdom, Solomon, on the throne. She was physically complete, and physical perfection—beauty—is very close to Wisdom. As we become more conscious of the Wisdom that is God, our bodies change and become more perfect; and the beauty from within—the Light—shines through the physical and the mental. Real beauty comes from within.

Bathsheba as a woman in Old Testament times is more a shadow figure than a leading character. Only when she arranged for Solomon to become king was she able to show her true worth. She suffered as she lost her first husband. She suffered with David as they lost their first child. We see that she developed courage and was a greater woman as she grew older. She was a blessing to her husband. She was still not perfect, but she had advanced immeasurably.

Bathsheba continued to obey David and rose in her consciousness growth. What caused them both to grow in higher consciousness? Of course, their devotion to the One God, and also the suffering they experienced. For personal love must give way to love of God and our fellowman in Universal Love.

I do not agree that we must suffer to become more holy. The idea that we must "pick up our cross" may be necessary in the early part of our spiritual trek, when we have already become embroiled in the sensual desires of the world. To get out of the predicaments we have gotten ourselves into, we suffer. Letting go of the encrustations of years of living from sensual pleasure and attachment to earth consciousness and ego hurts. So it was for Bathsheba and David. They had to pay the price for their choices. When they were forgiven, they had four other sons.

We need to cleanse our conscious and unconscious mind. Some suffering will be mental, some physical, some emotional. Finally, however, as our consciousness of spiritual essence becomes greater, we are forgiven, and we do not have to suffer the karma of our past. Centeredness on the Will of God and having faith in His Love overcomes all karma.

We are supposed to enjoy life. What beauty lies around us to enjoy, provided by the energy, the Love, of God! By the nature of the race consciousness of mankind, however, we will be put in places of suffering. But this state of affairs can be alleviated when we recognize that all that happens to us is for our spiritual growth. Then we understand and do not hurt so much. We cheerfully do what needs to be done, learn what we need to, and leave the rest in God's care and keeping. We are meant to be happy. And as we go through our time of repentance, we find at-one-ment.

Repentance in the metaphysical sense is not groveling in guilt and regret. True repentance is turning from a belief in error and sin and keeping our attention on God and what is Truth. It is a reversal of mind from the negative in our life to the positive. To repent, we turn from mortal thought to thought directed to the Highest Good. Turning from past error and putting our attention on the Good is true repentance.

Bathsheba and David did not continually berate themselves. Bathsheba learned forgiveness as she tried to help Adonijah. She was loved and respected by her son Solomon who seated her on a throne on the same level as his own. Nathan, the prophet, thought highly of her and helped her intercede on behalf of Solomon. Yes, she grew through suffering. She expressed impersonal Love in forgiveness, loyalty, following the prophet's advice, and in bearing Solomon, the peaceful and wise.

If you read the entire account of David, you will see how his personal love was sometimes his downfall. But he also loved with the Highest Love. Impersonal Love and Wisdom are the same. Both are attributes of God.

So from adultery and murder this royal couple grew in awareness of the Divine, and Bathsheba went down in history as the mother of a great king. David had the vision of the great temple to be built in Jerusalem and gathered the material for the building of it. Then Solomon built it. They both added immeasurably to the people of Israel. We, too, can overcome our past, and we may suffer in order to be cleansed.

Esoteric: BEAUTY AND LOVE BRING FORTH WISDOM

As we look at the teaching of this account for our spiritual growth, we must realize that David and Bathsheba did not demonstrate the highest consciousness level. It is true that Bathsheba symbolized feminine beauty. *Sheba* means seven, and seven is physical completion. With David symbolizing love, and Uriah, Bathsheba's husband, symbolizing light, we can see how David's having the light killed because of his lust may be our story too. When we kill the light, we suffer and lose other light (the child's death). The birth of Solomon shows that David's life was changed. Wisdom is sometimes learned through suffering, and Universal Love is contained in Wisdom.

When we have Wisdom, we are very close to spiritual completion. However, repentance is necessary before Wisdom comes. Repentance is an admission to God of our past mistakes, our separation from God. We all need to repent.

Wisdom is understanding, intuition, pure knowing, and is everywhere as pure mind. Wisdom is God. Wisdom, according to Jesus, is hearing the Word of God and acting on it. Wisdom is love and intellect in balance. True Wisdom is understanding why we are on earth, and that comes from many hard knocks for some of us.

Wisdom also comes as we study the words and ideas of those who came before us. The Bible has much Wisdom in it. We need to study it more and more. "Listen to advice and accept instruction that you may gain wisdom for the future" (Prov. 19:20). We also read: "Happy is the man who finds wisdom and the man who gets understanding, for the gain from it is better than gain from silver and its profit better than gold" (Prov. 3:13, 14).

Do not be deceived: Wisdom does not come by reading books, by training the mind. Wisdom is above logic and reasoning. It is the voice of God, the Word of God.

When we have Wisdom, we are close to our goal but still have to know with the mystic St. John of the Cross that "The soul, when it shall have driven away from itself all that is contrary to the divine will, becomes transformed in God by love."

When we have feminine beauty with lust, we will probably bring suffering and sorrow although at first it seems pure pleasure. When feminine beauty and love come together their offspring is Wisdom (Solomon), and high ideas of Truth (Shimea), and potential for turning from faith (Shobab), and spiritual power and understanding (Nathan). These four sons are the result. Three are uplifting. And the greatest result is Wisdom.

David had other wives and concubines and many children. We have learned that he was very much like us. He was human and divine. He showed one side and the other. His crowning achievement was Solomon, who built the Temple which symbolizes the spiritual body. We too can build our Temple as we love the Light and let it shine into our lives.

And Bathsheba, his wife, was an important part of all of this. We must give her credit for mothering that which mankind has searched for eternally, Wisdom.

18

Two Mothers of Solomon's Time

(I Kings 3:16-27)

"Give Her the Living Child": Abortion

This legend from the Old Testament has long lived in the minds of Christians and Jews as a demonstration of the wonderful wisdom of Solomon. It has probably been used as an example of great wisdom in churches and church schools more often than any other verses in the Bible. It strikes a very deep note in the psyche of the masses, for it deals with motherhood and babies. It demonstrates, so we have been taught, the good mother and the bad. It demonstrates also the wisdom of the male and the love of a mother for her child, as well as the selfish mother and her choice. So we have a number of routes to follow in understanding what this has to do with us as mothers, as women, as sojourners on our Path.

Briefly, the story is that two harlots came to Solomon (the common people had more ready access to the king in those days) to settle a dispute over who was the mother of a particular baby. It seems that these two women lived together and each had a baby. One woman smothered her baby accidentally while she slept. She arose and placed the dead baby in bed with the other woman and took the live baby for her own. When the second mother awoke, she realized that the dead baby was not hers—and the argument ensued. They came to the wise king for a decision. He ordered a sword to be brought in order to cut the live baby in two. The real mother protested and relinquished the baby when it was evident that the other woman was quite willing to see the king go ahead and divide it: "It shall be neither mine or yours." Thereupon the king knew who the real mother was and ordered the child restored to the woman who had urged him to give the child to the other woman rather than kill it.

In our present "psychological" age, the role of motherhood has been dethroned, and mothers have been blamed for everything that goes wrong in an individual's life. Freudian psychology was chiefly responsible for blaming our personality ills on the mother. The father, according to Freud, had much less effect on the child. For years the idea of "blaming the mother" has reigned supreme, and the religious teaching of Western Christianity, with its male God, lent support to this concept.

More and more we are realizing that the balance of masculine and feminine in a child requires the involvement of both father and mother, or surrogate parents, in the rearing of that child. And it is no longer popular to blame mothers for all the ills of the world. We are moving toward a more balanced concept of parenting when we realize that what each individual becomes is in his/her own control, and that blaming the mother, God, or the government only leads to a dead end.

Not all women are the perfect, loving, caring, nurturing type, however. And more and more, as women seek equality with men at home and in the marketplace, we shall see more confusion over the mother role. Many fathers are developing their mothering side and filling in the gap.

These two Bible women demonstrate two very different types of mother. In the second woman, we see a demonstration of real love for her child when she protests the dividing of it. The first woman demonstrates another side of motherhood and, out of her own need to have a child, is willing to use dishonest means, separating a child from its real mother, in order to satisfy her small self. Unfortunately, there are many mothers who correspond to this mothering model. These are the mothers who have not matured into the role of the loving mother. They have a child to fulfill their own needs only, without consideration for the child's needs. These mothers become very controlling, domineering, punishing, and believe that the child belongs to them and not to itself.

As long as mothers do not realize that their children are not owned by them but belong to God, to themselves, and to society, they will cling to them to fulfill their emotional—and sometimes physical—needs. This inevitably brings grief to them as well as to their spouses and children. At some point we must realize that children are their own person, they have a unique soul, and their own journey. If we can let go gracefully as they mature into adulthood, all will be well. If we cling too long, we are bound to reap grief.

The second woman, to whom Solomon gave the child, was willing to let go of the child rather than have it killed. In our case, it is more like psychological death. Out of her pure love she let go of the child; and even though she would grieve, she knew that it had the right to life.

The abortion issue is rampant today, and the courts have made laws that give a mother the right to have her pregnancy terminated by abortion. Allowing the woman to make this decision herself is a real switch from control of such a decision by the men of our society. It is really a very personal decision. For some, abortion is the same as murder. For others, if the fetus is aborted before a certain date, then it is only a thing and not a living human being. I suspect this whole issue is connected to the coming balance or equality between men and women. In one sense, it gives the mother precedence over the father to make the decision.

Perhaps our biblical story could give us pause in our haste to make shallow decisions about this important issue. The one mother said, "Kill the child." The other said, "Save the child and give it to the adoptive mother." Consideration against abortion carries the option of bringing the fetus to full term, birthing the child, and either raising it or giving it up for adoption. The other choice, abortion, may cause a deep feeling of guilt within the mother, a regret for losing the child, and a possibility of sterility as the guilt memories affect the functioning of the body. So many young teenage girls are having abortions, and I know from experience in counseling some of them that it is very difficult to rid themselves of a feeling of guilt.

The issue is a moral one, in my opinion. The moral issue begins at the time of intercourse, many times in a fit of passion, without consideration of the potential consequences. That is immaturity, and it usually carries the pall of secrecy, often producing a condition of shame and fear. The man, in most cases, is free from the results. The woman carries the greater moral responsibility and pain. And she it is who must make the decision what to do.

The issue of when life begins in the womb has not been settled by scientific methods. Each one of us knows the answer for herself. I believe that life begins at conception. The spirit or soul gathers to it the physical body that it will use in expressing in this lifetime.

When the body is killed, the soul will reincarnate another time. If this is true, is it not taking a life when the soul and body are together in the womb? A deep question for many. This problem has been addressed by many religions. However, the spiritual aspect is seldom addressed by the courts. It should be considered by each of us personally.

If a woman has had an abortion and feels some guilt, she should not carry these feelings around for life. Through self-forgiveness, prayer, asking pardon of the child and of God, one can leave this heavy burden behind. Centeredness in God's Will can release her.

Back to our biblical account. Wisdom in the form of Solomon directed the killing of this baby in order to test the mothers. Wisdom did not dictate killing to get rid of the baby, and I doubt if he would have carried out the order. Wisdom, or understanding, was given to Solomon by God. He was in touch with Him. That is where Wisdom resides, and what a woman needs before she makes a decision about abortion is a deep seeking for God's answer. Going to her inner Center in meditation will direct her in the right path. Jesus said, "My Father is working still, and I am working" (John 5:17). Believe this and turn to His Wisdom. Appeal directly to your heart, as Solomon did, and get truth quickly. What we feel and what we think are equally important.

Esoteric: DOUBLE-MINDEDNESS TO ONENESS

"For those who live according to the flesh set their minds on things of the flesh, but those who live according to the Spirit set their minds on things of the Spirit" (Rom. 8:5).

This scripture is the setting for the spiritual growth that we are seeking. For we all carry within us two minds until we are one-pointed in "You shall love the Lord your God with all your heart, and with all your soul, and with all your mind" (Matt. 22:37).

We bring to birth each day, each moment, duality of thought. The more often this happens, the more confused we become and the more in chaos our lives become. Because we are uncomfortable, without peace, we may choose to think in one way and then make our decision on quite the opposite foundation. We can live this way for a while, but eventually we turn to one set of moral decisions or another. Our choice will make the direction of our life.

Let me see if I can give you an illustration.

I was just an average person trying to work my way out of delusion, which had caught me up when I was very young. I had divorced, gained two degrees, had a secure job, and thought I was living the good life. But my life had very little spiritual foundation.

My only son enlisted in the army during the Vietnam war. Six months later he was in Vietnam as a foot soldier. Six months after that an Army messenger was knocking at my door with the devastating news: he had lost his physical life. Just two nights before I had had a beautiful precognitive dream that I now realized had been to prepare me for the message. That dream and the grace of God carried me through the first grief-stricken days.

Many who came to me expressed bitterness and anger that this fine young man had lost his life in a meaningless war. I too felt the same at times. But I knew through the grace of God that to hate, to be angry, would not bring him back. So I wondered what would make meaning out of his death.

I knew that I had never honestly come to grips with my own belief in spiritual matters. So I started my search, not knowing where it would lead, but knowing it was the right direction. It was exciting, satisfying, and I felt good about it. My spiritual journey would take a book to tell, but the Path led to my writing one book and publishing it, then writing this book. I feel I am doing what I was born to do. So the death of my son has brought blessings to me as well as many others. The glory of it is that I did not know where I was going or how I would get there, but I knew God Is and I AM. That made all the difference.

And yet I have this dichotomy of decision, of separation for my direction at times—but less and less as I become one-pointed in His Will.

Let us connect this double-mindedness with our story.

Two harlots had a child each. We are harlots in the sense that our mind is so often focused on the physical rather than the spiritual. Our mind is occupied by duality. And our thoughts, which are birthed, are doubled-minded.

Sometimes when we appear to be awake, though asleep, we smother a thought that is good. Sometimes we use denial and get rid of a thought that is negative. Thoughts of lack, of need, of illness, of tragedy need to be transformed, not smothered. Then we look around for another thought to fill the vacancy, and we may borrow from another person his or her thought and claim it for our own. Or we remember a positive thought and fill the vacancy. But it doesn't satisfy us. We are not at peace. There is a quarrel going on within us. Thinking has not satisfied our need.

If we turn within to the Wisdom of God to settle the matter, we shall be satisfied. If we turn toward a more selfish, less spiritual source, we shall continue to be confused and make the wrong choice. For when we are really uncertain whether we have made the right choice, we haven't.

When we turn toward God in prayer and have decided we will flow in His Will, we have started the healing. But if God's Will is something opposite to our intellectual choices, we can either say from our selfishness, "Go ahead and kill the idea, for I do not want it any more," or we can say, "I can transform this idea, this experience, into something good. Let it live. Let the idea mature even though I may gain nothing from it. It must live." Then we are of one mind.

Is this too abstract for you? Well, just hang on to the idea and I think you will find it demonstrated in your life.

The only way out of our dilemma is through reliance on the Spirit to settle all our problems, our tragedies, our unhappiness. We cannot continue to give more obeisance to the flesh, to sense desires, than we do to Spirit-centered desires. Desires of the flesh have their place but have been condemned by all religions; they frequently lead to destruction. Desires of the Spirit lead to perfection and joy.

So be of one mind, steadfastly following the lead of your inner Guide, and the thoughts that are born to you will survive—and all will be right in your world.

Wisdom will guide you. Jesus said, "In the world you have tribulation, but be of good cheer, I have overcome the world" (John 16:33). And he said we could do what he did and more, for he was here to help us. Rely on Wisdom and live!

19

The Queen of Sheba

(I Kings 10:1-13; II Chronicles 9:1-12; Matt. 12:42;
Luke 11:31; Song of Solomon)

RELATIONSHIPS BETWEEN MEN AND WOMEN

The reference to the Queen of Sheba is contained in thirteen verses of Chapter 10 of I Kings and twelve verses of Chapter 9 of II Chronicles, and is mentioned by Jesus; it is a story or legend that has captured the attention of most people who have read or heard it. And I think the attention it has been given is unique. I wonder why this account has so captured the imagination and thought of so many. It is not an unusual story—a story that depicts the meeting of a very rich queen with a very wise and rich king. So then why? What is in the archetype of our own unconscious that responds to this story? Let us find some answers.

This account, like the myths that have followed mankind through the ages, has a deep esoteric truth as well as a truth that can help us understand our own path to perfection.

According to the account, the Queen of Sheba had heard about Solomon and his wisdom, his fame, concerning the name of the Lord. She wanted to test him with "hard questions." She came from a great distance; some legends report that it took her two to three years to get to Jerusalem, where Solomon reigned. She brought much wealth with her, a huge retinue, and many gifts for Solomon.

She met Solomon and asked him many questions, and "Solomon answered all her questions; there was nothing hidden from the king which he could not explain to her." After she had heard his answers, observed his house, and seen his offerings in the Temple, "she was breathless and amazed."*

*Good News Bible.

Her response to the king indicated her conviction that he was indeed wise. She said that she had to come see for herself if the reports she had heard about him were true, and she mentions the indications of this Truth in his outer circumstances. Then she declared that his God should be blessed who had "delighted in you and set you on the throne of Israel." She gave him great gifts; he gave her whatever she desired; and she returned to her own land.

Solomon was wise from the Spirit and in his intellect. His name means name of God. He was at a high point of power, intellect, judgment, reasoning, understanding. God had given him wealth and peace also, since Wisdom brings these. One writer says his name means: *Sol* ("light"), *o* ("glory"), *mon* ("truth") and that this name predicted his path—light, glory, truth.

We usually look to men to have these characteristics, i.e. reasoning, judgment, understanding. In fact, as women we are searching for men who personify the perfection of these masculine qualities, for we know that as women we need this steadiness of the logical reasoning mind to balance our emotions. However, we have these characteristics also but may not have activated them. Education and responsibility in careers have released them for many women.

So often we expect more than our chosen mates can give. We come to them expecting that our needs will be met, and instead we may find them not having many of these characteristics that we have dreamed about. Disappointment then can lead us on or defeat us. The disappointment may lead us to helping men exemplify more of these characteristics and thus we lift them and ourselves higher. Or we may try, be unsuccessful, and have to move on to another experience. But we should not be too hasty in moving on. Perhaps the years it takes to help them raise their consciousness are necessary for our own path. The queen traveled years over a hot desert with many camels and people to reach Solomon. And our path can lead us to the "name of God" which is our inner awareness of Divinity if we patiently continue on.

We as women may bring to a relationship the qualities that the man is seeking. These qualities may be conducive to his happiness and they may not. He may not be ready for them. We bring intuitive wisdom, which supersedes intellectual wisdom. If the man allows a partnership that balances his reasoning with intuition, it can be a win-win experience. Sometimes we as women have to

be as inquisitive as Sheba in order to bring to the man the importance of intuition in his life. If he is truly wise, he will be able to
answer his mate's questions and hide nothing from her. This is true
communication.

It was Leo Buscaglia who, in his book *Loving Each Other,*
reported on a research project which indicated that communication
between people, especially married people, was at the top of the
qualities that enhanced a relationship and continued growth in
love. The second was affection, the third compassion and forgiveness. In this legend we have demonstrated communication, affection, compassion. All of these are spiritual qualities that need
expression and acceptance if we are to love in the highest sense.

Solomon and Sheba talked, listened, and responded. Their
affection was demonstrated in the gifts they gave to each other.
She gave gold (truth at the highest level), camels (material gifts),
and spices (things of the Spirit or immortality). Solomon gave
Sheba "all that she desired, whatever she asked besides what was
given her by the bounty of King Solomon." Now her accepting
these gifts means that his high spiritual consciousness gave her
spiritual gifts and she returned home "blessing the Lord your
God," which may mean she accepted the belief in the One God,
for "she was breathless and amazed." This indicates deep humility
based on a new understanding. Sheba came from a country that
worshiped "heathen" gods. Returning home is coming to rest.
Perhaps she returned with a God that gave her that. Sheba symbolizes "return to original state."

Notice also her praise of Solomon. This is one of the qualities
we need to express more and more in our loving relationships.
Men need this support from their wives openly expressed. It is
appreciation and praise of God and of those closest to us on a
daily basis that overcomes many of the tensions that may arise
in our outer activities.

We know that man and woman need each other in so many
ways besides the sexual. Our disappointment in the sexual is often
based on our disappointment in those areas of the relationship
that really count. The sexual adjustment becomes a glorious experience when we handle the other areas of the relationship in an
open manner: communication, affection, compassion, forgiveness,
honesty, patience, freedom, dependability, acceptance. Many of

these are needed first, depending on the needs of the individuals, before the sexual needs can be fully met. How odd that we in this age are inclined to put the sex act first, before the relationship is established! But that will change.

So as women we need to realize that the knight in shining armor on the white horse that we are searching for may develop rust and creaking joints unless we bring to him the same characteristics we expect of him. We have more spiritual intuition, which he needs; and we need his logically measured knowledge. The two needs draw us together, and we advance on our Path of Holiness as we remove more and more barriers from the total meshing of the two personalities.

It is a tall order, and it may take a lifetime. The two must be committed and work at the task together openly and in harmony. The man has much to teach the woman. We must be open to that also. When we reach oneness with each other, we are closer to Oneness with God. And Oneness in Spirit brings the happiest relationships. In fact, Oneness in thought and desire for a deeper understanding of God's Truth is the only path to follow for a perfect relationship between a man and a woman.

Esoteric: THE MYSTICAL PATH

As we go into the hidden meaning of this legend, we need to look at The Song of Solomon, or the Song of Songs. Herein lies the clue to the deeper teaching.

On the surface, this great book seems to be a very confused account of a lover and the beloved, and so it is. But the surface meaning is for the profane, the ignorant. The deeper is for the pilgrim.

The Song of Songs is a cry of ecstasy from the mind of a human being attempting to describe the route of purification, of returning to the Godhead, and the final achievement of pure balance of duality in the Oneness of ecstasy.

Solomon, it is said by the esotericist, was one of the most highly advanced souls to rule over Israel, perhaps one of the most highly advanced in the annals of history. This description reminds us of Hermes, the ancient Egyptian who, like Solomon, had close contact with God and Wisdom, which means that he was well versed in mathematics, music, chemistry, philosophy, agriculture, astronomy, the arts, and poetry. Solomon was what we call a mystic, one who is centered in and guided by the Word of God. His meeting with the Queen of Sheba was symbolic of his reaching the high state of the Mystical Marriage.

It is difficult for those who are on the Path of Truth to understand the Mystical Way, for our aim at first is to have a better life in this world, i.e. health, prosperity, right relationships, things. The leap from the Path of Truth to the beginning of the Mystical Way may take years or possibly lifetimes, but when one decides to achieve unity with God, or at-one-ment, the focus is on spiritual Truth of the Inner. Following the Will of God is paramount. Then our experiences change, and we are aware that we have made a great step forward.

Many have already started on the Mystical Path in a former life. However, it may take years of living and many difficult experiences before one realizes that what one wants to be is a mystic. The dis-ease we feel, the depths to which we sink to find satisfaction for our unrest, our depression, may indicate how high we are really capable of going. Perhaps the alcoholic and the drug addict are attempting to avoid the Truth that the Soul is speaking. Perhaps dis-ease of the Soul causes their deep need to obliterate their discontent by use of alcohol or drugs. Many alcoholics and drug addicts experience a feeling of deep ecstasy when under the influence. Later, if they are healed, they have the experience based on Spirit.

The mystic is heart and intellect. The mystic knows from the heart center what is Truth and uses the intellect to demonstrate it. The Eastern mystic is often quiet in his attainment, using his high consciousness to serve and teach others, but in a quiet way. The Western mystic needs to be active and serves his fellow man by various good works in the outer. To be both is the apex of our seeking and serving.

The beginner on the Truth Path looks for fruits in the outer. If health seems to be needed, the Truth student uses the mind to heal. The mystic, on the other hand, has the fruits of the Spirit in a larger measure and recognizes that poor health, to take an example, is to be taken cheerfully and with the realization that this challenge must be transformed in order to reach the other side of at-one-ment. In so doing, he is healed. Many saints who are aspiring mystics have physical illnesses. The fruits of the Spirit according to Paul (in Gal. 5:22) are love, joy, peace, patience, kindness, goodness, faithfulness, gentleness, self-control. Those who have these, he says, inherit the kingdom of God. These are the mystics.

Illness of the body means, to the saint, that the consciousness is moving faster than the body has adjusted. All three—body, mind, and spiritual awareness—must be in balance. And so the body needs time to catch up. The faith of the mystic is not moved by race consciousness, the beliefs and the actions of the many, but he/she understands and rises above these. The mystic knows that the body is healthy no matter what the outward signs.

Solomon symbolizes that person who is aspiring to have the Mystical Marriage. To him comes the Queen of Sheba, or the Light shining in the perfection that is his potential. When our body and mind have reached a certain level of perfection in the Spirit, our consciousness joins with perfection of body (Sheba, "seven," is perfection of body), and the two together bring the ecstasy of completion as Solomon describes in the Song of Songs. His body has become celestial and immortal, and the seven chakra centers are filled with Light—the seventh being the queen.

The Eastern teaching on the chakras is foreign to many Westerners. The Hindu teaching on the Kundalini energy, the Serpent Energy, is beginning to appear in our Western books. This divine energy is spoken of in nearly all world religions under other names. The word *Kundalini* may not appear in their teachings, but the concept is there. Some of these other names are life energy, divine energy, evolutionary energy, holy spirit, precious jewel, crystallized energy. There are centers in this country where the process of raising the Kundalini is taught. If, however, the raising is for any other reason than spiritual development, it is very, very dangerous to mental as well as physical health.

It is taught that this energy rises up through the central spine and affects different nerves that lead to the seven chakra centers. The seven centers are in the ethereal body and are located at the base of the spine, at the sex organs, at the solar plexus, the heart, the throat, the forehead, and the crown of the head. When these are all vibrating with pure Light, the physical body is changed to the spiritual. The pituitary and pineal glands in the head come together when the energy is raised to that level and cause the great feeling of ecstasy and out-of-this-world experience that is called Unity, Cosmic Consciousness, Mystical Marriage, Enlightenment. One who is totally spiritual will be able to express on different planes of existence in the required body, either physical or spiritual. And service to mankind is the reason for reaching this high consummation of Oneness.

If you are interested in the Mystical Path, I would suggest you read *Mysticism,* by Evelyn Underhill. On the chakras, read any of the books by Gopi Krishna, as well as my book *Revelation: For a New Age,* which goes into this more deeply.

Solomon needed the feminine side of Wisdom to be whole, and Sheba needed the masculine. The almug wood that Hiram brought is symbolic of the Tree of Life or eternal Life (I Kings 10:11, 12). The insertion about Hiram seems to enrich this interpretation of the meeting of Solomon and the Queen of Sheba. Hiram represents building the Truth in mind and body.

There are stages along the Way of the Mystic that may reveal where one is. Corinne Heline lists them thus:

1. The Quest
2. The Awakening of Love (the Mystic)
3. The Attainment of Knowledge (the Occult)
4. Detachment
5. Unification (the Blending of Human and Divine)
6. Annihilation
7. Consummation*

Consummation, the highest state, seems to be what Solomon and his Beloved are describing in the Song of Songs. It is so far beyond our experience, and we find the words chosen to be so esoteric, that we can scarcely grasp the meaning. Thus it will be when we reach that stage—we shall not be able to describe it but only experience it. Solomon's Song is telling us about a more perfect experience and a complete demonstration of the Way. Jesus Christ is our example. Immortality is won when we follow Jesus' Way.

---

*Corinne Heline, *New Age Bible Interpretation,* vol. 2 (Los Angeles: New Age Press, 1975), p. 153.

We again have the feminine and the masculine. Each speaks to the other. Each is balanced in the other. We need to have this balance consciously so that unconsciously there will also be balance. The "old" soul,* if incarnated in a male body, will show many feminine characteristics of gentleness, tenderness, compassion, and a deep appreciation of the beautiful in art. (Could the homosexual be the incarnation of an "old" soul?) The "old" soul in the female body shows forth as strength, independence, spiritual courage, and attainment. There are many of these women around today. Corinne Heline says that each of us has incarnated in either male or female body many times. Thus we can have understanding for the other sex. The "old" soul may incarnate in either hetero- or homo-sexual or in a celibate person.

So with the Queen of Sheba coming to Solomon we have a description of the Mystical Path. Let us pursue the way that is best for us.

---

*"Old" soul: a mature soul, a product of evolution rich in wisdom of the ages learned in former lives or through "special" instruction.

20

Jezebel

(I Kings 16:31, 18, 19, 21; II Kings 9; Rev. 2:20–23)

THE RELIGIOUS FANATIC

We have in the annals of history few women who compare with Jezebel as being synonymous with the worst that woman represents. Some suggest that Catherine de' Medici and Jezebel are in the same category. In any case, our Christian heritage has used the name Jezebel to connote the base level in a woman's character. She is mentioned in Revelation 2:20–23. The speaker, Jesus Christ, makes an allusion to her teaching the church in Thyatira to eat food sacrificed to idols and to practice immorality. She never repents and goes to her death in pride as a queen. She never heeded the prophecy of Elijah but went her stubborn way. And so we ask, "What motivated this woman?" Well, it could have been religious fanaticism.

Jezebel was married to Ahab, King of Israel. She supported the religion of Baal as Queen of Israel. Her husband, King Ahab, did not stop her; he also followed Baal worship. Baal, a heathen god of nature, along with his consort goddess, Astarte or Asherah, and other goddesses, was worshiped. Jezebel turned the altar to the One God into an altar to Astarte and erected the pillar of Baal (a phallic symbol). She appointed priests of the religion and supported them. She killed the priests of the One God.

It is said by Bible historians that Israel was subject to this nature religion of Baal because it dealt with fertility and nature worship. When the Israelites took Canaan, the natives of the region practiced this religion and taught them how to farm. The gods in nature had to be propitiated. Even fertility of the race was improved by the temple virgin ceremonies and the early spring ceremonies of orgiastic worship with the temple virgins. This religious practice was common in many other primitive religions. The Celts in Britain had many of the same ceremonies. So Jezebel, from this viewpoint, was helping the people by assuring fertility, controlling the weather, and introducing Astarte—the goddess of love—into their worship. But the One God religion was being decimated.

Many crimes have been committed by religious fanatics in all religions, yet their conscience was clear, for they believed they were doing good. We know some personally, don't we?

Elijah, the prophet, became alarmed at Jezebel's influence on the people of Israel and so decided to make a demonstration of the power of the One God. He invited the Baal priests to a contest. Each group gathered wood on which to sacrifice a bull. The people watched. Elijah told the priests to lay the cut-up bull on their wood and call on their god, Baal, to light it with his fire. They did as he told them but it was not lighted even though they called to Baal all day. Then Elijah poured water over his wood and the bull and called to God. The wood took fire and burnt up the bull and all the water that had been poured on the offering. The people bowed down and cried, "The Lord, He is God; the Lord, He is God" (I Kings 18:39). Then Elijah had all the priests of Baal brought down to the brook Kishon and had them killed. When Jezebel heard about it she said she would kill Elijah, and he fled to Judah, where he was protected by God.

Then there was the case of the land owned by Naboth, which King Ahab wanted for an herb garden. Ahab tried to purchase the land but Naboth refused. Ahab then sulked and cried when he could not have what he wanted. Jezebel arranged for the murder of Naboth and all his sons and so obtained the land. Elijah told Ahab that he would die and his sons also, and that Jezebel would die and be eaten by dogs. Ahab repented, and so the tragedies did not befall his family until after his death. But all that Elijah had prophesied came true.

It was years after Ahab's death that Jezebel was slain by her eunuchs commanded by Jehu, who had been anointed king by Elisha. Jezebel's daughter, Athaliah, who married Jehoram, King of Judah, took Baalism into Judah also. Her dominance and cruelty were evidenced by the destruction of the royal family when she was queen. She was eventually slain.

What great tragedies came out of the life of this woman, Jezebel!

We may say that this story has nothing to do with us. We are not situated as queen of a country and thus do not have the power in the first place. Further, we are not inclined toward such evil dealings. All of this is true; but could it be that we are domineering toward others through our religious belief? Do we act in the name of religion with complete confidence that we are right? Do we dictate to others how they should conduct their religious life? Are we afire with zeal for our own beliefs, and do we try to impose them on others? Women are in a strong position in the home to overwhelm their husbands and children with a faith that does not fit their needs.

It has been assumed by many, many religious leaders that they have all the answers for everyone. History is replete with these accounts. And, of course, our own Christian teaching has often been touted as the only answer for all the people of the world. But the metaphysical view is quite different. It is based on the following:

Each human being, having a soul that is unique, needs to find his/her own path. Each must tread his own way back to the perfection of the Garden. Each is responsible for his/her own life and can, through Oneness in thought and Spirit with the Father, be directed rightly. Each has a destiny to fulfill. Each has special lessons to learn. Each is at a different level of evolution and so cannot follow anyone, or be just like another. So a group religion, a religion dictated by a leader, a religion that is best for the political or social realm may not be right for each individual—although for some it may be perfect in this lifetime.

The above is, I believe, nearer to the teaching of Jesus as he spoke to each heart personally. Each must stand alone with his God. It is through our indwelling Christ that we are to be guided. Jesus did not appoint any head of the Church. The head was the Father. Each of his disciples grew individually in understanding. Paul's teaching took away a lot of this autonomy and established a church organization. And fanatics have taken over through the ages.

When you and I first learn of Truth, as it is called in metaphysical circles, we are so on fire with zeal and enthusiasm that we want to tell the whole world and so convert it. At the same time, our friends, family, and relatives may become weary of our continuous attempts to convert them.

We may go further and dominate our husbands and children and require them to follow. Now with this new-found spiritual knowledge we may do lots of good, or think we do. But we must be careful, for if the family is not ready for this outpouring and requirement to follow us, we may antagonize them, and they may close their minds to the whole idea.

Our best route is to continue to grow in our new-found spiritual understanding, put it to work in our own lives, show by our words and actions the improvement in our own personality, and let those who observe make their own decision. Our dear ones need freedom from pressure so that they can make the choice best suited for their spiritual development.

The fanatic, the domineering woman or man, the absolutist—all often end up angry and at odds with everyone. There is no one way, I believe, but as many ways as there are souls. When a person is ready for the teaching that we hold dear, he/she will be drawn to it. Each needs to have the freedom to find his or her own.

Jezebel was doing what she considered right. She was leading the people to more fertility in the field. She was teaching them about the goddess of love, of good fortune. She never seemed to have a twinge of conscience over her murderous deeds. She was possessed by a demon, some would say. She was extreme and that, of course, is our "red flag" too. When we become too extreme about anything, we should search out a balance. Harmony does not come from extremes.

Many have faulted her for dominating her husband. It has been popular to blame the woman for being domineering. Ahab showed his lack of force and strength, and he lacked devotion to the One God. He allowed her to take over. The man who is not well grounded in his masculine power will often do this to keep the peace. And peace at any price is not peace for long. Ahab contributed to Jezebel's campaign to turn the Israelites from the One God. The woman who is the domineering element in a family sometimes loses her husband and her children, although daughters are more apt to follow their mothers, as did Jezebel's.

How wrong we can be sometimes when we think we are so right! If we follow the admonition of Ecclesiastes 3:1 that "For everything there is a season, and a time for every matter under heaven," we will not push so hard. If we can learn to "Let go and let God," we will be far more peaceful, as will those around us. When we believe we have to do it all ourselves, then our ego is in command, and that separates us from God. That was Jezebel's downfall, and it can be ours.

Esoteric: THE NEGATIVE ANIMUS

Jezebel has another, deeper, meaning for me—a more personal meaning. I prefer to see her as beset by the archetype called the negative animus by Carl Jung. So we will study her from this perspective, as she can teach many of us women something about ourselves.

Carl Jung designated the feminine aspect of a man as the *anima* and the masculine aspect of a woman as the *animus.* The animus is, for a woman, that masculine drive which enables her to break through the limitations that being a woman has imposed for centuries. But it is the *positive* animus that does this. If she is beset by a *negative* animus, she becomes repressed, hostile, loses her femininity, is subject to illogical conclusions, becomes domineering, acts on impulsive whimsy—and her determination becomes stubbornness. I think if you study Jezebel's life you will see many of these characteristics. On the other hand, the positive animus is helpful, supportive, strength-giving, and allows a balance to the feminine that makes the woman harmonious with her world and all in it. The positive animus might be called the spirit of love.

Now, how did Jezebel become this type of woman, or how do any of us become this way?—for the negative animus is not visited upon us; we bring it to ourselves. Usually, our relationships with the important males in our lives establish this characteristic, and it is up to us to get rid of it. We may be affected in our body, in our social activities, in our thinking, and certainly in the relationships that are most important to us.

Ahab, her husband, was weak and showed a negative anima, which causes men to deny the masculine part of themselves and become overly feminine. He often projects his masculine needs and finds a woman who is out of balance to fulfill his needs. Or he may find a woman who exemplifies the same qualities of his negative anima. And that won't work, either.

Often when we are beset by a negative animus, a person comes into our life and tries to teach us the error of our ways. So it was with Elijah, who symbolizes the spiritual I AM of our consciousness. Elijah, however, was violent and destructive at this point, and instead of converting Jezebel antagonized her. She was under the control of the negative animus.

Later, after Elijah gave his mantle of power to Elisha and ascended, Elisha was able to get rid of the negativity of Jezebel by anointing Jehu (signifying the expressed power of divine Mind) as king. Jehu was commanded to strike down the house of Ahab, which he did. Elisha symbolizes the I AM in its highest form, and he has been called the forerunner of Jesus Christ. This is the only way to get rid of the negative animus or anima, to convert the energy in it to a balance of the feminine and masculine within each of us. This brings us to individuation (Jung's term), or oneness with the Father.

When a woman is possessed by a negative animus, she is very unhappy. Her sons and daughters are affected by her dominance and especially her control of the men in her life. She, like Jezebel, may believe that she *must* act as she does, for someone has to be in authority. Her husband often "flees the field" and allows her to take over, as did Ahab. But she is miserable and eventually pays a penalty.

Confronting the negative in our conscious and unconscious mind is to realize that the situation exists; then we should stop running from this demon that seems to be chasing us. Certain of Carl Jung's teachings can help us. Often we may want to interpret our dreams or have a Jungian analyst help us. On a personal note, I learned of my negative animus through my dreams and then consciously went to work to overcome it.

Most women are beset by a negative animus to one degree or another unless all of their experience has been of a very positive kind with the men in their lives. Controlling others may not be the way it expresses itself. If you suspect that you are beset by a negative animus, you might like to study further in Jungian literature about it.

We know that if our will is really centered in the Will of God, all of these negativities will flee. To heal the unconscious, we need to do some denial and affirmations, to change our thinking from negative to positive, to follow the guidance of Love, and to praise and thank God for our healing. Unless we do heal this condition in the unconscious, we may have physical ills that cannot be explained. (See Chapter 6, *Esoteric:* Anima and Animus.)

Poor Jezebel never learned. She has gone down in history as a byword of wickedness in the thoughts of those who see a woman acting out her masculine side without the balance of the feminine. She has much to teach us, however, and we can learn if we want to. It is never too late. When we are balanced in God, we are androgynous, and the positive will express in our lives.

So let us look at Jezebel with gratitude, for she has brought to our awareness the excessive masculinity that may destroy us as well as those near to us. Let us dethrone the queen that deceives so easily. Let us look to ourselves and to God for our balance.

21

Esther

(The Book of Esther)

TRUTH AND DIVINE LOVE DEFEAT EVIL

This chapter will not be divided into exoteric and esoteric but will include both together. It is also written for both men and women. After all, the division is becoming less and less, and all that affects one affects the other.

Esther is the last woman of the Old Testament that we shall discuss. She it is that brings together all the foregoing chapters.

Some say that this legend has not been proven historically factual. Therefore it can best be understood from its symbology. It is a description of the fall and rise of the divine feminine. Vashti, the first queen, fell because she would not follow the orders of the king. Esther, the second queen, rose, for she depended on her God to strengthen her as she stood against the king. Esther is the resurrected divine Love or divine feminine.

The events of this book are supposed to have taken place about 485 B.C., when the Persians and the Medes were in control of 127 provinces reaching from India to Ethiopia. The exiled Jews had been released from Persia to return to Jerusalem to live and rebuild the temple. Many of the Jews remained in Persia, however. King Ahasuerus was emperor. He was a good king and gave festivals and banquets for those in the top echelons of government, as well as for the people of the palace.

After one of his banquets, when he had had a great deal of wine, he sent for his queen, Vashti, and commanded her to come to show off her beauty to all present; she would be unveiled. She refused to come.

According to some commentators on this story, Vashti was the first woman whose self-respect and courage enabled her to act against a husband's will, to say nothing of a king's. She was an example to women of the higher unfoldment of woman. She was

117

ahead of her time. We women of today might learn from her that to express our own desires with respect to our own dignity is more important than to satisfy the sensuality of our husband. She was willing to take the results of her defiance in order to be true to her self.

The king was very angry and, upon the advice of his chamberlains, removed her from her position as queen.

When the king became lonely, many beautiful virgins were gathered in, given beauty treatments for a year, and then each went in to the king for a night. From them he made his choice of a new queen.

Mordecai—a cousin of Esther, and who had reared her—suggested that she enter into the contest. They were Jews. She was very beautiful. She was brought to court with the other virgins and did not tell anyone that she was Jewish. When she went in to the king, she pleased him very much and he made her queen.

Mordecai often sat at the king's gate to hear what he could. He discovered that two of the king's eunuchs were planning to assassinate the king. He told Esther, she told the king, and the eunuchs were hanged. Then Mordecai was given a responsible job in the court and forgotten by the king. However, a record of his having saved the king's life was made in the court chronicles.

The king promoted Haman the Agagite, and his seat was above all the princes. All the king's servants bowed down to him except Mordecai, who refused to. This roused Haman's wrath, and when he found out that Mordecai was a Jew, he decided to get the king's permission to have all the Jews of the provinces killed—men, women, and children.

He told the king that there was a certain group of people in all the provinces who did not keep the king's laws. He asked to be allowed to destroy them, for which he would pay 10,000 talents of silver into the king's treasury. The king gave his permission and allowed Haman to use the king's official ring to seal the decree. Thus the law went out that all Jews must be killed. Haman cast lots, called Pur, to determine what month and day would be best. The thirteenth day of the month Adar in the Jewish calendar was the date chosen and announced to the authorities of the provinces.

Mordecai heard about this and asked Esther to go to the king and try to dissuade him, since Esther, herself a Jewess, would also be subject to death. She resisted at first because of the law that the king must first summon her before she could enter his presence or she would be killed. Mordecai sent her another message reminding her that if all the Jews were killed, she and her father's house would also be destroyed, to which he added, "And who knows whether you have not come to the kingdom for such a time as this" (Esther 4:14).

This quote has inspired many and should inspire us. For we all have come "to the kingdom," to this place we occupy on earth, for a purpose. And our goal should be to find our purpose for living, God's purpose for our living, and then serve that purpose— or we shall surely die to our Good.

What purpose are you serving? Is it a greater purpose than your own small-self desires? Are you in a difficult position and do not know why? Perhaps it is for a greater purpose than you can imagine. If it seems the right place for you and the right time, dress yourself beautifully (your consciousness) and go to the king (God) and make your request for help to live out your purpose. The glory that will come to you may not be celebrated by others, but you will celebrate with pure joy as you complete your task. You have come to this life for a purpose. Be open, recognize it, and fulfill your destiny.

Esther dressed beautifully, fasted and prayed and asked other Jews to do the same, and stood in the hall near the throne, for no one was to see the king who was not invited. He saw her and invited her in; she touched the top of the scepter, which gave her higher powers according to esoteric teaching. The king told her she could have anything she asked for up to half his kingdom. She then invited him and Haman to a banquet.

Haman was very puffed up after the banquet that Esther prepared, because only the king and he had been invited. She also asked them to return for a second banquet. Haman had only one "fly in his ointment": Mordecai, who would not bow to him. He planned to hang him and set about having a scaffold built.

That same night the king could not sleep and had the chronicles read to him. He was reminded, in the reading, of what a great thing Mordecai had done in saving his life. He sent for Haman and asked how he could honor someone whom he wanted to bring before the people as honorable. Haman immediately thought that he was the one to be honored (the Adversary or ego readily believes this) and described how it should be done. The king liked his

ideas and told him to carry them out. He told Haman to find
Mordecai, dress him in the royal robes, put him on a white horse,
and lead the horse through the public square, showing that the
king delighted in this man. Haman did so and was ashamed, and
his wife and friends predicted that Haman would fall before Mordecai did.

At the second banquet, as they were drinking wine, the king
asked Queen Esther again what she petitioned.

She asked that her life be spared and the lives of her people.
(The king did not know she was a Jewess.) He immediately asked,
"Who is he, and where is he, that would presume to do this?"
She replied, "The wicked Haman." The king was greatly perturbed
and went into the garden. When he returned Haman was kneeling
at Esther's side asking her to intercede for him. The king thought
that he was assaulting Queen Esther and ordered him hanged on
the gallows that Haman had prepared for Mordecai.

The king gave Esther all of Haman's property; Mordecai was
given the king's signet ring and had the same power as Haman.

Since the letter had gone out with the order that all Jews be
killed, it was law and so could not be changed. The king gave
permission for Mordecai to issue a new edict from the king after
Esther begged him to do something about the first order. This
letter allowed all Jews to gather and defend themselves, to destroy,
to annihilate, to slay any armed force of men who attacked them
on the thirteenth day of the twelfth month, which is the month
of Adar and may be February or March.

Mordecai put on royal robes of blue and white with a golden
crown and a mantle of fine linen of white and purple. The people
shouted and rejoiced, and they had a feast and a holiday.

When the 13th of Adar came, the Jews killed many of their
attackers. The princes and governors of the provinces helped
them, for they feared Mordecai, who had become very powerful.
All ten sons of Haman were killed. However there was no plunder.

Esther then asked that another day be allotted to the defense
of the Jews, the 14th day of the month. Later the fourteenth
and fifteenth days of Adar were declared feast days celebrating
the time when all the Jews were saved. They were to send choice
portions to one another and gifts to the poor. They called these
days *Purim* after the term *pur* ("to cast lots"). This day was to be
honored by all generations forever. To this day Purim is celebrated

with the reading of the Book of Esther. Her command had fixed these feast days.

To many this legend may appear on the surface as just another interesting story about Persia and the Jews. We will find that it goes much deeper. According to historians, it was almost left out of the Bible, for the word *God* does not appear in it. But those seers who helped compile the Bible saw the deeper meaning. It is an account of the battle of the opposites, of duality, and the victory by the good forces.

The king, Ahasuerus, symbolizes the will puffed up with faith in the small self. In fact the king depicts our own small self or ego and the will that seems to be in control. Awareness of the spiritual will is nonexistent; thus Ahasuerus continually asks others for advice, acts on it without thought, and learns later he was wrong to do so. Our self-will rests on the authority of our thoughts and not on the authority of the Spirit. The will becomes balanced when it allows divine Love to guide it.

Queen Vashti is personal love to which the will was wedded. However, personal love is short-lived unless based on the Spirit. Thus when the puffed-up ego based on self-will used its authority to command the queen to come and show herself, she refused.

Our personal will is easily upset. We become angry, we hate, we kill, we strike, we withdraw from others, we rant and rave. Thus did the king, and he banished the queen. Now he was left with his intellectual ravings and became lonely.

How like us the king! We feel we command all we survey in our little world and use all of our arsenal of self-will to have our way. When we are frustrated, we banish that which challenges our position, but then we become lonely.

In the opening chapter we have a description of a beautiful palace and gardens; the richness of the appointments and all the gold goblets indicate great wealth. The palace, decorated with gold, silver, precious stones, marble, and mother-of-pearl, showed the bounty of the king. This could be a place of high spiritual consciousness. We are surrounded by the spirit and often are not aware of it because of our self-will and egotistic love of the small self.

When Ahasuerus became lonely, he arranged to interview all the beauties of the kingdom, the virgins. Frequently in our search for a way out of loneliness we reach for the best available. The virgins indicate innocence and freshness of consciousness. The virgin is one who is perfect and filled with great potential. He chose Esther, for she symbolizes divine Love to balance out our intellectual will—both men and women. All need the balance of head and heart to reach perfection.

Mordecai, Esther's guardian, means "turning to Truth with humility"—the very opposite of Ahasuerus. He was a Jew, which means "divine ideas or spiritual consciousness." Within each of us is this Divinity, which is silently guiding us to our good. Mordecai and Esther are good examples of Truth and divine Love, which carry us into a higher level of knowing His Will.

The Truth within the palace gates—high consciousness—saved the self-will (the king) from annihilation; for we must maintain our ego to some extent as long as we live on earth. Mordecai (Truth) as a result was written up in the records (the unconscious mind) of the king. This record is what finally saved the Jews, or spiritual consciousness.

Then the king—you or I—allows evil, which is negativity or opposition to good, or activity of carnal sense consciousness (but not a power), to enter into the spiritual setting of his good. Haman was the name ("arrogance; inner commotion; trouble"). He was given much authority and became very egotistical and self-assured. This is always a danger to us when we believe we are perfect and can do no wrong, have all the seeming good of the world surrounding us, have great power. When all of this is based on self-will and not God's Will, then belief in evil will come in.

Evil, Haman, was of such note in the kingdom that everyone bowed down to him except Mordecai (Truth with humility). Mordecai had been sitting at the palace gates to keep track of what was happening to Esther, divine Love. Truth and Divine Love go hand in hand. So Haman came to hate Mordecai and searched for a way to get rid of him as well as all the Jews (spiritual consciousness) in all 127 provinces (numerologically, 127 = 10, the highest level in the Old Testament; 12 is the highest level in the New Testament).

How often when sense consciousness is in control of our life do we take it for granted that we are wonderful and that the way of the world, of the carnal mind, is right for us! But deep within our consciousness there still linger Truth and Love, and we cannot shake them off. We are all divine, and although the Light may shrink to a pinpoint during some of our earthly escapades, it cannot be obliterated, for it shall eventually expand and expand, until it takes over our whole being, just as Mordecai and Esther eventually gained control of all the provinces.

Haman went to the king to get permission to kill the Jews, offering the king more worldly wealth if he would agree. How often we sell out for more earthly possessions even though we already have so many! How often our greed controls us! How often we think that to accumulate more and more is excuse enough to allow dastardly deeds to be done in our name! This self-will is weak in the face of carnal lust or bad advice from the negative side of our personality. So the king gave Haman, the Adversary, full authority to strike down spiritual consciousness.

When Mordecai, Truth, learned of the plan, he sent word to Esther. The feminine aspect of Esther responded with fear, for divine Love was not to go into the presence of the king (sense consciousness, without Spirit) without invitation.

Many believe that we bring to ourselves everything that happens to us. Some teach that if we do not have the right thoughts that no good will come to us. But divine Love opens many doors to our good without our ever thinking about it or doing anything, or even asking for it. It comes to us by Grace.

Since divine Love is spiritual consciousness (a Jewess), she had to approach the king, the ego, for she wanted to save spiritual consciousness and herself, Love. She robed herself most beautifully, she fasted and prayed and asked others to do so, and approached the king. When the king saw her, he invited her to his throne. And that was the turning-point in his life, the life of our spiritual consciousness, for as we open ourselves to divine Love, we are truly in the divine setting of our life, the palace.

The intellect has power to allow the good to flow. Esther invited the intellect, beset by the ego, and evil to a banquet. Now when the intellect and evil sit down to eat and drink wine (symbolizes blood and sacrifice or youth and eternal life) and they begin feeling godlike, something will happen!

The self-will (intellect) told divine Love to ask whatever she wanted and it would be given to her. She openly accused Haman of planning to slay her (divine Love) and her people, the Jews (spiritual consciousness). The king was so shocked he "rose from the feast in wrath and went into the palace garden."

The palace gardens of the Persians were the most beautiful gardens in the kingdom. The Persian gardens were religious shrines and symbolized spiritual consciousness. This palace garden was the highest spiritual consciousness, and the king went alone into it. (This symbolizes our going into the silence or meditation.) He was no doubt angry because he had been "taken in" by evil, angry at himself for being duped. He was a good king. He followed Cyrus, who helped the Jews return to Jerusalem and rebuild the Temple, and Darius, who further supported the Jews. He was not antagonistic toward spiritual consciousness. He just did not pay attention to it. He had been duped! And so when we see evil seemingly attacking divine Love, which we have become aware of, we must get rid of it. Evil was hanged on the scaffold of his own doing—hate and greed for power.

Evil is often strong in our worldly consciousness. Evil is an absence of good, not a power, but it infiltrates our life as smog infiltrates our houses and bodies. It manifests in race consciousness. It is subtle, and where there is a lack of good thoughts based on God's teachings and Love, it becomes very forceful and egotistical and believes it has control. We are tried by evil, but eventually we come to our senses and our spiritual center and overcome it. We realize that only good exists for us. Evil, as a power, is hanged.

Before the banquets Haman had decided to hang Mordecai, for he could not tolerate Truth's not bowing down to him. So he had a scaffold built to hang him. He boasted to his wife and friends that he had full control of the kingdom. However, when the king honored Mordecai (Truth), Haman was selected to put the royal robes on him and lead him among the people. This was the beginning of evil's downfall, for the king lifted up Truth. How this applies to us! Egocentricity must honor Truth. Evil, or erroneous thought, is defeated.

Haman, sensual carnal consciousness, was hanged, and divine Love and Truth were set high in the consciousness of the king (you and me), and the Jews (spiritual consciousness) were saved.

Divine Love, Esther, is a great heroine. If she had not taken charge and had the courage to approach the king, the story would have ended very differently. We see what divine Love does for us.

This is also true of us individually. It takes courage and belief in Truth to make a difference in our life. Esther could not escape Truth, as It was part of her life. Mordecai had raised her. Our parent, our Father, is God, and Truth dwells in Him. Spiritually, He dwells within us, and the Truth is always in our unconscious and will break through eventually. It takes Truth and Love to bring us to a higher awareness of our Divinity, and we carry both within us. Truth helps divine Love lay down Its life for others. We too can do no less.

Spiritual consciousness can always protect itself from attack by its enemies. We fight these attackers with our thoughts, with our affirmations of good, with our meditation and prayers, with our study of religious books—the Bible particularly—listening to teachers, being open to the Truth and practicing Love. Our spiritual consciousness will then thrive. And we have someone the Jews did not have: we have Jesus Christ and his Presence.

The festival of Purim is celebrated at about the same time that we celebrate the resurrection of Jesus Christ. Many religions have festivals and celebrations at this time of the year. We celebrate the resurrection of Truth and Love as they do. The Spring Equinox has been celebrated by primitive religions for centuries. It is the time when the earth energy, the dragon (so called by the Druids) begins to show again in crops, fruits, and energy for growth. The whole earth is resurrected.

Divine Love is the heroine, for she was in the palace of the self-will, and spiritual consciousness was saved. Divine Love is always present in our kingdom. We, like the king, govern our life with the help of many "experts" until we are made aware of the primrose path we are being led down. Eventually evil is deposed and Truth and Love guide us. They become one, and the opposites are overcome.

The end of the account in the King James and Revised Standard versions of the Bible extols the greatness of Mordecai. However, in the Jerusalem Bible an addendum, which was probably written after 300 B.C. by the Greeks, brings Esther in as equally great. It reads in part, "All this is God's doing . . . a little spring became a river, the light that shone, the sun, the flood of water. Esther is the river, whom the king married and made queen. . . . Yes, the Lord has saved his people, the Lord has delivered us from all these evils.'' Esther is the queen in our personal kingdom. The king (intellect) and Esther (heart) are truly married. When all is Light, Love, Truth, there is no room for Haman (evil), and our way will be one of rejoicing and celebrating the rolling away of the stone and the resurrection of New Life. Thus Esther has entered into our lives and we are whole.

Part Two
NEW TESTAMENT WOMEN

22

Mary, Mother of Jesus

(Matthew 1, 2, 12:46–50; Mark 6; Luke 1, 2;
John 19:25–27; Acts 1:14)

THE GREAT MOTHER FREED HER SON

In this opening chapter of Women of the New Testament I am overwhelmed by the task of writing about the greatest mother of the New Dispensation. We as women can identify with her to a point, but we cannot place ourselves totally in her position, for it is difficult to envision or discuss this holy woman. Still, as we tell her story should we not also be aware of our own Divinity, of our giving birth to children who are divine? Should we not be aware of the Christ that is within us and our giving birth to this awareness? Are we so different?

That may be blasphemy to many who have Mary the mother of Jesus on a pedestal and worship her. But Mary is also a symbol of the deeper teachings of Jesus, which raised the feminine archetype and which are affecting our world today. We are in the time of balancing the masculine and feminine, and this divine feminine called Mary is our pattern. For the femininity of God brought forth the Son of God. The feminine is on the ascendancy. Mary's "immaculate conception" represents an ideal of purity that we all will emulate some day. We will all have pure and sinless bodies for the incarnation of the Christ awareness. Then we shall be free from death, disease, tears—and all evil (which is illusion) will be overcome.

Before the time of Mary the Virgin there had been other virgin births recounted in history and mythology. In various accounts all of the great religious leaders had miraculous births, divine beginnings; the Buddha, Krishna, Osiris, Zeus, Mithras, Dyonysius, Hermes are some of them. These do not diminish or otherwise affect our belief in the virgin birth of Jesus. On the contrary, they only reinforce our realization that mankind is capable of bringing forth Divinity from the physical.

Whether one believes that Mary was a virgin when she conceived Jesus is unimportant to many. It is not Jesus' beginnings on this earth, but his teachings, his resurrection, and his ascension that are most important for us. Those who believe that intercourse between a man and woman is sinful will find the virgin birth more important. Mary has for many women been the example to follow and so they have kept themselves chaste and sometimes celibate. What a wonderful example she is!

Anyone who has lived in a Christian nation knows the story of the divine Incarnation through the Holy Spirit and the birth of Jesus. It is recounted most clearly in Luke 1. In Luke 2 we have an account of Jesus' early childhood to age twelve. Rereading these chapters will help you understand what I am about to set forth. Be aware, as you read, that the feminine principle within you, man or woman, is being addressed. Mary is a part of each one of us.

As background to my discussion of Mary and also of Elizabeth, the mother of John the Baptist, I should like to share with you some information I have gathered about the Essenes—a group of Jews who lived before and during Jesus' time.

The Essenes are never mentioned in the Bible, but certain ancient historians—Josephus, Philo, and Pliny—have told us about this religious sect which occupied an area in Judea as well as Mount Carmel. (See Manly Palmer Hall's book *The Mystical Christ*.) They lived in two types of communities. One was monastic, where celibacy was practiced, and the other was a community of men, women, and children. They taught baptism by water for cleansing the body and the consciousness, for the forgiveness of sins and redemption. They taught that one could receive revelations or guidance directly from God. They believed in reincarnation, and they expected the coming of the Messiah—a vital part of their reason for being. They gave special training to specially chosen young girls in the temple to prepare them to be the possible mother of the expected Messiah. *Christ* and *Messiah* are the same Greek word.

One can see that their teachings would not follow the traditional Jewish teachings; thus they were looked down upon by the Jewish authorities. It is thought by some that the mothers of John the Baptist and of Jesus were of this community as well as their fathers, Zechariah and Joseph.

The use of baptism by both John and Jesus raises the question
of where this teaching derives from. The baptism by blood for
forgiveness of sins was a teaching of the Jews. In Exodus 30 and 40
we read of the need for the priests who came near the altar to wash
with water. The Mystery religions of ancient Egypt and Mesopotamia taught rituals that included trial by water and fire. Perhaps
these deep Mystery teachings were imparted to John and Jesus
during those "lost years" of their lives. The Essenes, as we have
seen, practiced water baptism.

The Dead Sea Scrolls were found in the ruins of Qumran in
1947, and the excavation of the ruins began in 1951. Speculation
arose whether these records were made by the Essenes and hidden
in the caves. We have heard much more about the Essenes since
then, although their name was not mentioned in the Scrolls. Some
of the teachings revealed there are in accordance with those described by the ancient historians mentioned above. It is thought
that the Essenes lived in the Qumran area. In any case, this might
explain some of the unknowns connected with John and Jesus
and their parents.

Now Mary, it is said by some, was reared in an Essene temple.
Her parents were Joachim and Hanna (Anna), who were of a high
degree in the Essenian Mysteries. Since Mary had been raised and
educated in the temple and had been taught that some girl from
the temple might be chosen as the mother of the Messiah, she was
better able to accept Gabriel's message when he made the Annunciation.

Gabriel greeted her with "Hail, O favored one, the Lord is with
you." She was startled, but he soothed her, told her that she would
conceive and bear a son and should call his name Jesus. She ques-
tioned this, since she had no husband. He told her that the Holy
Spirit would come upon her and the child would be called Jesus,
holy, the Son of God (Luke 1:26–38).

Now Mary was espoused (engaged) to Joseph and was not
married. However espousal, which lasted a year, was as binding
as marriage. Mary asked how this could be possible, since she
was not married. Gabriel replied, "For with God nothing will
be impossible."

Mary hurried to visit her cousin, Elizabeth, who Gabriel said
was with child. Because Elizabeth was past child-bearing age, this
too seemed miraculous. When Mary arrived, Elizabeth confirmed

her own pregnancy and greeted her warmly as the mother of her Lord. Mary then accepted her task and sang the great Magnificat which lives on in churches today. It begins: "My soul magnifies the Lord and my Spirit rejoices in God my Savior" (Luke 1:46–55).

Joseph was disturbed when he found out about Mary's pregnancy but through a dream was told that she had conceived by the Holy Spirit and that she would bear a son whose name would be Jesus and who would save his people from their sins. Joseph, coming from a priestly class also, accepted her and cared for her gently.

The baby Jesus was born in a stable with animals present. The shepherds and wise men found him there, all of which Mary "pondered in her heart." Because Herod was having all male babies under two years of age killed who were in Bethlehem and surrounding areas, the parents and babe escaped to Egypt. (Joseph listened to another dream, which warned him.) Then they came back to Nazareth, where Jesus grew up, "increasing in wisdom and in stature and in favor with God and man" (Luke 2:52).

At age twelve Jesus announced his mission. The family had gone to Jerusalem to the Temple, and when the parents set out for home, Jesus remained talking to the priests and scribes. When Mary found him after a three-day search, she rebuked him. His reply was couched in impersonal language; he called her woman, and said, "Did you not know that I must be in my Father's house," or, as the King James version puts it, "Wist ye not that I must be about my Father's business?" (Luke 2:49). He declared his independence— age twelve is often the age when children realize their reason for being born.

The mother Mary appears again when Jesus first begins his ministry, and we know that she had had much influence on him during his growing years, for she was trained in the Essene Temple and she knew that he was very, very special. She knew whereof he came. This in itself made her a mother to be adored. The "silent years" were certainly not silent for Mary and Jesus. Also, Joseph taught Jesus a useful trade.

Early in Jesus' ministry at the wedding feast at Cana, Mary pointed out that the wine had given out. His reply to her was again impersonal: "O woman, what have you to do with me? My hour has not yet come" (John 2:1–11). After this seeming rebuke she told the servants to do as he said, and he changed the water into wine. This whole story has deep esoteric meanings.

On one occasion Jesus was preaching in his home town and his family wanted to seize him and take him home, for the people were saying that he was possessed by Beelzebub, an evil spirit or Satan. When Jesus was told that his mother and brothers were standing outside asking for him, his reply was impersonal again. In a sense, he rejected them as family, for he said, "Here are my mother and brothers. Whoever does the will of God is my brother, my sister, my mother" (Matt. 12:46-50).

The next time Mary is mentioned is when Jesus was on the cross and she was among the women grieving at the foot of the cross. Jesus saw her and lovingly gave her to John as his mother (John 19:25-27).

Mary is not specifically mentioned as being at the tomb, nor do we hear of her during the time Jesus taught the apostles after his Resurrection; but after the Ascension she was in the upper room with his apostles and others (Acts 1). They each were visited by the Holy Spirit and their mission began. She was no doubt part of the early Church.

These are the simple facts as recorded in scripture, but how much more has been deduced from these accounts! How Mary is worshiped in most of the countries of the Western world! How she has been deified in art, music, poetry, architecture! Today she is given a more central place in many Catholic cathedrals than Jesus. We may wonder why. But then, if we see Mary as the divine feminine who represents the longing within each of us to lift up the feminine aspect of God and balance it with the masculine, which has held forth for thousands of years, we understand. It has been a long, hard evolutionary journey, but the human race is beginning to see the results of Jesus' lifting up woman to her rightful place and of Mary's truly immaculate conception. The feminine is on the ascendancy in our world and will rise still higher as the Aquarian Age of androgyny is ushered in.

And now as women, as mothers, potential mothers, surrogate mothers, let us look at Mary as a teacher for us. You may think that you could never aspire to be such a divine mother chosen by God to give birth to the Savior of the world. No, maybe you can't. But you have something she did not initially have. You have the teachings and example of Jesus Christ, her son. You are living in an age when women have more freedom, are looked up to, are seen as the prototype of love. You may not be the mother of *such* a Holy Son, but you are or can be the mother of a holy son and holy daughter, for we are all sons of God.

Mary, if we are to believe the ancient historians, had been reared in a holy atmosphere. She had the teachings of the prophets, the Psalms, and for teachers she had men and women devoted to God. Perhaps we will not raise our children in such a holy atmosphere, but we can teach them our values, our religious beliefs, to love the Bible, to be open and receptive to the inner Voice. We can spend time with them at work and play and open their hearts and minds to the Spirit of God that is in all and is All.

Are you interested in giving birth to a special soul? Consider the following: In the period of preparation before conceiving a child, both parents can be devoted to separation from the world, to prayer and study, and to thanksgiving for the future entity to be born through them. A period of celibacy might also be good. At conception, the mind and emotions should be filled with the highest level of love possible. The body, mind, and emotions in a high state of ecstasy, in Oneness, can bring forth an unusual soul, for those souls are waiting to incarnate and have parents who will lead them higher.

As our child grows, we teach—but we also liberate. The child is not for us; the child is for the world and for his or her own Christing. We gradually let the child find his own path. We do not cling or direct. We watch, we "ponder these things in our heart," and we know that some day this individual, a son or daughter of God, will find the way to her/his destiny. We will not be dragged to the depths of despair if our child strays for a period. Remember, Jesus had his temptations in the wilderness after he had reached a very high point, baptism by the Holy Spirit.

All this is not easy. For Mary it must have been hard to be told by a twelve-year-old boy that his business was somewhere else besides being with her. How would you have responded? Of course, she knew that he was special. Do *you* recognize *your* special children?

She knew of his miracle-making ability when she asked him to make more wine at the marriage feast. How would you have reacted if your son had said, "O Woman, what have you to do with me?" Would you have understood, or would you have drawn yourself up to full height and responded, "*I* am your *mother!*" It is not easy to let go of our primary position with our children. It is the feminine nurturing and caring for them that we enjoy. But we need to ask ourselves, "Is it myself or them I am nurturing and caring for?"

And then, when Mary and Jesus' brothers believed the rumor of their neighbors and friends that Jesus was possessed and wanted to take him home, care for him, keep him from exposing his insanity, and he rejected them—how would you have felt? Would you "wash your hands" of this strange son and put him out of your mind? Would you grieve? Would you feel guilty? Would you resent the ones he called his brothers, sisters, mother? Or would you know that he had to fulfill his destiny and that no matter how opposed he was to the race consciousness, he was doing what he had to do. She must have been aware of all the healings and raisings from the dead he had performed. Remember, she was trained to see the majesty of God at work in all lives.

And she, like us, was at the cross. She, like us, walked the miles with him to Calvary. She, like us, grieved and did not understand fully until he ascended. And then she, like us, received the Holy Spirit and carried on his work and helped others as best she could. When we lose a child from this earth plane, it may be the impetus for our greatest work. She knew he had fulfilled his mission.

We do not know how, when, or where she died. We assume that she made her home with John, the beloved apostle. We do know that she left a tremendous mark on mankind. All of us do the same as we realize our Divinity and sing the Magnificat with her, "My soul magnifies the Lord and my spirit rejoices in God my Savior." Ascension without going through death was certainly possible for this divine mother.

We are also sure that Jesus did not ignore his mother; he adored her. But he depended on her understanding that he had a great and difficult work to do. He loved her through it all, but he had to go away so that we could know that death can be overcome, that God is a loving, forgiving force in our lives, and that we have a Comforter, the Christ within. He had greater work to do than to remain a son of a woman. Let us free our sons and daughters to do what they came to do!!

Birthing of sons and daughters is a high and holy task. Men who are becoming "mothers" are learning that they have the capability of nurturing, caring for, loving their children. And as they have this experience, they are becoming more in harmony with the great design for humanity. Mary, the divine feminine, is rising in our consciousness today, in both men and women. Let us hold her up as one to whom we can look as we go our way as mothers, would-be mothers, or surrogate mothers.

Esoteric: BIRTH OF OUR CHRIST

This birth of Jesus, or the Christ Child as some call him, is a mystery for us humans. I doubt whether we shall fully understand it until we have reached a much higher level of spiritual awareness. Many believe they understand from the literal viewpoint, as they interpret all the Bible. I do not understand how they literally interpret the virgin birth, since science has determined that the conception of a child occurs when a man's seed and a woman's egg conjoin. This conception without physical intercourse is accepted by many as the Truth taken on faith in all that is written in God's Holy Word. Who of us can say for sure that it is impossible? We praise God for those who have carried this torch for hundreds of years.

It is of no consequence to many whether Jesus was born of the Holy Spirit and Mary, for the teachings that Jesus gave are of the highest that we have been exposed to and are most important. Also his resurrection and ascension, his presence on this planet now as attested to by many, and his raising of the vibrations of this planet to higher spiritual levels seem to be more important. So whatever your position, I should like to offer an inner or esoteric interpretation of Mary's life and her son Jesus.

Let us see Mary as symbolizing the heart, love, the divine feminine. Let us see Joseph as symbolizing the intellect. Let us see Jesus as symbolizing Savior, Deliverer. Now let us see how all of these qualities can be a part of us.

Born within each of us thousands of times a day are thoughts. We have freedom to choose what we think, and that makes all the difference. We are not victims! We are creators of our life, for it is through our marvelous creative thoughts that we bring forth our experiences. And so we too can bring forth the Christ, which is the Savior of our own life and which can affect the lives of many others.

The Annunciation may come to us by the Word, by teaching, by reading and studying holy books, by our own needs and desires. When it comes, we may discount it as did Zechariah when the angel announced the prospective birth of John the Baptist. An angel represents intuition that is spiritual. Our intuition is alive and often gives us thoughts that we are unready to accept. But they will keep coming back until we do accept.

The verification of our great message may not come for years. We may get an insight, we may birth the Christ awareness, but we may go down into Egypt (home of sensual living) for a while before we come back to our spiritual guide. Herod, the ego, may want to kill our new Christ awareness, so we escape to another state of consciousness until a more propitious time. Thus we save our new-born babe. When the ego (Herod) is dead or inactive, we can return to our spiritual home for our development. We may make a rough, laborious journey on the back of a donkey over desert wastes before we realize we must return. Perhaps the intuition will break through in a dream (Joseph was guided by several dreams), but inevitably we will grow in wisdom of God and of man. This Christ awareness is our inheritance, and intellect (Joseph) and love (Mary) will protect it until its maturity. After twelve years (twelve is symbolic of spiritual completion), we will know our destiny and will follow it.

Mary, the divine feminine, is the progenitor and with the Holy Spirit protects the Christ awareness. Mary, the divine feminine, brings forth this Truth, and the human race advances on its spiral of evolution. We evolve to a high level of Christ consciousness and live in our Father's house as we put into action, words, and thoughts this Truth: God is incarnate in our own subconscious and will break through into conscious awareness in due time.

This birth of the Christ awareness within our own consciousness will be a great event filled with joy. It may happen at a time when our life is replete with sensual needs or with illness or with sorrows and defeats or with loss of identity. For the sorrows of this world often open us to the realization that God is ever ready to help us. The rejoicing over our "born again" status is attended by shepherds (protecting entities of God that watch over us) and wise men (the stored resources of the soul that will present gifts without price). There may be past-life rewards that are being brought to our consciousness. All is joy as we birth the Christ Child awareness.

The birthing is just the beginning, and as Mary and Joseph combined to raise Jesus, so our intellect and our feelings must combine to establish this "child" as the Savior of our own world as well as of others. Sometimes this "birthing" occurs many times before it is firmly established in our awareness.

Often a new religious insight that comes to an individual is considered inferior by church authorities and put down and ignored. Church leaders are often so captured by the law and past practices that they cannot accept any teaching that deviates from it. Our Christ awareness, the inner God voice, is often decried by established religion. The Jews in Jesus' time were much the same.

When we take our Christ to the church or temple we will find a few who will bless our new awareness. Simeon, the priest, saw Jesus and realized that he was the Messiah, as did Anna, the prophetess. So we shall find more advanced souls who will recognize our new-found Truth.

Jesus in the Temple questioning and talking with the priests we can see as symbolizing our own need to question and talk with the leaders of our organized church. Sometimes we will need to leave that church and find a new group. We may find that we need a group to share with, to study with, to meditate with. Sometimes coming together accentuates the new Truth as well as raises the spiritual vibrations of each member of the group. Jesus had his own group of twelve apostles.

The inner meaning of the marriage feast has been missed by many, for any time marriage is mentioned in the Bible it bears the esoteric connotation of the Mystical Marriage, when the individual reaches a high state of Oneness and his body, mind, emotions, and spirit are one with God.

The divine feminine and the Savior were at the marriage feast. The six jars represent the six chakras. The water represents physical life and the wine represents the divine energy that flows through our body and changes the physical to the spiritual. Mary, the divine feminine, starts the process, but the masculine is necessary to complete it. The balance must be reached. (See Chapter 19, "The Queen of Sheba," for more details on the Kundalini and the chakras.)

Mary, the divine feminine, knows all of these inner secrets. She ponders them in her heart and tells no one. So should we. There are times when we should keep secret the insights and intuitive understandings we receive. Spreading them before unbelievers may weaken the energy that we need.

As important as the divine feminine is, it must not take over our lives. It needs balance with the divine masculine. Feeling and reasoning are both needed. Jesus, the Christ, personified an androgynous figure who expressed to perfection both the feminine and the masculine. He was not aggressive but peaceful. He was not weak but strong in his opinions and denunciation of evil. He was filled with compassion yet he could reject and deny some requests. So when he used the impersonal with his mother, he was teaching us that the divine feminine must not take control. The Christ, the balance of love and intellect, must direct our life. For too long we may have been under the sway of the masculine identity. Let us not as women swing too far toward the masculine ourselves by way of compensation and lose our feminine balance.

Letting go of attachment to our relatives is necessary when we reach a certain level in our Mystical Path. The mystic is centered on the Father's Will and nothing else.

Our Divinity will ever be with us as we tread our path to Calvary. It is said by some that we each must go through our Garden of Gethsemane, our Calvary, our Resurrection, and our Ascension. Love accompanies us all the way. And love serves others as we realize that Impersonal Love, the Love of God.

Carl Jung in his book *Psychology and Religion: West and East* refers to the Roman Catholic dogma of the Assumption of Mary. Assumption means the lifting of body and spirit to the throne of God. He considered it a very important movement in traditional religion, for it gave the feminine a rightful, equal place with the masculine concept of God. This resolution of the opposites in an individual is what Jung calls *individuation,* and what we call *wholeness,* Oneness with the Spirit. The Catholic church's pronouncement of the Assumption in 1950 brought this idea to the world as a whole and began a change in the collective unconscious, according to Jung. As we observe women reaching toward equality as human beings, we can see the results.

The churches, both Protestant and Catholic, are still struggling over the issue of woman's position in the organized church. Some are being divided or split asunder over the issue of the feminist movement. Little by little, I believe, women will take their place and be allowed to become great leaders. The New Thought movement gives equal status to both men and women.

Mary, the divine feminine, was and is the mother of the Prince of Peace. It is the loving, compassionate heart that brings peace to this world. But the peace of the world is different from the peace that Jesus brought. He said in John 14:27, "Peace I leave with you, my peace I give unto you; not as the world gives do I give to you. Let not your hearts be troubled, neither let them be afraid."

Again it is the heart, the feminine principle of love, that he is speaking of. It is fear that causes us to be troubled, that takes away our peace. It is love that casts out fear and brings Peace.

Isaiah prophesied that a child would be born: "The government shall be upon his shoulder . . . his name will be called 'Wonderful Counselor, Mighty God, Everlasting Father, Prince of Peace.' " (Is. 9:6). And so Jesus was and is the Prince of Peace. And within our consciousness is the Christ, the Prince of Peace, for our lives and the lives of those surrounding us—indeed, of the world.

When Jesus came to the apostles after his resurrection, his first words to them were "Peace be with you. As the Father has sent me, even so I send you." He sent them out in peace. How the Christian world has misinterpreted Jesus' mission and his commission to us!

Mankind has ever been embroiled in anything but peace. Now that the nations have an arsenal large enough to destroy the earth, it is imperative that we have peace, and it must be woman's task, the feminine's, to lead the march for peace. It is through love for every man, woman, and child on earth that peace will be established. And Love is the peace that Jesus gave. Peace in man's terms is lack of war. But peace in Jesus' terms is Love.

Yes, Mary is the Mother of him who teaches us to "Love the Lord our God with all your heart, with all your soul and with all your mind." and to "love your neighbor as yourself." Through these two commandments and only through these will we have "peace that passeth all understanding," and then the peace of the world and the peace of Jesus will be the same, will be one.

The feminine principle within each of us, man or woman, must lead the way to peace for the world. Peace within each of us will bring peace to the world.

And so Mary, Our Lady, is our Savior also, for it is through her that the Christ is born. And the Christ has much work to do, as we shall see in the lives of other women of the New Testament. Our Christ can also heal, lift from death (sleep), bring peace, teach the good news, and lead us to pure Being. Jesus said, "In my Father's house are many mansions" and "Truly, truly, I say to you, he who believes in me will also do the works that I do, and greater works than these will he do, because I go to the Father" (John 14:12). The Spirit within Jesus is speaking to our Spirit within, the Christ. And love, the divine feminine, leads us upward.

23

Elizabeth

(Luke 1, 3)

BIRTHING AN ADVANCED SOUL

In writing of Elizabeth we must of necessity learn much about John the Baptist for, as his mother, she helped prepare the way for Jesus to do his teaching.

In our growth and development to higher consciousness we go from stage to stage. As we study the biblical accounts of the Jews, John the Baptist, and the teachings of Jesus and the first Church, we see these as stages in our own development. Thus John the Baptist becomes a bridge from the Jewish Law to the Love and compassion of the teachings of Jesus Christ.

As mentioned in the chapter on Mary, the mother of Jesus, there is a distinct possibility that Jesus and John came from parents who were members of the Essene sect. Zechariah, the father of John the Baptist, served as a priest in the Temple. He was of a high spiritual caste, from the division of Abijah. His wife, Elizabeth, was from a priestly class also, her genealogy going back to Aaron, Moses' brother and the first high priest. She was deeply spiritual and may have been reared in the Essene temple.

While Zechariah was offering incense on the altar one day, he was visited by the angel Gabriel. Now he and Elizabeth were well advanced in years and without children. The angel announced to Zechariah that Elizabeth would conceive and bear a son whose name should be John and who should be raised as a Nazarite, drinking neither wine nor strong drink. "He will be filled with the Holy Spirit . . . and he shall make ready for the Lord a people prepared."

Zechariah could not immediately believe the heavenly messenger. His masculine centeredness on logic and reasoning and not on intuition made him skeptical. So he was struck dumb, probably deaf also, and did not speak again until the baby was born and named John. Meanwhile Elizabeth conceived and for five months hid herself away, saying, "Thus the Lord has done to me to take away my reproach among men." She must have been an unusually spiritual woman to bring to life the great prophet John the Baptist. Since she was advanced in age and past the time of child-bearing, we can assume that this birth was also miraculous.

Elizabeth, as we know, was cousin to Mary the mother of Jesus (in some translations she is called a kinswoman). When Mary received the annunciation of her pregnancy, you will remember, the angel Gabriel told her that Elizabeth had also conceived. Mary at first could not receive his prediction for her, but after he told her about the Holy Spirit being upon her kinswoman Elizabeth, she began to believe. And he left a very important message for all of us: "For with God nothing is impossible." Then she accepted the message and her service to the Lord. However, she was so overcome by the news that she had to go visit her cousin. She knew that Elizabeth would understand because she, Elizabeth, had had a high spiritual experience too.

When Mary greeted her cousin, Elizabeth immediately recognized that Mary was pregnant and carrying a special child. Elizabeth was clairvoyant, a special trait, else she would not have discerned Mary's mission. She was the first woman to recognize the Christ, the Messiah. She said to Mary, "And why is this granted to me, that the mother of my Lord should come to me? For behold, when the voice of your greeting came to my ears, the babe in my womb leaped for joy. And blessed is she who believed that there would be fulfillment of what was spoke to her from the Lord" (Luke 1:42-45). Mary then accepted fully the message from Gabriel, her concern and doubt laid to rest by Elizabeth, and she sang the glorious Magnificat—"My soul magnifies the Lord, and my spirit rejoices in God my Savior."

Elizabeth helped Mary accept her gift from God. Mary remained with Elizabeth for three months, the end of which would be about the time for the birth of John. When finally Elizabeth delivered, her relatives and friends rejoiced with her and wanted to name the baby after his father, as was the custom. However his parents named him John, whereupon Zechariah's speech was restored. He was filled with the Holy Spirit and prophesied the coming of the Messiah as well as John's duty: "You, child, will be called the prophet of the Most High; for you will go before the Lord to prepare his ways, to give knowledge of salvation to his people in the forgiveness of their sins, through the tender mercy of our God, when the day shall dawn upon us from on high to give light to those who sit in darkness and in shadow of death, to guide our feet into the way of peace" (Luke 1:76–79).

For us of the New Age, the story seems very speculative, especially in view of our scientific knowledge of the biological process —that Elizabeth could bear a child in her advanced age. There have been many great religious leaders throughout the ages who have had such a birthing. But what does Elizabeth mean for us of this modern age?

Elizabeth was advanced in age when she conceived. Many of us think that we are too old to take up a new truth, to study the metaphysical philosophy. But we, like Elizabeth, must accept the messages that come from God and allow to happen what otherwise seems impossible. She birthed a child in her advanced age because she was being blessed by God. She had earned the joy and privilege. *Birthing a child is symbolic of birthing an idea.*

Elizabeth and Zechariah had earned the happiness that came to them in the birth of John. He was advanced spiritually and his life portrayed this. What does it take for us to birth a great soul? It is thought by many that if we are to improve our world by birthing children who are advanced spiritually, the mothers and fathers of our physical children must devote themselves to a spiritually pure life. Attention to things spiritual; meditation; study— all enhance this possibility for our modern parents. They must prepare the way. Certainly Zechariah and Elizabeth did so.

The world needed John the Baptist, or at least that part of the world that was preparing for the Messiah. Perhaps Elizabeth had prayed for such a son. As we look at the children that are being born today we can see those who are more alert, healthier, more intelligent, and more spiritually aware. These children are being born for an important purpose, and the advance of humanity on our planet depends on them. These children will often lead the way.

Elizabeth must have also been prepared for a child who was very different. It is said that John "grew and became strong in spirit, and he was in the wilderness till the day of his manifestation to Israel" (Luke 1:80). We wonder how she accepted his going to the wilderness to learn his lessons. Did she want to be protective, as so many of us mothers are today?

There is very little said about Elizabeth in the scripture, but we are reminded of that great mother, Sarah, who like Elizabeth bore her special son, Isaac, in her advanced age. And we know that mothers, in their rearing of these special sons, have much to do with the outcome of the lives of those sons. Elizabeth is reflected in her son's mission of preparing the way for the Lord, as she predicted when she saw Mary.

John always claimed that he had come to prepare the way for the Messiah. Perhaps Elizabeth had taught this to him. It was necessary for someone to come to move the people from the old Jewish Law to the Law of Love. And John fulfilled this mission. John, although seeming to be a haranguing, absolutist preacher, was also humble enough to recognize the higher being that Jesus was. As Jesus came to him to be baptised, John proclaimed, "Behold the Lamb of God" (John 1:35). And we admire Elizabeth, for we know that her spirituality shone through John.

Elizabeth gave the world John the Baptist through a miraculous birth. Some say he was Elijah reincarnated. Elizabeth no doubt knew the scriptures well and may have known that his mission was as great as Elijah's. She raised John to be aware of the God of his salvation. We should do no less for our children.

There is only one woman in the Bible named Elizabeth, and she it is who gave birth to this great harbinger of Truth. The metaphysical meaning of her name is the soul in the feminine, or love consciousness. She carries the letters *El* in her name, which stand for God. She brought forth a great prophet. We have much to be grateful for.

Esoteric: THE BRIDGE FROM LAW TO LOVE

Let us see the inner meaning now.

Zechariah (the entrance of spiritual thought into man's consciousness) affords a beginning. This entrance of a spiritual thought into our consciousness can change our life forever. John the Baptist symbolizes intellectual acceptance of the Truth.

Elizabeth means "my God is my oath" or "the fullness of God." It is well to remember that *beth* means seven, which is the number of physical completion. Elizabeth, a high level of spiritual understanding, lies within us also. When a spiritual thought enters our conscious mind, the Divine is waiting. We are helped in our birthing by an intellectual acceptance of God. Then the Christ that dwells within our unconscious is born. Once we have had an experience of touching that Divinity through hearing, either from a teacher or from our inner Knowing, we give birth to the grace and mercy of the Lord (Jesus). Our repentance follows, sometimes baptism of water or the Holy Spirit, or both, and our life is centered on our spiritual growth and development. We are not finished. We have just begun, for it takes many years and possibly lifetimes to overcome the false beliefs we have held based on intellectual teachings and the Law passed down by our predecessors.

Being like Elizabeth, "in the fullness of God," we may bring forth the awareness of our God at a different level of consciousness than Mary brought forth. We each bring forth from our own level of consciousness. But each step in our evolution back to the Father is necessary, and John, or the intellect, goes before us and leads us on to higher and higher Knowing. Elizabeth taught him to express his fullness in his own way as we too must express our Truth.

Often we start out by being an absolutist. It seems the right way. Many of us carry the shadow of memories of former lives when we were in a more absolutist place, and it feels comfortable to remain there. But we also have the teaching of Jesus on love, and this will come forth at the proper time. Then we are not comfortable with the teachings of guilt, fear of Hell, belief in a wrathful, punishing God. John the Baptist, intellect, precedes the Christ, spiritual awareness.

Many of us coming from a Christian background of "hellfire and damnation" may have had parents who were very moralistic, based on reason, the intellect, without much forgiveness and love of God included. They often taught that we must follow their laws with no regard for our own choices. Like John the Baptist, the intellectual haranguing brought us to baptism and a feeling of being cleansed of our sins. But we must remember, as John taught, that there is another who teaches fuller Truth, the teaching of Jesus Christ. So much of our Christian heritage is based on the teachings of St. Paul and the Law of the Old Testament, and not on the teachings of Jesus. We of the New Thought are trying to restore the true meanings of the Sermon on the Mount and the Kingdom of Heaven. We are trying to free people from their burden of guilt.

Elizabeth was complete and whole. We too are complete and whole, but we do not always realize this. I am sure that she learned many lessons from her son, her intellect. This is the proper sequence for us. But eventually we come to the teaching of Jesus and are less dogmatic, more accepting of the choices of others for themselves. And then Jesus' teaching—to love the Lord our God with all our heart, with all our soul, and with all our mind, and to love our neighbor as ourself—becomes real.

So Elizabeth, the perfection of the Lord, abides in us all, awaiting the birth of the intellect, the New Thought, that will lead us from the Law of the past to the awareness of our inner Divinity, the Christ.

24

Anna

(Luke 2:36–38)

THE PATH

To some women is given the opportunity of separating from the world and, through prayer and fasting, rising in strength and love to a divine place of omniscience. Thus it was with the widow Anna, a prophetess, who was the first woman to proclaim Jesus, after his birth, as the Christ or Messiah. There are women today who have done likewise and who proclaim the Christ in their daily duties.

Many women who are divorced or widowed, after rearing their children, have turned within to prayer and meditation (fasting from thinking) and grown in conscious awareness of God the Father. They have worked in the Church or have allowed their creative powers to express in art, music, writing, or caring for others. These, like Anna, are given the Word to proclaim in many areas and are a great blessing to mankind.

Three small verses are given to her account, but she has lived through history as an insightful woman. She taps our imagination.

The account is that seven years after her wedding she became a widow. She began devoting herself to temple work and was a prophetess—the only one mentioned in the New Testament. She served and prayed and fasted. She was standing by when Simeon, the priest, blessed Jesus and proclaimed, "Behold, this child is set for the fall and rising of many in Israel, and for a sign that is spoken against (and a sword will pierce through your own soul also) that thoughts out of many hearts may be revealed" (Luke 2:34,35). As Anna observed the ritual, she *knew* and she "gave thanks to God, and spoke of him to all who were looking for the redemption of Jerusalem." The redemption of Jerusalem was the coming of the Messiah.

We, as women of the New Age, can do likewise. Now we have financial security; now through education and a career we can be self-supporting. Maybe we will have to wait until we retire from our job but we still have twenty years or more to devote more fully to our spiritual growth and expression. Hopefully through our career years we have been devoted to prayer and fasting and "do not depart from the temple" nor forsake our spiritual development for sense appetites.

There are few women who are ready for this spiritual devotion, and until one is ready, one should not try it. Remember, there is only one prophetess in the entire New Testament. Jesus said, "Many are called but few are chosen" (Matt. 22:14). But when a woman is ready for this devotion, she will know it. Then her heart, her hands, her feet, her mind will be devoted to God, and she will "see" the Christ.

Anna also proclaimed the Christ "to all who were looking for the redemption of Jerusalem." If you choose to devote yourself to Anna's way, then you will proclaim what you see and know to the right people. Often we are so excited about our discovery that we try to tell everyone about it and succeed in antagonizing not a few. No, we proclaim to those who are "looking" for the Christ. Sometimes they may be looking in the outer, as the Jews were. We may be able to help them look within for this Savior of mankind. Jesus expressed his inner Christ in all his teachings, and others can do the same.

Devotion to this Path is a lonely choice for those who are able to give up attachment to children, spouses, relatives, things, and friends. When we start the Path, we do not realize what things we may be required to sacrifice, but as we drop them off one by one, we are ready to let them go—that is, letting go of what we have been so attached to that we felt we could not live without it. Of course we will continue to love all in our circle, but we put the Christ first when choices must be made. Even though married to a very understanding husband, we must tread our own lonely path, for each consciousness must manifest in its own way. This is what being a mystic means.

We shall then recognize the Christ in each person we meet. We love and adore each soul. We express our love by giving thanks to God for each one and by proclaiming the appearance of that Christ in him or her.

All this is a deep responsibility, but the rewards are so great that words cannot describe them. "A sword may pierce your soul," as Simeon proclaimed to Mary, Jesus' mother. Yes, there will be pain. But to nurture and care for this Christ will be the greatest Joy of your Soul.

Esoteric: GRACIOUSLY TURNING TOWARD GOD

Anna was born of Phanuel. Anna means "gracious" and Phanuel means "turned toward God" or "beholder of the face of God." Often we have a phenomenal experience that turns us in the direction of devoting our lives to God and His people. Mine came through a vision, but because I was not ready to give up attachment to physical happiness, it was some eighteen years later, when a "sword pierced my soul" at the death of my twenty-year-old son in Vietnam, that I was turned. But I had in my past experience "seen" God, and I was turned toward Him. The result was a secret decision to devote my life to God and His work.

So often we do not understand what happens to us, but all experiences are really meant to help us manifest our spiritual understanding in one degree or another. By being alert and aware to serendipity (good coming from unexpected experiences) we will rejoice. These experiences, when recognized, give us our first toehold on the ladder of ascension.

The two numbers used in these three verses are 7 and 12. "Seven years from her virginity" and "a widow of about eighty-four years" (= 12 in numerology). Both numbers represent completion. Seven = physical completion (she left the world of marriage and conserved her divine energy for the work of the temple, or spiritually changing from the physical). Twelve denotes spiritual completion (twelve disciples, twelve gates to the Kingdom of Heaven). Anna's prophetic awareness of who Jesus really was indicates her spiritual perfection. When we reach this high level we too shall be able to prophesy and teach the ultimate realities of God's kingdom.

Anna, a true teacher for our generation, is to be meditated upon. Her life of devotion and her reward of seeing the Christ before he was proclaimed may lead some of us to separate from the world and serve in the spiritual realm. Jesus said to his apostles, "Come away by yourselves to a lonely place, and rest awhile" (Mark 6:31). We too need to come apart from the scramble of the world so that we can recognize the Christ.

25

Mary and Martha

(*Martha:* Luke 10; John 11, 12.
Mary: Luke 10; John 11, 12; Mark 14)

There is so much wonderful teaching in the accounts of Mary and Martha and Jesus that this will be a rather lengthy chapter. These two women, the inner and outer devotion to the Christ, and their brother, Lazarus, the Christ initiate, all come together as exemplifying what Jesus taught. Service and silent devotion bring us to the ultimate of Wisdom, the Kingdom of Heaven; and the Christ (Jesus Christ) is our teacher, our revealer, our resurrection and our Savior.

There are three significant accounts of this family. Each event is a bead strung on our own consciousness to act as a rosary for our awareness. So many interpretations have been given them. I hope that this one will strike a note that will reverberate throughout your earth life and beyond into eternity.

Activity or Meditation: One Thing Is Needed (Luke 10: 38-42)

This family—Lazarus, Mary, and Martha—were often hosts to Jesus and his apostles, so they must all have been of very high consciousness of God the Father. Although Mary and Martha confessed their belief that Jesus was the Messiah or Christ, Lazarus never spoke, or so the scriptures seem to imply. These two women alone declared their faith.

One day Jesus came to their home in Bethany (house of palms or fig trees). Martha, it is said, received him into *her* house. "House" symbolizes consciousness, so we know that Martha was spiritually centered. Mary sat at Jesus' feet in a humble manner and listened to his teaching. Martha was busy preparing the food and serving it and became irritated when Mary did not help her, so she complained to Jesus. His reply was that she was

too anxious about many things when only one thing was necessary, and that Mary had chosen and recognized this one thing:
listening and learning what the Christ had to say.

Martha's service to others was her way of expressing her
spirituality. Now this is laudable, and our Christian teaching
has always emphasized service to others. We have interpreted
Paul's teaching to care for the prisoners, the orphans, and the
widows as our primary task, and much good has resulted. But
somewhere along the way in our busyness we may have lost
direct contact with God and let the priest or the preachers do
our praying and listening to the Christ. As a result, we lost our
focus on the "one thing needed" and became irritated and
impatient with those not so busily engaged in the world's activities but who have chosen to withdraw from the world in order
to enrich their own souls.

However, too much of either gets us out of balance. We must
serve as well as study and meditate. When we are enriched by
our awareness of the Presence, we need to channel it into our
daily active life—but knowing all the while that to be engaged
in study and meditation and prayer is central to our serving in the
right amount and in the right way.

We can make life much simpler if we really look for ways to
center on God. How many times I have heard women say, "I
would like to meditate and study and pray more, but I just do
not have the time. My club needs this, my husband demands
that, my children and house take up the rest of my time." And
what did Jesus say about not following him because of these
responsibilities? When a disciple asked that he be allowed to
first go and bury his father before he followed him, Jesus said,
"Follow me; and let the dead bury the dead" (Matt. 8:22). Not
having time is only an excuse and usually indicates lack of
devotion.

As women, we can enrich our own life and the lives of our
families if we choose to spend our time balanced between service
to others and Christ awareness, remembering that Christ awareness is choosing the good portion.

We are all subject to race consciousness, which today finds
its principal base in consumerism. But we can rise above that if
we are truly dedicated to our soul's advancement. Doing too
much for children and husband deprives them of the oppor-

tunity of growing and of giving to each other and to us. How many selfish teenagers we see coming from homes where mother uses the time that modern mechanical conveniences have spared her to spoil her children and husband. This time, which is truly God-given, might be better used to develop her consciousness, which would raise the others of her household to a higher level. We are all faced with the choice of whether to minister to the physical or to the spiritual.

The female aspect of our being, both men and women, longs for the wholeness that can be had only through faith in God and reliance on the highest teachings ever brought to earth. If you have everything and are still dissatisfied with your life, unhappy without real joy, you have probably chosen to be anxious and troubled about many things, like Martha, when only one thing is needed: centeredness in God's Will and knowing that all is in Divine Order in your life. This will bring peace beyond understanding. Real and effective service needs to be preceded by knowledge of Truth. The practice of It will bring Joy.

Esoteric: THE MYSTICAL AND OCCULT PATHS

In the area of consciousness development Corinne Heline defines the Mystical Path as one of a spontaneous and unplanned experience of God, of the Christ within. She defines the Occult Path as one that is planned in advance and scientifically worked out. It is the path of knowledge and works. The Mystical Path eventually requires the casting off of the personal life for the impersonal one, and the occultist will cast off knowledge as the only answer, for it does not satisfy. Mary, we could say, represents the Mystical Path, while Martha represents the Occult Path through her works and knowledge. The combination of the two was needed.

We are all capable of being the mystic, one who centers his/her life on the activity of the Spirit. Or we may be an occultist—one who centers on knowledge, perhaps a more scientific approach to consciousness expansion.

In the metaphysical movement we have both philosophies, although seeking knowledge through books, lectures, and seminars seems to be on the rise at present. And this is only proper, for most of us must grow through this phase before we realize that we need more. The two are combined in the following scripture, although the italicized portion is often left off by teachers of this movement. "I go to the Father" is the Mystical Path (John 14:12): "Truly, truly, I say to you, he who believes in me will also do the works that I do, and greater works than these shall he do, *because I go to the Father.*" Works and knowledge, yes, but it is consciousness of the Christ, which is God manifest, that moves us from knowledge and works alone to Spirit-centeredness.

One or the other is neither right nor wrong. They are only sides of the same coin, and if it is your destiny to be a Mary in this life, you will know it. If it is to be a Martha, so be it. But when you accept the Mystical Path as your destiny, your consciousness will be turned more and more to your spiritual Center and you will sit at the feet of Jesus and give to your Christ the best you have to offer.

At the same time, we need to be well grounded in knowledge of the scriptures, of the Law, of the way of Jesus. Then our next step of "knowing because I *know*" will come. When knowledge and spiritual experiences come together, we are wise in the best sense. But it takes both. Do not die at the stage of knowledge and works. Go to the highest.

And so within our own being we balance the work on the inner and on the outer, the masculine and the feminine, the opposites, and reach beyond the reason and come awake, rise from the dead, and allow wisdom or intuition to lead us. It is this resurrection we will speak of next. In resurrecting wisdom we will raise our divine energy from the dead, and as we are crucified we rise again. Our body changes to pure spirit. We live in the ethers, in the Kingdom of Heaven, as John prophesied in the Book of Revelation. Jesus demonstrated all of this for us.

Jesus said that Mary had chosen the better way. She was the mystic.

THE RAISING FROM THE DEAD: FOREVER YOUNG
(John 11:1–46)

We have just touched on the first important incident in the account of Mary and Martha. The other two are the resurrection of Lazarus and the anointing of Jesus' feet by Mary. One follows the other to a higher and higher level.

Briefly, Jesus received word that Lazarus was ill. He remarked, "This illness is not unto death; it is for the glory of God." And we have the setting for his actions. Then the scripture says that Jesus loved Mary, Martha, and Lazarus and so he stayed two days longer where he was. That is intriguing. If he loved Lazarus, why did he not go immediately and heal him? Then he suggested they go to Judea, where Lazarus dwelt and where the Jews were antagonistic to Jesus. His apostles remonstrated. Jesus declared that he was protected; besides, Lazarus was only asleep, and he would awaken him. Then he said, "Lazarus is dead," and he said he was glad he had not been there when he died, "so that you may believe."

As they approached the house, Martha met him and declared her faith in his healing power by saying, "If you had been here my brother would not have died; but I know that whatever you ask from God, God will give you." She opened the door to her brother's resurrection. Jesus replied "Your brother will rise again." Then he said that he, the Christ, was the resurrection and the life. "He who believes in me, though he die, yet shall he live, and whoever lives and believes in me shall never die. Do you believe this?" Martha replied, "Yes, Lord, I believe that you are the Christ, the son of God, he who is coming into the world." Remember: the Christ within Jesus, not Jesus the man, spoke the above words.

When Mary, who was being still and at home, learned he had come, she too went to meet him and said, "Lord, if you had been here my brother would not have died," thus declaring her faith in his healing power and the need for the I AM in healing.

Jesus showed emotion: "Jesus wept" when he saw the grief of those around Mary and Martha. Why he wept has been discussed for centuries. Perhaps he was moved by their grief. Perhaps he was showing his Jewish heritage of great emotionality. Perhaps the movement of emotion is most important for the doing of any great spiritual work. Perhaps he knew that this act—raising Lazarus from the dead—would hurry the Jewish authorities to condemn him.

He went to the tomb, he ordered the stone removed from the tomb's mouth, he prayed and thanked God for hearing him and declared he was doing this act to influence others to see the glory of God; and then he *commanded:* "Lazarus, come forth." And

Lazarus appeared still bound in his grave bandages, and Jesus said, "Unbind him, and let him go." Some Jews who were in attendance believed in him. Others went to tell the Pharisees, who immediately were fearful of Jesus' power and influence and planned how to get rid of him.

What a marvelous account and how many directions we could go! However, I will discuss it from the viewpoint of overcoming death and unfettering our youthful spirit so that we may live again.

Many of us live to what earth consciousness calls old age before we take time and give attention to the Christ that lies "quietly stretched out in sweet repose" waiting for our attention. Many believe they are too old to "take up their cross and follow Jesus." But we are never too old. Even though we long for eternal youth, we give in to race consciousness, which says, "You will grow old and die," speaking of the physical. We often equate our mind and our spirit with this same conviction.

Charles Fillmore taught that the resurrection of Lazarus symbolized restoring the consciousness to the idea of youth, which is asleep in the subconscious or tomb of the mind. He says, "The awakening of youthful energies is necessary to one in the regeneration"* These youthful energies are spiritual and physical.

Now in order to bring this youthful consciousness, eternal youth, alive many are dieting, exercising, using cosmetics, thinking positive and youthful thoughts, declaring and living faith in their own ability to take care of themselves—but these do not retain youth, for most become wrinkled and physically weak as the years pile up. The spirit, the consciousness of God, is dead and bound in the physical body. All attention is focused on caring for the body. And it doesn't work.

The three—Mary, Martha and Lazarus—with a fourth, Jesus, make wholeness and life, and not death.

Mary symbolizes deep attunement to the teachings of Jesus Christ, to inner devotion, probably through meditation and prayer. Martha symbolizes outer (physical) activity based on spiritual association. Lazarus, who is silent, symbolizes wisdom or intuition, which comes to us through feelings and unconscious knowing. Jesus symbolizes the Spirit, the Christ that uses the I AM, the

*Metaphysical Bible Dictionary, p. 398, under "Lazarus."

Father, to awaken the person to the awareness of the beloved child, the youth, that lies dormant in his or her dead consciousness. In order to awaken or resurrect it, the higher Self, God Incarnate, must be appealed to. And so all of the faculties—body, mind, emotions, and spirit—come together, and we are rejuvenated and have eternal youth.

Jesus affirmed his belief in God's power to resurrect Lazarus when he said, "Father, I thank thee that thou hast heard me. I knew that thou hearest me always, but I have said this on account of the people standing by, that they may believe that thou didst send me" (John 11:41,42).

Lazarus, the wisdom or consciousness of God which never grows old and dies, is within each of us. We are all blessed with this potential. For it to come fully alive, to be resurrected, we may need to practice service and loving devotion to our Christ Presence for many lives. But as we begin a new life, we start at a higher level. And then, when we completely believe that God is capable of doing *all* things, we finally demonstrate our faith in the Ultimate. Our Spirit is fully resurrected and we do not need earth experiences again to convince us of this great Truth. We are eternally young.

Do not believe you are too old to start this new but old quest for oneness with God. The "stone" or belief in old age and death can be rolled away with the teaching and the power of Christ consciousness. Your consciousness is not dead; it is just sleeping.

Jesus said, "He who believes in me shall never die." It is on this scripture that Christian faith and practice have been built, sometimes to the exclusion of awareness of God as the Father that Jesus always said was his Source. This level of consciousness has led us all higher at one time or another. But there are higher and still higher ways of looking at this scripture. Let us explore "shall not die."

Esoteric: ETERNAL LIFE, NOT DEATH

This seems to be a planet of death. We see it all around us. The creatures of this planet survive upon the death of another. And man seems to be irrationally afraid of death. Jesus came and demonstrated that death can be overcome, that there is no death but only Life. He taught us how to overcome and he spoke not only of spiritual death but also of physical death. More often, however, he spoke of eternal Life. Scriptural references include John 11:25,26: "I am the resurrection and the life; he who believes in me, though he die, yet shall he live, and whoever lives and believes in me shall never die"; John 8:51: "If anyone keeps my word he will never see death"; John 10:27,28: "My sheep hear my voice, and I know them, and they follow me; and I give them eternal life, and they shall never perish"; John 17:2,3: ". . . since thou hast given him power over all flesh, to give eternal life to all whom thou hast given him. And this is eternal life, that they know thee the only God, and Jesus Christ whom thou hast sent."

Now it is said that there are two deaths. The first death is to spiritual life. We are dead when we are not recognizing God as the source of Wisdom and Life. The second death is dissolution of the body. But Jesus taught that they can both be overcome.

In resurrecting Lazarus he showed that if one is of a high enough spiritual understanding, one can be resurrected even though one seems dead. This of course was Jesus' demonstration also.

A teaching that comes from Eastern Mysteries is difficult for us to accept. But I believe it is what the resurrection of Jesus was to teach us. With many lifetimes we can raise our conscious awareness of God to such a high point that our body is changed into pure energy. The great Masters have achieved this. Then the soul can manifest in either the physical or the spiritual body. Jesus showed this at his meetings with his apostles after his resurrection. And then in his ascension he demonstrated the manifestation of his body as pure Life. This is eternal Life. In Luke 20:34f. he states that those who are resurrected and are Sons of God cannot die any more.

Charles Fillmore (in *Atom-Smashing Power of Mind*) and Thomas Troward (in *The Law and the Word*) both taught that we do not need to die and wrote extensively on it. Our final challenge seems to be to overcome this race belief that all must die. And Jesus was teaching this, I believe, in his resurrection of Lazarus.

The Egyptian Mysteries have some basic truths that we have been trying to understand for hundreds of years. One of these has to do with the Mystery of Initiation, which is said to have been held in the Great Pyramid. After an initiate had studied many years and was assessed as being ready for his final test, he was taken into the pyramid, laid in the sarcophagus, and left alone.

Through exercises that he had been taught, his spirit, or astral body, was able to leave the physical body as he slept, and he learned the great Mysteries beyond this planet or this level of consciousness. After three and a half days, when the astral body, which was still attached to the physical, returned to the physical body, he was resurrected at the highest level of achievement of an initiate.

It has been suggested by one writer that Lazarus was going through this initiation, for which Jesus had trained him. He had achieved eternal life, for he had followed Jesus and had great faith in God. Perhaps this is what Jesus was alluding to when he told his disciples that Lazarus was asleep. This could explain why he did not awaken him until the fourth day of his entombment. We need not be reminded that Jesus was resurrected on the third day. One author has suggested that because Jesus revealed and demonstrated these deep secrets to the populace, he had to be put to death by the priests—for, as of old, none of these secrets was to be revealed or the revealer would die. Jesus revealed this great secret as well as many others to all of us.

The great Mystery of overcoming death was one of Jesus' greatest teachings. He repeatedly said that we could have eternal Life. Do we believe him or not? Basically, if we believe in the Christ Spirit within as a spark of God, we cannot die. We all have eternal Life; we just need to recognize it. Trial by fire, water, air, and earth was a part of the great Mysteries. Going through the death experience with full faith and no fear is said to be another test. Then it is that we *know* that death is an illusion.

Jesus' teachings are much deeper than we are able to grasp. Some day our understanding will be opened and the great Light will shine forth and we will know eternal Life. "O Death, where is thy victory? O death, where is thy sting?" (I Cor. 15:55). And Revelation: "And death shall be no more" (21:4). What a promise! What Truth!

The Anointing: Blocks on Our Path
(John 12:1–8)

In the outer world we are beset by cares for the physical, for the body needs. In our inner we are often disturbed by negative thoughts that cause chaos in our lives. Each of us must find that center of peace and anoint it with our oil of love if we are to be at one with God. Mary did this anointing of Jesus' feet as an example of what we should do with our spiritual consciousness.

To have the Christ within and not to be aware of it is the Hell that Judas went through. He did not understand that Jesus was teaching about the Kingdom of Heaven and so wanted to see Jesus made king of Judea. There is within us this same Judas—we must be aware of it.

I have used the account of the anointing that is recorded in John 12:1-8 as my source, since the other references do not make clear who the woman was, although the accounts are similar (Matt. 26:6-13; Mark 14:3-9; Luke 7:37,38).

Jesus, we are told, came again to the home of Lazarus, Martha, and Mary. This was following the great resurrection of Lazarus. They had supper and Martha served as usual. Mary took a box of costly ointment and anointed the feet of Jesus and wiped them with her hair. (The washing or anointing of feet was a usual custom performed for guests in that day.) Judas Iscariot protested and said that she should have sold the ointment and given the 300 denarii to the poor. Jesus said, "Let her alone, let her keep it for the day of my burial. The poor you always have with you, but you do not always have me."

What great love there must have been at that table that night! What rejoicing and gratitude! For Lazarus, the beloved brother, had come to life, and Jesus the great Savior was with them. His presence must have been so holy and uplifting that the vibrations all around were peaceful and joyous, so that Mary had to celebrate. She had to give to Jesus as he had given so richly to them. And the best was none too good. Not cheap oil, but the very best—with a wonderful fragrance that pervaded the entire house, just as his vibrations were doing.

Mary, the quiet one, felt deeply and perhaps anticipated that Jesus might not always be with them. So she gave him her full attention and with love cleansed his feet and used her hair to dry them. What humility!

There are always those in our company who do not understand our devotion to the Christ principle. Judas was focused on the outer. He found the purse more important than devotion to the principle, although it would appear he was very charitable. When others do not understand our spirituality, they often find a perfectly acceptable (to them) reason why we should not do what we are doing. And they often try to make us feel guilty.

Questions such as, Why do you spend so much time at class and studying when the children need you? or, How much are you giving to that church? Don't you know we cannot afford it? or, All that quiet prayer and meditation do no good; why do you waste time at it? And our reply must essentially be as Jesus gave it. "The house can wait, the children are at school, I need to give as I have received, I must have my quiet time." We must be firm as Jesus was and know that the Christ cannot wait. It needs our attention *now.*

Judas is often our own habits. The habit of saying "I don't have time to anoint my inner Christ" is only an excuse for our lack of devotion. When we are too busy, there is no anointing for our inner Christ. If we are to grow spiritually, we must give our first attention to God and the other things will be provided. Centeredness in our spiritual growth will make our outer life easier to live.

From the vantage point of inner Truth we can see the ointment as pure love that Mary was pouring on Jesus' understanding. And as she used it, she and the others in the house were able to share it through the fragrance of the love she poured out. All benefit in our circle of friends, children, spouse, relatives, and indeed the world when we give love unselfishly and give our very best.

This was done just previous to Jesus' triumphal entry into Jerusalem for the last Passover. Mary was getting him ready for his great commission. He said, "If anyone serves me, he must follow me; and where I am, there shall my servant be also; if anyone serves me, the Father will honor him" (John 12:26). He was speaking of the Christ within him and within each of us.

Esoteric: LOVE—THE MYSTIC'S DEVOTION

Mary being the mystic is that within us which knows that our Christ should have the very best. Judas is that within us that is not quite honest, not quite dedicated to the Truth. The human and the Divine; the sensual and the spiritual; the opposites. And how do we redeem this part of our consciousness that fears and covers up the fear with alibis and untruths?

The answer of course is to affirm our unity with Truth. Affirmations and denials are a good starting place, calling on God and in faith believing that He will help.

Sometimes our Judas is covetousness, greed, the need to lay up treasures on earth. All of these will also separate us from our Mystical Path. If our commitment to Truth is strong enough, we will be shown the way to overcome those thoughts that keep us from being devoted to the Mystical Path.

Mary may have been accused of being a dreamer, a ne'er-do-well, lazy, unsuccessful. After all, she was not married, and she followed this itinerant teacher. But she had chosen the better way for herself. We must each choose our best way, too.

The Christ loves us. Such love bubbles up from our inner Being when we give it extensive attention. This reward of meditation may not happen overnight, but with continued devotion such ecstasy can be ours. We may be alone so far as other people are concerned, but we are never really alone, for this living Presence, the Christ, is our constant companion.

Jesus said, in response to Judas' suggestion,"The poor you will always have with you. In physical form I will not always be with you." This was another hint he gave of his future sacrifice, but many did not understand him. And when Mary Magdalene went to the tomb "toward the dawn of the first day of the week," the "other Mary" was with her. Could this not have been Mary the sister of Martha? In our pouring out of love, we continue on, even in the face of seeming death. Her love was taken to the tomb.

These three—Mary, the mystic; Martha, the mind; and Lazarus, Wisdom—meant much to Jesus in his ministry. Our ministry needs all three also. Sitting at table and eating with the Source of all Light, our inner Christ, brings us the reward we so diligently seek. We can seek in peace now, for we know that Love poured out on the Spirit will bring us more joy than we can imagine. "Choose the better way."

There are so many rich spiritual truths in this account of Mary and Martha, and I have not begun to cover them. Seek them out for yourself. And your interpretation is right for you. Learn from them how you can best serve and love the Christ.

26

The Three Women Who Were Healed

(Matt. 8:14, 15; Luke 13:10–17; Mark 5:25–34)

SPIRITUAL HEALING

These three women—the one infirm, the one with fever, the one with the issue of blood—represent the faculties within us that are separated from our good. They find their good through the intercession of Jesus. For us our Christ Spirit represents Jesus and is the instrument for healing. It was the Christ of Jesus or the power of God that did the healing. His hand, his voice, and his love were directed by God. To God is all the praise, he said.

As we discuss spiritual healing, many of us have a tentative faith in it, would like to believe that it works, but are unsure due to the scientific medical approach to healing. If we can realize that it is not the doctor or the surgery or the medication that heals, but our faith in those scientific instruments, we will begin to understand faith healing. For faith healing and healing in outer medicine have the same source. It is the combination of the power of God and our faith that perfects, and until we rest in that belief, we will continue to have maladies and pain. Permanent healing comes through "preaching the gospel and healing the sick." Preaching the gospel is to understand the laws of life, living them, and teaching them. It is the Good News.

Through the ages we have had many faith healers—witch doctors, medicine men, Egyptian Mystery healers, Hippocrates, Asclepius, Jesus and his apostles of the early Christian Church. All taught that the spirit of the sick one must be touched if complete healing is to occur. The early Christian Church gave much emphasis to healing and to exorcising evil demons. Paracelsus, the European doctor and mystic who lived in the early 1500s, influenced the practice of medicine then and for many years later.

With the advent of the scientific age, these close ties with Spirit became lost. The intellect took over. With the coming of the nineteenth century, religion, medicine, and mysticism parted ways. The Christian religion let go of its original healing ceremonies and materialistic science had its way. (This brief history is expanded in *Healing, the Divine Art,* by Manly P. Hall, cited in the Bibliography.)

Then in the latter part of the nineteenth century metaphysical groups began to arise in the West. In America three were begun by women who had been sick and who were healed by spiritual methods. Three sick women again! Mary Baker Eddy began the Christian Science movement. Myrtle Fillmore healed herself of tuberculosis by spiritual methods, and she and her husband, Charles, founded the Unity movement. And Nona Brooks, also healed, founded the Divine Science movement. There were also traditional Christian church groups that taught and practiced the laying on of hands and prayer for health. (See *Spirits in Rebellion,* by Charles Braden, cited in the Bibliography.)

Jesus' ability to heal through spiritual methods has never been doubted by the spiritually minded. Time after time we are told in the gospels that he healed many. We are given accounts of over twenty specific healings. Hundreds of others occurred. All of these were performed not only to prove his ability to heal and to alleviate suffering, but also to teach his disciples how to heal. He knew the secret. We have been trying to learn it ever since.

Today we have many medical doctors who are combining the scientific as well as the intuitive spiritual practice of healing and are being most successful. However, most medical doctors treat the symptoms and do not bother with the cause. There is a movement toward holistic medicine, which takes into consideration the whole person—body, mind, emotions, and spirit. I believe this is the medicine of the future. It takes courage for a doctor to step out of the safe circle of scientific research and reach up to the spiritual; but more and more doctors will be doing this.

There are several methods used by those who are classified as spiritual healers. *Occult healing* uses magic, exorcism, astrology, magnetism, and extrasensory perception. *Magnetic healing* uses instruments that store up magnetic currents or else uses the magnetism of the healer's body, which he or she directs with motions of the hands. *Mystical healing* comes through direct knowledge of God and Truth and can be performed as the healer and the healee get in touch with the essence of Divinity. *Mental healing,* which is not new, is practiced by witch doctors, shamans, and priest-physicians as well as by such psychologists as Freud, Adler, and Jung. Mental healing is extremely popular in the metaphysical movement. Psychology and religion are combined to affect this healing. It is the healing of the healer's consciousness that affects the condition of the patient. Since the One Mind is everywhere present, It is the medium that heals. Some metaphysicians teach denial and affirmation as necessary for healing. But it is the at-one-ness that brings about the healing, all agree.

The first woman healed was Peter's mother-in-law, who was sick with a fever (Matt. 8:14-15). A festival breakfast was planned and Jesus and some of his apostles came to eat. She was probably the main organizer. Jesus saw her, touched her, and she was healed. And she "rose and served them." Peter symbolizes faith, and so through his faith the woman was healed. And later Peter became a great healer. Faith is a must.

A fever indicates an infection, and we assume that it is in the body. But if we went deeper, we might find that our thinking or emotional life has been beset by some kind of disturbance, perhaps deeply buried, that has changed the body vibrations. The fever is good, just as the feeling of disturbance or of pain is good. Then we are led to do the cleansing. And our spiritual work does much of the cleansing.

In Luke 13:10-17 we read of the second woman, who was healed in a synagogue. Jesus was teaching there on the Sabbath and saw the woman, who was bent over and could not fully straighten herself. For eighteen years she had been infirm. Jesus called to her and said, "Woman you are freed from your infirmity." He laid his hands on her and she "was made straight and praised God." She knew whereof the healing came. She had faith. He spoke and he touched. She praised God.

Our medical world is doing much research on the cause and cure of arthritis at the present time. It strikes many people, seldom brings immediate death, and is a pain that people live with for years. It causes stiffening of joints. This seems to relate to stiffness of attitude of mind. Or perhaps it is rigidity of life, looking back to the past (remember Lot's wife), inability to move with the times. In any case, again we have the Spirit healing. How wonderful when our medical doctors will take into consideration the flow of energy in the body and the release of its blockages. Many have received healing with acupuncture, which is releasing the divine energy to do its work. And Jesus taught us how.

The third woman (Mark 5:25-34) was the one with the issue of blood for twelve years. We do not know whether it was external or internal bleeding. Perhaps cancer was the malady. She found Jesus in a crowd and pushed her way forward, thinking, "If I can only touch his garment I shall be healed." She did it silently and timidly. It is said that she was healed upon touching only the fringe of his garment. Oh, the mightiness of the Spirit! He was immediately aware of the healing and turned to find her. She came and fell at his feet (humility) and confessed (Truth). She was fearful, but he removed her fear by saying, "Daughter, your faith has made you well; go in peace, and be healed of your disease."

Through faith which removes fear; through imaging (she saw herself touching him); through persistence of effort to get to the Source of all healing; through action on her part; through humility and through Truth she was healed, and Jesus said, "Go in peace," have no fear. We hear of this happening every day and wonder how. We know that it is the Spirit interceding when we are ready. Perhaps it is fear that causes our illness. Faith alleviates fear.

We all learn much from our physical pains. Do not decry such an experience. It may bring you the greatest awakening of this lifetime. Jesus comes to us through our Christ, and healings do take place. We may need to have the intercession of a healer, of a person trained in spiritual healing available from all the metaphysical churches. Some of these groups seem to emphasize spiritual healing more than others. But if you feel this is the route for you to take, find one of them. Prayer heals!

And so Jesus used touch, the spoken word, omniscience in thought and deed. Forgiveness, faith, humility, praise and thanksgiving, compassion, love—all of these and more he demonstrated as he gave special attention to women and lifted them up from

their slave-like condition. He is our greatest friend. He gives
women courage to be whole!

If you have a calling to be a healer—follow it. Many nurses
who have been trained in the medical world are now using one
or more of these spiritual methods to heal their patients. Many
doctors, especially chiropractors and osteopaths, are practicing
holistic methods with great success. More and more medical doctors will bring the Spirit "priest" back into their practice. I believe
one must be called to be a spiritual healer, for it is a great gift
and comes from the Spirit's nudging a person on to greater service.

There is so much fine material written today on how to remain
healthy that I will not go into that. I would like to suggest, however, that diet, exercise, and the practice of the highest spiritual
principles will help. A balanced, harmonized life; faith in the
Goodness of God; proper use of your divine energy to promote
health and not pleasure of the senses; thanksgiving for health;
forgiveness of one's self and others for their mistakes; eradication
of guilt feelings based on past performance; humility in the face
of the great blessings that come; and of course prayer and meditation will all be conducive to better health. The list is endless. Go
to your inner Guide in the silence and learn what you must do for
your own health.

I must add something about *chemicalization* of the body. As
our consciousness of the Divine changes, our thoughts change, our
emotions change and our bodies change. As we allow the Divine
to become more conscious, our body may take on the appearance
of ill health. A cleansing process is taking place. As the body is
cleansed, it may throw up some illness that seems to be our downfall. However, we must remember that all is for our good if our
life is centered on God's Will.

And so we pray. We examine our thoughts and feelings to see
if we are holding resentment, guilt, anger, lack of self-esteem,
covetousness, negativities of all kinds. We then cleanse these and
wait for our healing. It may not come suddenly, but as long as we
stay centered on the Christ, we know that it will come. Slowly
the body will heal.

Do not think of an illness as punishment. Know that it is for
your divine Christing. Use the medical help needed, pray without

ceasing, wait for your healing. You can rest assured that you will finally come up over this lack of perfection, and it will be of no account in your pursuit of the True Light.

Esoteric: Trial by Fire, Earth, Water, and Air

Each one of these accounts can be seen as a rung on the ladder of our own spiritual evolution, for evolving spiritually is really becoming 100 percent healed. Let us see what we can learn.

As we have seen, the esotericist teaches that we need to be challenged by testing. The four elements, a very important concept throughout the ages, are our testing ground. Air, water, earth, and fire can all be seen symbolically, which is how we will approach the three tests given here. When we study the Mystery religions, we are often reminded that our trials or tests by fire, earth, air, and water are a part of our Path to Ascension. Most of the accounts included in the Bible have to do with our evolution.

The first woman, Peter's mother-in-law, had a fever. Fever is heat, of the *fire* principle. Fire can cleanse, purify, or destroy. A fever can burn up the body, or the divine fire, the Kundalini, can cleanse the body of impurities and change the physical to pure Light. We have no idea what caused her fever. In fact, Jesus never seemed to be interested in the cause. He was interested in whether the patient believed, had faith, wanted to be healed.

The feminine principle, Peter's mother-in-law, within each of us is tried in many ways. It is through the lifting up of ourselves out of the negative use of fire that we can "arise and serve him." We serve the Spirit at a higher level after we are healed, having passed the test of fire.

Let us see this account as symbolizing something within Peter or ourselves. Let us see Peter as being sick with fever.

Peter symbolizes faith. His house symbolizes his body or consciousness. The feminine within him was out of balance. Being touched by Christ consciousness healed this imbalance. The passion of his emotions was neutralized and the fire within, the divine energy, was channeled to allow him to rise, to get up from his misdirected position and serve the Spirit of all Knowing. Thus Peter or faith was lifted up.

So it can be with us also. The feminine may be sick within us. It needs healing before we can find our true Self. This is the Age of Feminine Ascendancy. Men and women alike are experiencing it.

The second woman, called the infirm woman by many, represents the trial by *earth:* for eighteen years she had been bent over and directing her vision to the earth. She had not been able, under her own power, to straighten her body and look up to the heavens. She was an older woman, and her spine had been straight and upright at one time. Now she was imprisoned in her own body and consciousness.

The woman was in the synagogue where God was, for that was her belief—that God resided in the holy place. She was probably no stranger there and she did not ask for healing, but because she was where God was, it came to her by grace. Never underestimate grace. Inexplicable healings come many times.

Being bound to earth seems to be a test we all go through. It is part of our soul's experience. Most of us have to learn through experience that keeping our tunnel vision on the material does not bring joy, much less the happiness we seek. But we are tried. When we are freed, it is because we realize from our deepest Knowing that there is something else more important. Then we can detach from things and people, lose our desire, overcome pain, live a God-centered life, and look up. Our paralysis is healed. We are free.

Jesus called her (God knocked loudly and she heard). Woman (feminine principle) is infirm (attached to senses) 18 years (1 + 8 = 9, numerologically symbolic of the highest and most noble, and associated with great spiritual experiences; it approaches the state of wholeness, or 1). He laid his hands upon her (she allowed the power of God to come into her life through Jesus' teaching). She was made straight (the feminine principle flowed freely through her body and consciousness). She praised God (she immediately recognized the Source).

This could also be our path to overcome sense attachment. The grace of God is always working for us, for God is Love, and we are Love, and God Is.

Womankind is straightening up and looking ahead and upwards as she takes her rightful place next to men in an upright position.

After this healing, Jesus taught the correct use of the Sabbath and also expounded on his most popular theme—the Kingdom of Heaven (Luke 13:14-21). The healing of earth attachment is so connected with our regeneration that the healing prepares the way. The Kingdom of Heaven is that final spiritual state of a mankind that has lifted its eyes to the Divine and lives wholly within the Spirit.

The third woman is identified as "the woman who touched Jesus' garment." To be healed by merely touching the outer clothing of a mystic seems strange to us, but the esotericist knows that the effulgent light that surrounds a highly evolved being imparts this characteristic to all that he or she touches.

This humble woman, who did not have the courage to walk up to Jesus and ask for healing, knew that she could be healed by his Presence. She pushed through the crowd (negative ideas) to get the healing.

The physician had not healed her. *Physician* symbolizes outer means of healing. She had spent her substance (her energy) and had no more. She was at a very low point in both body and mind and still she had faith.

Blood (water) is symbolic of life. Blood is also symbolic of sacrifice for a higher good. Trial by loss of blood to the point of death often occurs before a person is to do a great spiritual work. Faith carries us through these trials.

She had been tried for twelve years. Twelve is the esoteric number of completion. Instead of defeat, she pushed her way through the negative thoughts against her healing and came to the Light. She overcame her trial by blood (*water*). However she was still fearful, and Jesus knew this. He located her in the crowd, and she came forward in fear. He said to her, "Daughter, your faith has made you well [whole]; go in peace, and be healed of your disease." Now she was whole—no more fear.

Her feminine principle had been misused for twelve years, but through faith, at the end of this period the flow was stopped and peace presided in the consciousness. The right use of the feminine is required. It can be lost in too much compassion, too much loving of the masculine, too much misuse of feelings and sensitive emotions expended on the outer things and people of our life. She was tried by the loss of water or passing through the time of loss of blood. She was healed by the Spirit or *air,* as were the other two.

Jesus, the Spirit, healed. Air is related to the creative breath of life. Light, lightness, is also related to the general symbolism of air. Air is our very life. It is the Spirit. Our faith in Spirit is tried.

Now each of these women was tried by the element of air, but each was also healed by it. Faith is a mental and spiritual as well as an emotional condition. Air is related to our thoughts and our imagination. Each woman, or the feminine principle, had been tested over and over by her thoughts, for when we are ill, our divine thoughts are often strangled, and it takes a healer who images us as healthy and whole to overcome these negative ideas.

The teachings of Jesus, the power of the word, the directions from our inner Christ are all related to air. The spiritual body that evolves from the physical is like air—light in weight and able to move anywhere. We live on air (the Spirit). Our trial is the misuse of this element. We learn to use it rightly as we do also fire, water, and earth.

Jesus images these women as whole and well. He used his divine energy (fire) to lift them up. His blood (water) was shed, which is the forerunner of the cleansing of this planet. He came to earth for our benefit. He looked up always to his Father and ours. "Look up and raise your heads, because your redemption is drawing near" (Luke 21:28). Our healing is nigh. It can be ours.

27

Herodias

(Matt. 14:1–12; Mark 6:14–29; Luke 3)

A WIFE'S INFLUENCE

Herodias is for us an extreme example of the depths of vindic-tiveness that a woman can fall into. She was of a family not known for their virtues, the Herods. She affected the lives of many good people of her day in an adverse way. She was responsible for the death of a servant of God who had come to prepare the way for the Messiah. She may have had a hand in the decision Herod, her husband, made about Jesus when he sent him back to Pontius Pilate to be sentenced. She symbolizes that side of human nature that is selfish and unforgiving, unable to admit the negative thoughts and actions of the human condition.

Herodias had been married to Herod's half-brother, Phillip. For unknown reasons—perhaps for power—she developed a rela-tionship with Herod, divorced her husband, and married Herod after he divorced his wife. John the Baptist, not being the most discreet prophet, openly and publicly denounced her and Herod. John, coming more from the intellect than from Love, the Spirit, had antagonized many with his self-righteous attitude, and Hero-dias waited for revenge. Herod imprisoned John the Baptist for his haranguing and accusations. At a banquet held on Herod's birthday, Herodias' daughter danced and pleased Herod and his guests. He offered her anything she wanted up to one-half of his kingdom. Her mother suggested she ask for the head of John the Baptist. Herod did not want to do this as he was somewhat in awe of John. But out of pride he agreed. John's head was brought to the daughter and she passed it to Herodias. Because John was a holy man, it is suggested by some that Herodias wanted his blood as it contained a power that she could use. (This is a very old, primitive belief.) John's life and ministry were ended as were his good works—all because of the unforgiving spirit of a woman.

This story is brief, but it has gone down in Bible history as an example of a malicious deed. Herod, through his desire to please Herodias, was the actor in the tragedy. Herodias was the cause. The daughter (the name Salome was given to her by Josephus, the ancient historian) had her part to play too, as she must have danced in a very suggestive manner.

As we all know, our actions have an effect on many among our acquaintances. We cannot help affecting many by our thoughts and actions, for we are truly one, although we may not understand that. Our highest ethical actions *and* our lowest affect many. And the higher our position in society, either on a national or a family scale, the more effect we have.

Herodias, being wife of the tetrarch of Galilee, was not thinking of her effect on others but was instead thinking of her own selfish needs. She was drunk with power and would not abide any criticism even though it was the truth. She knew that John the Baptist had power over the people. She also knew that he was right in his accusation. Oh, how violently we often respond to criticism of our actions, especially if our ego is bruised! She had her way with Herod, who was in the number one position. Many a wife has this same power in the life of a man who is a leader, a ruler, a despot, or just one of the mass of humanity.

How important is a wife's position in the life of her husband! A man in a powerful position often feels compelled to play the "macho" role of the strong he-man as he goes about his duties. Then his wife fills that vacancy of the feminine aspect lacking in his personality. He depends on her for the softness, the love, the sensitivity of the feminine. If she is a spiritually centered woman, she can handle this role with ease and compassion. If she has a need to control, to have power, she can ruin him, for as he trusts her and needs her, she has much power over him.

And so we as women must look to our own basic beliefs and philosophies. We must examine our motives as we talk with our husbands and help them with their problems. We can exert much power even in the family, which causes an imbalance and disharmony if we take the position of both father and mother. Our children will resent us, and ultimately their healthy personalities may be killed if we become domineering and controlling. (Salome was under the power of her mother; we do not know what her feelings were after she received the head of John the Baptist.) A woman's power is mighty! Who said she is the weaker sex?

Herodias' daughter appears in only a few verses of this vast book, but her name, Salome, has gone down as the epitome of sexual temptation. The opera *Salome* by Richard Strauss portrays this very graphically. Coming from the environment she did—her blood line came from Herods on both sides—we would expect her to find it difficult not to follow her mother's orders. Many a daughter has made devastating choices due to her mother's domination. Perhaps her dance was more innocent than has been portrayed through the ages. Who knows? She was really a pawn in the powerful setting, totally under the control of her mother.

Thus we as women must realize our power and serve the Spirit within and not our own selfish needs. For Herodias to have forgiven John the Baptist, to have looked at herself and her actions honestly, to have made amends where she could, and to have changed her way would have been the path of repentance that John taught. But she has portrayed for us the opposite. We know that the law of cause and effect caught up with her when, according to Josephus, the historian, she and her husband were banished to Gaul and all power was taken away from them.

Esoteric: EGO VERSUS THE CHRIST

Herod (symbolizing ego) and Herodias (symbolizing the feminine side of sense thought) were a team that was bound to bring disaster to many. This Herod, the ego, was the tetrarch who might have saved Jesus, the Light that came into the world, from death. How we allow our own ego to kill our spiritual leanings!

Ego, the controlling element in our personality based on a limited belief in our own power, causes us to make many decisions that are disastrous to our life. It is based upon fear, although it seems to be filled with courage. When we believe that we are totally and independently responsible for the good in our life, we are controlled by the ego. Some day we come to the realization that it is our Lord who gives us the opportunities, the intelligence, the love that brings success. We bring to ourselves our success as we open to the Spirit that goes before us. We also bring to ourselves our lack of success.

Herodias must be seen as an instigator of the aroused passion in the ego that made the decision to have a holy man killed. John the Baptist symbolizes the intellectual belief in God and the need to cleanse our thoughts and action so that the Christ can enter in. Herodias was sense-centered. When our life is centered on feeding the appetites of our senses, whether it is with food, drink, riches, power, sex, we can be sure that the holiness in our life will be crippled if not killed. Thus the ego and sense pleasure are a couple that cannot choose the spiritual way, for the focus is on the opposite. Any thoughts we have that might criticize our way of life are immediately imprisoned, and if our guilt has been aroused by a preacher or teacher, we may kill the thought and be done with it.

Many of us live long enough to realize the trap we have fallen into and go through repentance and change. We then deny the negatives in our lives, the ego and sensual attachment as our control, and find our way to a more spiritual center. Everyone makes some progress on his or her path in each life, the judgment of others notwithstanding.

The intellectual acceptance of the Lord's love and favor is not enough. Cleansing the unconscious through denial is not enough. We must go on to a feeling of spiritual love and devotion. The intellectual must fall and the spiritual must take over. John the Baptist lost his head (the intellectual) so that his prophecy could be fulfilled (Jesus will baptize with the Holy Spirit). Thus it will be with each of us. Symbolically, John had to become less so that Jesus' teaching could become more.

Search yourself, John taught. And so we should. For to know the presence of the Christ in our undefiled consciousness is to know all that we can grasp. We can be healed and know the Divinity of His Presence.

Herodias, our sensual attachment to our pride or ego, will finally be banished to Gaul without power. Her husband, Herod (the ego), and she (the sensual attachment) were together. We too will banish this pair. Our banishment may seem a punishment, but to rid ourselves of the ego and our sensual pride may be our saving grace. We often are in pain before we change our ways. The ego is a fighter against the Christ.

Some may point out that in having John killed, Herodias opened the way for Jesus to be the leader he was meant to be. On the other hand, John prepared many for Jesus' teaching and would probably have given all leadership to Jesus over time. He said, "He must increase while I decrease." She in her cruelty deprived many seekers who needed John's preparation.

We must not too suddenly let go of our reasoning, intellectual awareness of the Spirit. It will happen gradually as we fill our heart and mind with the presence of God through meditation. We then transform the ego and it "becomes less and less." Gradual growth of consciousness is sounder.

Herodias has taught us also.

28

The Syro-Phoenician Woman

(Mark 7:24–30; Matt. 15:21–28)

HUMILITY BRINGS HEALING

The account of the Syro-Phoenician woman is laid in Tyre and Sidon, cities of the Canaanites. In Mark the woman is identified as Syro-Phoenician (Greek from Syria); in Matthew she is a Canaanite woman. Both refer to people of the Gentile clan or race. She was not of a Jewish background.

Jesus had come here to rest, for he had been healing and ministering. But the woman, in desperation and humility, pushed her way to him and asked him to heal her daughter of a demon possession. He refused, for he said that he should feed the children (the Jews) first before the dogs (Gentiles). She replied that even the puppies under the table are given scraps from the children's plates (Mark 7: 28).* Then Jesus said to her, "For this saying you may go your way, the demon has left your daughter." And she found the child healed when she got home.

I think that this has a very vital lesson for us who are "on fire" with having discovered a great religious Truth for ourselves—for so many of us who have discovered New Thought think everyone should be told. Often we tell all to any and everyone and go so far as to believe that the Truth that we have discovered is the *only* Truth and that it is needed by everyone. And so we spread it abroad. Sometimes we antagonize friends and relatives by doing this. Sometimes it drives them away from ever being interested. Sometimes our absolutism creates a schism in our family and our spouse and children are divided from us. Yes, we in metaphysics can reach the belief that there is no other way but our way. We forget that each of us must find his or her own way, and it may not be our way.

It is very important that we listen and wait for the right time to teach. Sometimes we may wait years. But we can most effectively demonstrate our new-found Truth in our own life and thus

*Living New Testament.

affect those around us. When they ask to be taught, then we know they are ready. The Syro-Phoenician woman was ready.

Jesus may have been testing the woman, for it is hard to believe that he was unaware of her readiness. On other occasions he had spoken well of the Gentiles. But he had to find out if her faith was strong enough. So many must have come to him begging for healing who did not believe. She showed her faith by her reply.

The puppies are those who are still of the earth and have not really started the Path. The children are those who are using their faith in a small way and being fed. So, yes, we have a responsibility to teach others, to heal others, to love others, but they may not be ready for strong food or strong drink. Be careful how you share, and how much, at the first attempt to teach.

Jesus, all compassion, saw that intuitively the woman realized the Truth. Her humility and faith were apparent. Out of his compassion and love he gave to her because he saw she understood, and he healed her daughter.

Jesus healed on several occasions at a distance. His consciousness, one with God, lifted the sick daughter up. Our consciousness, when one with the Creator, is one with the sick person. When we are One, we are the healer. Healers have different methods, but generally someone has to ask for the healing and have faith in spiritual healing and the healer. Then the person who is emotionally attached to the asker is affected. The Spirit knows no space or time. "The wind [spirit] blows where it wills, and you hear the sound of it, but you do not know whence it comes or whither it goes; so it is with everyone who is born of the Spirit." (John 3:8).

Jesus came from the house of Israel. His disciples also had many arguments over whether they should teach anyone besides Jews. Jesus before he ascended admitted his mission and ours to all on the earth: "Go into all the world and preach the gospel to the whole creation" (Mark 16:15). Paul argues that all were included in Jesus' message. We, too, have a responsibility to help circulate the news of the "New Thought" movement if we believe in it. And those who are ready will hear and be healed.

Esoteric: SEEK YOUR PATH

Tyre and Sidon symbolize fixed states of thought but a willingness to admit error and repent. The Syro-Phoenician woman symbolizes the feminine intuition that knows the Truth. Gentile symbolizes thoughts based on sense needs, an unregenerate state of mind. Dog is a term used to mean Gentiles. Daughter is the beginnings of realization of Truth that is caught in a negative consciousness.

We are not of One Mind usually. Our intellect presents several sides of an issue. Our intuition may give us glimpses of Truth while our intellect pulls away because our religious belief does not teach what our intuition is telling us. We may be living in a place where the gods of materialism are worshiped. And still we have a nudging to a different basis for our life. How do we bring peace to our life? How do we exorcize the evil spirit (opposition to Truth)?

We can seek a teacher who demonstrates the ideas that our intuition tells us are Truth. We can study the Bible from a metaphysical and not a literal viewpoint. We can pray that someone be sent to us to heal us. We can through meditation contact that inner Guide that Jesus followed. We can pray that books will fall into our hands that will support our intuitive idea. Books are great teachers! And so many are available now.

When I started to realize that my deep beliefs did not fit the traditional Christian teaching, I thought I was alone. Then an assistant Methodist minister came to call and I told him some of my doubts and my tentative beliefs. He agreed and opened to me the realization that I was not alone and that my ideas had credibility. He, like Jesus, gave me healing. However, it was several years before I earnestly sought out more metaphysical teaching and put my foot on the Path.

Be open, be committed, and have faith that God's grace is always guiding you. Your dedication will be instantly accepted and you will be healed, as Jesus did for the woman and her daughter. "Great is thy faith, be it done unto you thee as thou wilt." Later we discover that a church group had been organized and was meeting in Tyre when Paul did his teaching. Could this woman have been one of the early members?

She, like all women of the Bible, has her message, and it is humility, faith, and devotion. Thus our lives are happier and fulfilled when we accept the true way for our own salvation.

29

The Mother of James and John

(Matt. 20:20–28; Mark 16:1–8)

AN AMBITIOUS MOTHER

Many people have rejected the Bible as a great teacher and as an inspired book because they believe that God's Word should recount the lives of saints, not sinners. The intent of the holy books of all religions is to help us see ourselves as human and then show us our potential as pure Spirit and how to become the mystic that we unconsciously yearn for. We are all at one stage or another. As for myself, the Bible is a great mirror that helps me look at myself and then gives me the guidance to become more Christ-like. Thus it is with this story.

It is assumed that the father of James and John, Zebedee, was a leader in the community and a successful fisherman. James and John were fishermen when Jesus called them to follow him. He had developed a great following, and many believed that he would take over the reins of government, depose the hated Roman rule, and be King of the Jews. Although he had tried to explain his mission to his apostles, they did not understand. And certainly this mother did not understand.

Jesus, the apostles, and others were walking to Jerusalem to celebrate the Passover. Jesus had just told his disciples what was going to happen to him, but they did not understand. Then the young men and their mother came to Jesus and bowed before him. She asked that her two sons, James and John, be allowed to sit on either side of the throne in Jesus' Kingdom. He asked the young men if they knew what they were asking and if they could drink the cup that he was to drink. They both replied that they could. Then he told them that they would indeed drink his cup, but that the honor of who was to sit at his left or right hand was not up to him; rather, "it is for those for whom it has been prepared by my Father." When the other ten apostles heard about their request, they were upset, and Jesus answered them with his famous saying, "But whoever will be great among you must be your servant, and whoever would be the first among you must be your slave, even as the Son of man came not to be served but to serve, and to give his life as a ransom for many."

Peter, James, and John seemed to be at a higher level of spiritual consciousness than the others. They were taken to the Mount of Transfiguration with Jesus and were able to see clairvoyantly Moses and Elijah with Jesus. It was also they who went to the Garden of Gethsemane. And on other occasions they seemed to be really close to the high spiritual consciousness of Jesus. But here they were still not understanding his mission. We, too, have misunderstood his mission.

We could blame their mother for this lack of discretion, but these were grown men. In Mark 10:35–40 they themselves ask for the special privilege. But their mother asks in this account.

How ambitious mothers often are for their sons! How often we treat our grown sons as children and intercede for them—and how often we are embarrassed when our petition is denied! How often we learn humility from such an assumption, as this mother did, for it was she who is mentioned as being with the other women at the foot of the cross and at the tomb. She had to go all the way before she truly understood Jesus' answer.

Clinging to our grown children, especially sons, can often cripple them for life. Until we realize that our sons are separate from us and have their own masculine way to pursue, they cannot fully function. Making them dependent on us for guidance and smoothing the way for them may make them overly feminine and less masculine. We cannot afford this mistake. No one, not even a mother, knows the soul's path of each of her children.

What this mother asked for lay far beyond her sons' ability. True, they both did drink of Jesus' cup of martyrdom, but this befell them years after the crucifixion. James was beheaded by Herod. John was exiled to the Isle of Patmos, where he composed the Book of Revelation, which depicts initiation into higher consciousness. A legend has it that he was translated without going through the experience of death. His body was changed to vibrations of Light and he disappeared from sight. He was not martyred.

Jesus' great compassion and kindness shows through in this incident. Instead of denying her request, he told her that he could not grant it. Each, he implied, must gain such an honor through his or her own serving of others and indeed of the world—for, he said, the Son of man did not come to be served but to serve. Thus should we follow his teaching.

These words give us our clue as mothers. The mother in this story was serving her sons. Perhaps they were a little shy about asking the question, or perhaps their having been chosen out of the twelve to experience some high moments with Jesus had produced spiritual pride in them. How easy that would have been! Certainly she felt that she had a position of grandeur to even ask such a favor. They all three learned much from their mistake, as have we and untold millions who have read or heard this story. The mother of James and John, so typical of many mothers in her ambition, has presented a mirror for us to see ourselves in.

Each of us must climb his or her own evolutionary spiral to the kingdom of Heaven; and we shall be great if we are servants and not ego-centered rulers. Jesus served. He is also our Master because he did so. We are blessed.

Esoteric: EGO IS LOST IN SERVICE

Zebedee, the father of James and John, means "Jehovah has given." The mother seems nameless, but scholars have given her the name of Salome ("whole," "sound," "perfect"). James means supplanter (James is the English form of Jacob). John means grace and mercy of the Lord. All of these four are very positive and spiritual. Peter, faith, was often included with John and James.

In the teaching of Charles Fillmore, each apostle represents a power that we have that needs to be strengthened before we can reach perfection. James symbolizes judgment or wisdom. John represents love. Peter represents faith.

As we reach for the various levels of spiritual attainment, wisdom, love, and faith are most necessary. These are the three qualities that Jesus kept near him. But sometimes judgment can be rash judgment without due intellectual consideration. Wisdom supplants critical judgment when coupled with love. And love, as we have seen, can be at a very personal level and not of the impersonal Love of God. Judgment, love, wisdom, perfection were yet to be gained in the fullest sense by these three.

We can then assume that even though we have wisdom and love, which come from Jehovah, and wholeness (Zebedee and the mother), we may misjudge our level of expression or what price we will be required to pay to sit with Jesus (Savior, Deliverer). Jesus called the two brothers Boanerges, or sons of thunder (Mark 3:17). This symbolizes fiery and destructive zeal.

They, like so many of us when on fire (lightning) with our new-found Truth, believe that they have all the answers. This is spiritual pride. And we may use hasty judgment and bigoted, limited love before we are well grounded in our belief. Jesus saw this in the two brothers and knew that their zeal could be turned around and used for the glory of God. So he pointed them toward the Father and away from themselves and him. Pride must diminish. Love—in the highest sense, service, nonresistance, and wisdom—must be developed.

The reactions of the other ten apostles show us also that none of them was ready for this honor and that James and John had not impressed them as being worthy of it either.

Now to the inner meaning of their mother's experience. Her request revealed so much about her, but it was not necessarily negative. What wonderful sons she had raised! As we follow their story after Jesus' ascension, we realize that they were truly great. Both worked to spread the gospel. Both were courageous and gave their lives for the cause. Both have taught us so much through the ages. Both wrote books that are included in our New Testament. And it was through her giving birth to love and wisdom that the world was lifted up, that the gospel was preached.

More importantly, we see how she grew in understanding, humility, and loyalty to Jesus, for she is mentioned as one of the women who stood at the foot of the cross with John and several women, one being Mary, Jesus' mother. She and the others were of a high consciousness. She was also one of the women with Mary Magdalene who were the first to come to the tomb to anoint Jesus' body and to know of his resurrection (Mark 16:1). So step by step she herself climbed in consciousness and served Jesus and followed him all the way. Love and perfection go all the way with Jesus and serve all of us today.

Such is our task. Our ego, our pride, may at first request more than we are capable of handling. But through our continued loyalty to Jesus' teaching we grow inch by inch. She must have been in his presence often. We, too, can have that experience through prayer and meditation. At the same time, we take up our own cross of materiality, of living on this planet, and through it learn what we need to learn in order to experience the overcoming of death. Witnessing this in the life of Jesus and others makes us know that there is no death but only eternal Life.

She may have started her climb at a low level, but she achieved that state of "he who is greatest among you shall be your servant." She served when it took great courage, and her sons James and John drank the cup that Jesus drank. They spread the Good News and died victorious. Jesus designated John as the beloved apostle and appointed him as the caretaker of his mother, Mary. By inference this meant that John was at Jesus' level of spiritual awareness and was to take his place as son to Mary. What higher honor could the mother of James and John—or any other mother—experience?

Our way is the way of humility, love, and faith. Our way is following the Christ Spirit. Our way will bring us to the Kingdom of Heaven here and now. Our way is God's Will. Our way is the Christ Way. "I am the way, and the truth, and the life; no one comes to the Father, but by me" (John 14:6). The Way is the Tao.

As women, we need love and wisdom as our offspring. And faith accompanies them. The mother of James and John is that feminine instinct within each of us that serves as we grow in divine consciousness. They—love, wisdom, and faith—must be tested. Until they are, we are not ready to take our place with Jesus Christ. Testing will bring our evolution to perfection.

30

The Samaritan Woman at the Well

(John 4:7-42)

CHOOSING A MARRIAGE PARTNER

The teachings of Jesus have raised womankind to a high place of adoration and love. They no longer are slaves to men, to society, to generation of the race. They are freed through the high teaching of that Son of God who came to this planet to lift us on our evolutionary journey back to the Kingdom of Heaven, the Father's house. This woman, to whom Jesus revealed such profound truth, is our example. She was worthy to receive his Truth even though she was not the highest moral example, and even though her culture was despised by the orthodox Jews. Her life was not complete, and she needed Jesus to befriend her. He lifted her to a place that was honorable, and the townspeople believed her report about the stranger; many listened and were converted. Indeed, women made some progress in her climb out of the pit with Jesus' advent. It has been slow and tedious, but progress is coming faster and faster.

The story is familiar to anyone who has studied the Bible. Jesus and his disciples were going from Judea ("spirit-minded") through Samaria ("mixed thoughts both worldly and spiritual") to Galilee ("life activity" or "manifestation"). At a well near Sychar ("confused state of mind") they paused to rest. Jesus remained near the well while the disciples went into the city to obtain food. The well was a social gathering place plus a place to fill the water jugs to take back home. Animals were also watered. The well symbolizes deep truths. Water symbolizes the feminine or the intuitive, love, imagination, the feeling nature.

A weary Samaritan woman came with her water jugs. The Samaritans were scorned by the orthodox Jew because they sprang from a mixture in marriage of Jew and Assyrian. No Jew traveled through that country. Jesus, of course, saw all men and women as equally worthy of the Truth. Jesus asked her for a drink; she was amazed that he would speak to her; then he told her that if she asked him for a drink, he would give her "living water."

The woman replied, "Sir, you have nothing to draw with, and the well is deep; where do you get that living water?" Jesus said, "Everyone who drinks of this water will thirst again, but whoever drinks of the water that I shall give him shall never thirst; the water that I give him will become in him a spring of water welling up to eternal life" (John 4:11-14). When she asked for his water, he told her to go get her husband. She said she had none, and he said that was true—that she had had *five* husbands and was now living with a man who was not her husband.

She, like so many others, believed that the Messiah, the Christ, was coming. He made the confession to her: "I who speak to you am he" (the Messiah or Christ). He also told her that the hour was coming when true worship of God would not be at Mount Gerizim (the Samaritan temple was built there) or in Jerusalem; rather, "God is Spirit and He seeks worshippers who will worship Him in *Spirit* and *Truth*" (italics mine).

The woman hurried back to the city. The people listened to her, for she related that Jesus had told her about her past. Many went to the well to hear him and invited him to stay with them and teach, which he did; and so the first Samaritans were converted to Jesus' teaching—all because a woman who was attached to sense pleasure and who had suffered the loss of five husbands was taught by the Master Teacher and had believed.

It is difficult to understand this account fully from the literal viewpoint. It is far more esoteric than literal. The book of John has many more metaphysical truths in it than the other three gospels. We shall see that there is a wonderful application to our modern lives.

Woman in her new-found freedom of divorce, living with a man though unmarried, sexually promiscuous, seems to believe that her happiness can be found in a relationship with a man. She is no longer bound to stay in an unhappy marriage nor will she be scorned by society if she divorces and remarries. This turn of events has allowed her to go from one relationship to another without censure. Her children are not objects of derision either, because many children are from divorced homes. The problems of children of divorced homes have proliferated, but society has provided the healing agents to help many of these children. So all should be rosy! But it isn't.

Woman or man can seldom find the entire answer to their haunting loneliness through another human being. The water of the earth or the senses will not bring that. Only the living water of the Spirit welling up to eternal Life assuages the thirst.

We do not know whether this woman was divorced or widowed from her five husbands. But we certainly know that her physical needs, her sexual needs, must have played a part in the suffering that the loss of five husbands brought to her.

The woman who believes she cannot be happy living alone will seldom be happy in a marriage. She expects too much of another human being. Her needs cannot be fulfilled by another. Her real needs are basically inner needs, which only the Christ can satisfy. Running from one man to another will only confuse her psychologically and emotionally. She begins to feel that she is inadequate and incapable of having a lasting relationship, and often she turns to hypochondria, drugs, alcohol, or complete withdrawal in mental illness. The ups and downs of getting another sexual relationship and then losing it keep her out of balance and harmony. The peace she gains with each relationship is short-lived. She is drinking of the water of Jacob's well.

Jesus told the woman the solution, and he did it in a loving, accepting way. He did not make her feel guilty. He acclaimed her honesty, and she believed—because he was able to "tell me all I ever did." Implied in that statement was no feeling of guilt.

Guilt over our past only enlarges the problem. If we have been searching for Truth in another human being without knowing the "living water" within ourself, we will make mistakes. Acknowledging our mistakes and digging our own well of deep Truth within our own consciousness will bring to us self-confidence and direction through worship of "the Father in Spirit and in Truth."

Jesus pointed out that the worship of God either in Jerusalem or on Mount Gerizim was passing and that individual worship of Spirit is the Way. Worshiping a statue, worshiping bread and wine, a scripture, an organization, a person who heads a church, a spiritual authority, or worshiping only in a building set aside for that purpose—these are the way of the beginner. As we advance, we realize the Center of worship within ourselves, and although Jesus Christ is our great teacher, we remember that he said we had a Comforter whom he would send (John 14; 16, 17). "And I will pray the Father and He will give you another Counselor [Comforter] to be with you forever, even the Spirit of truth." God is Spirit and Truth. That is the Christ, the Spirit, that abides within as our own personal Helper.

Young women who have become free financially through opportunities in education and work should realize that these steps will not lead them to the real freedom they seek. Finding freedom through Jesus' teachings and study of the Bible as well as other books will develop them into the kind of woman who will wisely choose her mate. About fifty percent of our Western marriages are ending in divorce. This is not to be wholly decried, as individuals often do not grow at the same rate or in the same direction; as they mature, their needs may change, and they can find more happiness and peace with another. Continued failure in choosing the right mate, however, should alert them to the personal problems they have. Perhaps they may choose to live alone, develop companionship with their inner Divinity, and eventually pass the stage of needing to live with a man or woman. At this point, I believe, they are ready to choose the ideal mate.

Woman's financial freedom is bringing her more opportunities to be spiritually free, if she so chooses. In the Ultimate, the androgynous state will free us from the need for a mate. The divine androgyny is the symbol of the New Age—male/female as One. All great world religions teach this concept. And all teach that we will become Christed or fully spiritual, that the corruptible will become Incorruptible.

We do not know what happened to the woman at the well, except that she wholly accepted Jesus Christ as the Messiah and influenced the people of that town to so accept him. The Messiah is a visible manifestation of the I AM of the Old Testament and the Christ of the New Testament. Jesus, of course, was a Messiah for the spiritual Kingdom, not for the physical kingdom. He is with us still in Spirit.

The haunting loneliness we feel is for that inner relationship with the Christ. That will lift us out of our confused state (Sychar) and bring us a constant companion. We are never alone when we realize that God is Spirit, not a spirit. Spirit is that effervescent quality that we can experience but cannot describe.

The "woman at the well" realized Jesus' Divinity, and he told her and us to worship God in Truth and in Spirit. In that lies our happiness. This woman led many to the well of "living water." Should we not do likewise?

Esoteric: LIFTING THE FEMININE

This inner teaching is equally if not more important. It is through understanding the inner meaning that we grow in closer awareness of our Lord.

The five husbands of the woman of Samaria symbolize the five senses. (Five in the scripture quite often refers to the senses.) Now this woman was Samaritan (mixed thoughts both worldly and spiritual) and came from Sychar (confused state of mind). Her spiritual allegiance was to the ancient teaching of Moses in the Pentateuch and had not changed. Her attachment to the five senses was very similar to our own beginnings and, for many of us, our endings. How fortunate that Jesus Christ came into her life and comes into ours!

Jesus (the Light) was traveling from Judea (spirit-minded) through Samaria (mixed thoughts) to Galilee (manifestation of spirit). This is our story too. We carry the Light but are not aware of it and so we are confused and often in chaos. When we see the Spirit manifesting, either with our spiritual or physical eyes, we then believe in It.

The woman came to Jacob's well. Jacob symbolizes the intellect without spiritual awakening. Jacob became Israel (spiritual thinking) when he wrestled with God face to face. This woman was attempting to assuage her thirst by the Law, by the intellect, and not by the Spirit. Jesus helped her see the difference.

How many students of metaphysics we know who have sat at the feet of many of the great teachers of metaphysics—Ralph Waldo Emerson, Phineas Quimby, Mary Baker Eddy, Emma Curtis

Hopkins, Ramakrishna, Yogananda, Charles Fillmore, Nona Brooks, Emmet Fox, Ernest Holmes, Ervin Seale—drank in the teaching and were lifted up for a period and then forgot it or failed to put it into action. They were elevated a little each time but did not make the great personal leap of faith. Or think of the great libraries of metaphysical books that have been read, the excitement engendered, the "Aha!" of Truth experienced—but the concepts were forgotten. The physical senses were delighted; the intellect was watered. But where was the spirit-centeredness? Where was the Truth lived out to completion in their lives? What went wrong?

Was it because the greatest Teacher of all, our inner Christ, was ignored? Were all of these experiences only living with the senses based on intellect? Were these serious students really committed to the spiritual essence? Were they unwilling to confess their mistakes, give up their old way of living, turn to a different way? Oh, yes, it was difficult to trust the "living water," the Spirit of God within. But until we do, our thirst will not be satisfied. As Jesus said, "Everyone that drinks of this water [Jacob's well] will thirst again, but whoever drinks of the water that I shall give him will never thirst." And she asked for the water he had to give. So must we—and accept it, and put it to work in our lives.

If we accept that each of her husbands symbolized one of the five senses and that they were with her no longer, then we would know that she was ready for the "living water." She was not committed to the man she was living with, but the senses were still being fed, and Jesus recognized this. The senses are so beautiful when directed by the spirit within and will cause us no harm. It is when they take over our life and we are focused on satisfying them that we have grief.

The senses then will be quieted. No longer will we need to continually feed our curiosity with the intellect. Our satisfaction will be complete as the Christ feeds us, leads us, teaches us, and assures us of eternal Life.

Jesus said to his disciples, when they returned with food, that he did not need anything to eat, for "I have food to eat of which you do not know." Not even his disciples understood that. And we who have this living spiritual Presence often do not understand. He also said, "My food is to do the will of him who sent me, and to accomplish his work." We are each one sent. Finding what work to accomplish will be revealed when we believe we are sent. And after we believe, we run and tell others who are also thirsting for eternal Life and not just the happiness of the senses. Then joy will come as a spring of living water.

I must again discuss the lifting up of the feminine polarity in the life of each individual and the people of the earth. Jesus, as previously mentioned, lifted up womankind. The work is still going on, and the lifting up of the feminine within the man is equally important.

The masculine has been in the ascendant in the West for thousands of years. In order for the race unconscious to be lifted up and balanced, the feminine must be given freedom to express both inwardly and outwardly. We must not miss the point of the need to lift the feminine inwardly.

The feminine symbolizes love, intuition, imagination, and nurturing. It will balance reasoning and logical thinking. Recognizing the feminine part of our personality comes before we recognize the Christ presence or before the Christ awareness is born. It behooves all of us to at first practice these characteristics intellectually, or, let us say, consciously—love, intuition, imagination—before we can accept the spiritual. Now for some, the rebirth occurs before they practice the feminine traits. But if you are seeking and not finding that deep allegiance to the Christ, perhaps you should begin with practicing some or all of the above.

Our imagination needs developing. Do not suppose that you do not image. Imaging is something we all do. Perhaps you do not think you do, but you do it unconsciously. We constantly image ourselves in different situations, saying certain words, being with certain people. It is necessary to use this ability consciously for success, for spiritual growth, and to reach our goals. Do not image the negative, however. Stay your mind on the good that waits to be unfolded.

To practice intuition we must "park" our intellect. The easiest way is to learn to meditate, which allows us to stop our meandering thoughts and take control of our mind. With a blank mind we let any feeling manifest that comes up. Practice helps you determine what comes from Jacob's well and what is "living water."

To love—we all know what that is but just do not always practice it. To be truly loving, we need to love ourselves, praise ourselves, forgive ourselves. Then we are free of many hang-ups and can love others more deeply and fully. It is a natural state, for we are truly loving, we are divine. God is Love; and to love is to nurture. To nurture is feminine. The feminine aspect of our personality leads us to higher awareness of who we really are.

Jesus, in his lifting womankind, started this process. He practiced all of the above—love, intuition, imagination, and nurturing —to the utmost. He gave the woman at the well the great gift of spiritual understanding. The Jacob well-water and the living water are both necessary. Intellect and spirit go hand in hand as we lift the feminine pole and become whole. The masculine intellect, combined with the feminine, love, brings Wisdom.

And the Samaritan woman left her water jug—she no longer needed the container for the well-water—and went into the city and said to the people, "Can this be the Christ?" And they came to him.

Jesus said to his disciples "Lift up your eyes, and see how the fields are already white for harvest" (John 4:35). We too must help harvest souls as Jesus did.

Jacob's well became Israel's well through Jesus Christ. Our Christ gives us this "living water."

31

The Woman Taken in Adultery

(John 8:3–11)

THE BATTERED WOMAN

Jesus came down from the Mount of Olives, from a time of meditation and silence, and went to the Temple to teach the people. He was interrupted by the scribes and Pharisees, the leaders, bringing a woman who had been taken in the act of adultery. They pointed out to Jesus that Moses' law directed that she be stoned to death. Jesus tried to avoid answering but finally said to the accusers, "Let him who is without sin among you be the first to throw a stone at her." He then turned away from them and the woman and waited. When he looked up no one was there except the woman. He asked the woman where her accusers were. "Has no one condemned you?" he asked. She replied, "No one, Lord." And Jesus said, "Neither do I condemn you. Go, and do not sin again."

In no way was Jesus condoning adultery. But he was astute in pointing out to the men that they had a part in the commitment of adultery by women. It is not for man to determine what is false in a woman until he has cleansed his own behavior and life experiences.

Men have for ages put upon woman the responsibility for the ills of the world. They have battered women with laws that they have made and enforced. They have kept women subservient to their needs without attention to the needs of women. But there are men today who, like Jesus, are realizing the inequity of the law and are changing it. Even today many women are not given equality in the divorce court. But judges are moving in the direction of compassion for a woman's unequal economic position in this society, and they are making decisions that benefit each person in the settlement.

At this time the battered wife is "coming out of the closet." For centuries a battered woman, physically battered or psychologically, has kept silent and, through fear and other reasons, has not revealed the cruel behavior of her husband. Now we have places for these women and their children to go for protection, for assessment of the situation, for support and comfort. It is a very complicated situation in most cases but there is help through the love, understanding, and strength of the professionals in these way-stations. A woman has help now and need not be ashamed to ask for it.

And what of the batterer? I think this account of Jesus has deep teaching for them. He said to the scribes and Pharisees who thought they were right to punish the woman, "Look within yourself. Why do you want to stone this woman? What causes you to want to punish her so severely? What have you done in your life that makes you such a judge? Have you never done the same thing?" And each had to examine his own life and admit his own shortcomings and guilt. Thus they left and could no longer accuse the woman.

The batterer should not be disregarded. The batterer needs help too. His feeling of inadequacy in the marriage situation which pushes him to resort to physical or psychological violence indicates his need for understanding, compassion, counseling. He is miserable also and is in great need. Jesus did not point the finger of derision at him. He only said, "Examine yourself." And when we understand ourselves, we have much more understanding for others.

Jesus looked at the woman and asked, "Has no one condemned thee?" She answered, "No one, Lord." And Jesus said, "Neither do I; go and sin no more." And she was released. She was not made to feel guilty.

Many a woman who is battered tends to blame herself. She batters herself with stones of guilt and fear. She also recognizes that after her husband has taken his own bad feelings out on her, the tension in him is somehow reduced, and he is all sweetness and light. This gives her hope that he has changed, but then the tension builds, and the scene is repeated. This is true also of a home where there is an alcoholic. It sometimes takes years of this before the realization comes that the bad times will come again and again, in cycles.

Counseling is needed by the battered wife. She has low self-esteem, is filled with fear and insecurity, and sees no way out. She needs a friend, and a home for battered women will offer her this friend. There are also women who batter their husbands. All of the above applies to the husband who is in this situation. The battered one is not free from responsibility, but battering will not solve the problem.

The woman taken in adultery was responsible for her act, as was the man she was caught with. Both needed Jesus' love and compassion, and his pointing out the Truth. And his last directive, "Go, and sin no more" must be taken seriously by both parties. The battered and the batterer need help and not censure. Freedom is available for both. Our society should provide a means of escape from such a situation.

Esoteric: BALANCING THE FEMININE

We are all guilty of throwing stones at others without examining our own behavior. For some reason it makes us feel superior. "Judge not, that you be not judged" (Matt. 7:1). But we feel differently when we throw stones at ourselves, for our self-esteem is battered, and we feel useless and inept. We forget that we are children of God, with the same potential for Light and Love available to us as Jesus manifested. Self-flagellation is the worst kind of battering.

Woman has battered herself for longing to express her capabilities and talents in an intellectual setting. She was told for years that it was unlawful for woman to be anything but a wife and mother. Men stoned her if she stepped out. But thank God there were those women courageous enough to stand tall, withstand the opposition, and express their whole self. We owe a debt to them.

We are all, men and women, born with the capability of being whole, of being balanced in expressing and in experiencing the masculine and feminine qualities in our mind, our emotions, our body, and our spirit. It is the balanced expression of both that brings joy to both men and women.

The feminine must express if we are to save the world. It should not be criticized too harshly when mistakes are made in this self-expression. The love expressed by Jesus in the scripture quoted will allow us to continue expressing the feminine, and eventually our accusers will be silenced.

The feminine must express, or disaster will come to our world, personally and worldwide. Stoning by the intellect and reason (masculine) will not silence the need for love and compassion (feminine). It is the intuitive voice of the Christ that will direct each of us, man and woman, and peace will reign in our hearts and in the world.

When a man attacks, scorns, batters a woman, he is probably expressing his own derision of, and dislike for, his feminine nature. He is controlled by his negative feminine, his negative anima. It is realization of the source of his harshness toward women that will heal him. He must look within his subconscious and realize why his feminine pole causes him to attack and batter women. "He who is without sin cast the first stone."

Battering the feminine, battering a woman, battering a man with the stones of reason and the law does not change any situation for the better. Only the love and compassion of Jesus expressed through our inner Christ can solve this dilemma. We are guided when we ask for help in the outer and eventually turn for guidance to the Inner.

32

Mary Magdalene

(Mark 15:40-47, 16:9-11; Luke 8:2, 3;
John 19:25, 20:11-18)

HEALING OF THOUGHTS AND EMOTIONS: PSYCHOTHERAPY

There are several Marys in the New Testament, and they are all important to us. This Mary is identified as coming from Magdala, which means elevation, tower, castle. Mary—contradiction, bitterness—describes her human side, but she came from a place in high consciousness, a "tower," as we do. We all come from God and return to Him.

As we come to the account of Mary Magdalene, we must first let go of the idea that she was a fallen woman, a prostitute who washed Jesus' feet with her tears, or the harlot brought to Jesus by the group of men who wanted to follow Moses' Law and stone her to death. According to most scholars, she was neither. She has been maligned for many years. Instead, we should see her as one of the greatest demonstrations of redemption, which means turning from the old, inadequate way of living to the Christ-directed way. She was one of the highest initiates who followed Jesus, and she was loved deeply by him. She followed him and served him. She is mentioned ten or more times in the New Testament, and on eight of these occasions her name is given first in a group of women. She recognized that all that she was she owed to the Christ.

In Luke 8:2 we have a reference to Jesus' healing her and some other women: "Mary, called Magdalene, from whom seven demons [evil spirits, diseases, infirmities, obsessions] had gone out."

The casting out of so-called demons from a personality was common in Jesus' time. Jesus illustrated this healing on several occasions. The behavior of those beset by demons was very abnormal according to the mores of the day. Scripture references include:

197

Mark 1:23-26 and Matt. 8:28-32; 9:32,33; 17:14-21. Because the primitive belief accepted that deviant, disembodied spirits could take possession of a living person and change his or her behavior, and because no one knew how to exorcise them, Jesus' healing was considered a miracle.

Spiritism has always been a part of human thinking, it would seem. The medicine man of primitive times had his way of releasing a member of the tribe from an evil spirit. Today there are those who appear to be possessed also. It is said that many who are considered insane and who are committed to institutions for the mentally deranged are possessed. However, one teacher, Manly Palmer Hall, believes that to be insane and to be possessed are not the same.

For our purposes, I should like to suggest that Mary Magdalene was possessed by memories, ideas, thoughts that had been buried in her personal unconscious and that affected her behavior adversely. All of us have some of these "demons," and we may have cleansed many from our unconscious. They may not depart all at once, as the scripture implies, but we do take care of them one by one if we are serious about our path.

Mary Magdalene demonstrated her growth potential as she followed Jesus, with other women, and served his needs. When Jesus spoke to her at the tomb, she was grieving for the loss of his body, grief which was based on personal love. When she saw him in his spiritual body, she finally reached the impersonal Love stage and recognized him as her Teacher, her high Master. She knew the vision was real and she was complete.

Emotional illness is a curse of our modern technological society. We as women are very sensitive to this in our children, in ourselves, in our husbands, and in society itself. To receive the right kind of help in these trying times is difficult when so much of our counseling help is based on intellectual understanding coming from scientific research. The use of chemicals does not heal either. However, these are helpful to a point, but until the spiritual need of the individual is recognized, the complete healing will not be forthcoming. This is why I am attracted to Jungian psychology— because it takes into primary account the spiritual needs of the person. This will be the New Age psychology.

By his power and word, Jesus was able to cast out those demons and free Mary Magdalene. His spiritual baptism gave her a new birth. But she needed to learn to live with this new consciousness and so stayed in his presence as much as possible and served him. To be completely healed, we too must stay as much as possible in the mindfulness of our God and in full faith in the healing power of God's grace. We cannot be healed without help from our God.

Often in our psychological treatment we are encouraged to get rid of the negatives that we have stored up. This brings to our conscious mind memories of pains and chaos that are better let go. But if we do empty our unconscious of these memories, we must fill it with the positive, the good, the beautiful. So often psychologists do not understand that this is necessary. And we must take responsibility for our own healing in the final analysis, and not leave it up to the expert. The responsibility is ours to reach through peace and stillness—engendered by meditation, that connection with all-Good—the Christ within. It is the healing of our guilt feelings and our fears that brings health.

And at last, when we reach the need to follow the Mystical Way, we must give up all and follow Christ. It is the direction through intuition from our inner Christ that brings us lasting happiness and joy. It is through faith that we reach out, and it is through experience that we learn to love, above all, the teachings of Jesus, as did Mary Magdalene. Prayer, service to our fellow beings, study of that which raises our consciousness, experiencing that which is good and true—all these will take us to the point of realizing that we can be resurrected from the grave of material existence and ascend to the highest form of spiritual experience. Most of us, however, have to be crucified before we are resurrected.

Mary, the devoted one, is our example as women. We may have to leave all personal attachments when the time is right and move to complete obedience to the voice of the Christ. Do not be fearful of this, for it will not happen until the right time and you will be ready. However, the most of humankind will continue to mix the Divine and the human and so stumble until they reach this high state.

Mary, the mother of Jesus, and Mary Magdalene are examples of those who have arrived and those who are still evolving. It was necessary for Mary Magdalene to follow closely because she was still subject to error. Jesus' mother had already arrived at perfection. They both are great examples to us.

Mary Magdalene is mentioned by name as one of the women who followed Jesus to the cross. She was also one of the first to go to the tomb. She loved him deeply. She was a truly restored soul. All infirmities, all demons were cleansed from her unconscious. She was made whole by the Christ.

Mary Magdalene's main honor comes from her being the first of Jesus' disciples to learn of the Resurrection. She was also the first one to whom Jesus spoke after this event. He said to her, "Woman, why are you weeping? Whom do you seek?" She then inquired where Jesus' body had been laid; she did not recognize him. Jesus said to her, "Mary." She turned and said to him in Hebrew, "Rabboni" (which means Teacher). Jesus said to her, "Do not hold me, for I have not yet ascended to the Father; but go to my brethren and say to them, I am ascending to my Father and your Father, to my God and your God" (John 20:11–17). Woman was chosen then and is chosen now to lead the world to Truth.

How this account stirs the love in our heart! How we visualize the scene! How joyful Mary Magdalene must have been! How important a mission he sent this woman on! She was lifted up again as this Jesus announced his ascension to her. How she must have wanted to touch him, but because he did not want her personal love to hold him back from his completion, he asked her not to.

Woman indeed had reached the spiritual heights. It is woman's loyalty and adherence to Christ principles that has lifted up the human race. Each of us is a Mary Magdalene.

As women, we have an immense responsibility. Not so much as teachers and preachers, although that is important, but as examples to our generation. It is for us to lead the way in showing the world that the feminine pole, raised to its full height, can bring more love, compassion, peace, and intuitive understanding into the lives of many and into the world at large. We, like Mary Magdalene, may have much to clean out of our own lives, but we are equal to the task with the help of our inner Christ and the love and teachings of Jesus Christ. And each of us will do it in an individual way and at his or her own pace. We are centered on the Presence and know our direction. As we each become more balanced in our masculine/feminine role, we shall be healed and become great examples to all.

Esoteric: THE PHYSICAL BECOMES SPIRITUAL

Luke 8:1,2: "And the twelve were with him, and also some women who had been healed of evil spirits and infirmities: Mary, called Magdalene, from whom seven demons had gone out, and Joanna, the wife of Chuza, Herod's steward, and Susanna, and many others, who provided for them out of their means."

The number seven gives us a clue as to the inner meaning of this account of Mary Magdalene. Seven, as stated before, is a number of completion. It indicates the depth of her affliction. Mary Magdalene also demonstrates this completion in her scene with Jesus as she greets him at the tomb. She started from the lowest and became so enlightened that she was able to talk with spirit beings, angels, and with the resurrected Jesus Christ. She became whole.

In Chapter 19 ("The Queen of Sheba") I have described the Eastern teaching on the transformation of the seven chakras in the ethereal body that changes the physical to pure Light. This is referred to by Paul in a very esoteric way in I Corinthians 15:40–55: "It is sown a physical body, it is raised a spiritual body. If there is a physical body, there is also a spiritual body. The first is the physical, then the spiritual. For this perishable nature must put on the imperishable. Then shall come to pass the saying that is written: 'Death is swallowed up in victory.'" We can put off the terrestrial for the celestial by activating these energy centers, chakras, through meditation, physical exercise, yoga, breathing exercises, diet, devotion to perfection, devotion to a particular Teacher, spiritual baptism, living on a higher plane. At the same time, the consciousness of a higher dimension of being must be activated. This comes about through the changing of our thoughts, words, actions, and centeredness from the outer to the Inner.

And so let us suppose that Jesus did this for Mary when he cast out the demons. His teachings, and our listening and following our inner Christ Spirit, can do the same. Mary still had to serve. Mary still suffered. Mary still did not understand who Jesus was. Mary grieved for the loss of his physical presence. Mary loved. But in the end, her spiritual eyes were opened and she saw Jesus the Christ as that pure Spirit. However, we have no account that she ascended. She, like us, had more cleansing to do.

Her story is our story. Jesus Christ can cleanse us also, and then through our effort and the grace of God we can come up higher to the realm of angels and we can know our Christ completely.

Mary Magdalene is womankind who has been possessed by race consciousness, is slowly being healed, and is going toward the light of freedom and equality that Jesus taught. She was chosen to make the great announcement to the world that death had been overcome. Believe that you as woman are also chosen! Jesus is our guide.

And so we have Mary Magdalene at the open tomb with the risen Christ. How wonderful when each of us shall have this experience! Many have it. Why shouldn't you?

33

Women of the Early Church

As we approach the section depicting the women of the early Church and the women who were with Paul in his ministry, we realize that we must remove some of the blocks that have arisen in our mind concerning the Church's teaching about women. As we come into the New Age of women's liberation, we must forgive and forget actions of the men who through the ages have put woman in a subservient role religiously, socially, economically, and politically. For the Truth will surface, and men and women will be on an equal basis.

According to The Acts of the Apostles, the early Church developed soon after the experience of the disciples and others in the upper room when they were visited by the Holy Spirit at Pentecost. They received all the powers that Jesus had demonstrated. There were women among that group but no mention of women is made when the early Church organization is described.

In the early Church all things—all property, all money—were held in common, with no one poor or rich. They practiced baptism for the forgiveness of sins as taught by John the Baptist and promised that the convert would receive the gift of the Holy Spirit. Communion was held with bread and wine, as they believed Jesus had taught. Prayer, teaching, and fellowship were all a part of the early Church. Many were converted, and the Church grew quickly. The apostles were able to heal and perform miracles. In Acts 2:46 we learn that "day by day, attending the temple together and breaking bread in their homes, they partook of food with glad and generous hearts, praising God and having favor with all people."

This was the Church for the Jews. They still followed the Mosaic Law in many ways. In Acts 3 we find Peter and John going to the Temple. Some of their greatest preaching was done there. The first mention of a woman member is in the account of Ananias and his wife, Sapphira, who withheld money from the common treasury after they had sold a piece of property.

The apostle Peter served as the spokesman and leader at the beginning. A division of labor within the Church was then begun, and with it an organization. Seven men were chosen to "serve tables" so that others could concentrate on preaching the Word of God. Later James the Just, not an apostle of Jesus, became leader of the Church. The apostles were dispersed to teach in other parts of Samaria, Phoenicia, Cyprus, and Antioch.

Then we have Saul of Tarsus entering the drama. His story is well known. He began preaching forgiveness of sins and baptizing the Gentiles without requiring the men to follow the Law of Moses, i.e. to be circumcised. He was criticized and brought before the early Church council. Peter had a vision indicating that all were worthy of receiving the teaching of Jesus and so agreed that the Gentiles should be accepted. Paul then developed the church of the Gentiles, although he also preached to, and converted, Jews. They were baptized and received the gift of the Holy Spirit.

This is a very sketchy history of the early Church as given in the Book of Acts. At the same time, there were other groups that seemed to be closely connected to the teachings of the early Church. Two were the Gnostics and the Essenes. I have described the Essenes in Chapter 22 ("Mary the Mother of Jesus").

I have also earlier raised the possibility that Jesus and John the Baptist came from the Essene sect. It is possible that many of the rules of the early Church sprang from this sect. Baptism and communion were central to the belief and practice of the Essenes, as was owning everything in common. They believed that the Messiah would be born from a woman of their sect. They existed to fulfill the prophecies of the Jewish prophets, especially Isaiah, that a Messiah was to come into the world. The Dead Sea Scrolls are assumed to have come from this sect and have added much to our understanding of the activities of the early Church.

We do not know the status of women in this sect, but we know that Jesus raised women to an equal status with men. Some believe that the Essenes gave selected girls special training to prepare them to be the mother of the forerunner of the "Anointed One," as the Messiah was called.

The other group, the Gnostics, was centered in Egypt. The Nag Hammadi Scrolls give us information about their beliefs. Theirs was a religion of a mixture of Egyptian and Christian beliefs. They taught that true knowledge (gnosis) comes from contacting the inner spark of Divinity, seeking intuition, following it. Baptism, they said, did not make Christians; rather, they required evidence that the pilgrim had received spiritual insight and personal holiness. Gnosis or direct communion with God had to be demonstrated before membership would be entertained. They taught that God was both masculine and feminine and that man and woman were equal. This was, of course, in direct contrast to the Catholic church's teaching of God's being "masculine." For many of the above reasons and others, this sect was finally declared heretical by the Church, and eventually it was silenced.

Accounts of women in the early Church are sparse. There seemed to be a variety of beliefs about women in religion, politics, and society that affected both the treatment of women and the record of information about women in the early Church. Some accounts may have been deleted when the Bible was rewritten.

Paul has been accused of demeaning women. If taken literally, much of what he is purported to have written in I Corinthians 11:4–16 and 14:34, 35; I Timothy 2:8–15; and Ephesians 5:21–32 seems to confirm this allegation. However, we must look for his meaning on a deeper level if we are to overcome our prejudice toward Paul. I shall later give you some of those esoteric insights.

The society of that time relegated women to a subservient position. Since Paul converted in many foreign places, he had to follow the social mores in order to be successful. Despite this "excuse," we know that the Church's interpretation of the biblical teaching has set women back immeasurably and has kept them slaves, unable to express their divine intelligence. The Catholic church and Eastern Orthodoxy to this day will not ordain women, but there are a few who are giving homilies in the churches. Jesus taught differently. Paul had many women followers, some of them named in Romans 16:1–16. Many women served in the churches he established and supported him in his efforts.

We should remember also that Jesus never established a church organization. Neither have his teachings been followed. Perhaps the overwhelming structure of social, political, and family life of the time was too much for the little Church to overcome as regards the status of women. In any case, it would appear that they did not "hear" Jesus' message about the value of the feminine in all of their affairs.

PAUL'S TEACHING ON WOMEN

In an effort to understand Paul's deeper meaning, please read I Timothy 2:8–15 and Ephesians 5:21–33.

In Ephesians 5:22 let us replace the word *husband* with *intellect; wives* with *intuition; Christ* with *inner Spirit; church* with *physical body.* This requires a great leap of thought but is necessary if we are to understand the secret teaching of Paul, which is foreign to most of us. We have, then, "For the *intellect* is the head of the *intuition* as our *inner Spirit* is the head of the *physical body* and is himself its Savior."

As we spiritualize the body, as it becomes pure Light, the Spirit must be in control of it. We must devote all its activities to consciousness-building, and the body, intellect, and Spirit will be in complete harmony. The intellect guides the body and the search for Oneness for a while. When the intuition, the feminine, begins to function, we say, "Ah, that came from my intuition" and feel pleased that we have listened to our inner Spirit, the Christ. Ultimately, however, we will be so close to our intuition, which is the Spirit guiding us, that we will be unaware of its functioning in our thinking, in our choices. Then the feminine (wives) will be silent, and the masculine will seem to be guiding us in all that pertains to our awareness of the Spirit and our earthly life. Actually, however, the Spirit is guiding us through our intuition (wife). The intellect is then the carrier at this level.

Ephesians 5:25–27 reads: "Husbands [masculine], love your wives [feminine], as Christ loved the church [the Spirit loved the body] and gave himself for her [the Spirit took over the physical body], that he might sanctify [cleanse] her, having cleansed her by the washing of water with the word [God], that he might present the church [body] to himself in splendor [fully spiritual], without spot or wrinkle. . . ."

Verse 28: "Even so husbands [the masculine] should love their wives [the feminine] as their own bodies."

I don't know whether this is clear. It is difficult to describe such an exalted spiritual position. When the feminine and masculine are in balance, they are lost in each other and become one. No division exists between the conscious and unconscious, between the opposites. Thus: "For this reason a man [intellect] shall leave his father and mother [the opposites in its nature] and be joined to his wife [intuition and love], and the two shall become one [total Oneness]" (Eph. 5:31). This is the highest level.

Thus the feminine is exalted as well as the masculine. Neither is above the other. So intuition needs the intellect. The intellect needs intuition. Each is one half without the other. In I Timothy 2:11: "Let a woman learn in silence with all submissiveness" means that the silencing of the intellect, submission to the Spirit, gives us the intuitive ideas we need to be creative, to live a pure life, to be happy and joyful. But intuition needs intellect to express. If we lived purely on intuition, we would not be in this world. We could not exist on a material plane. In the silence, intuition functions.

First God created the earth (the physical), then man (the intellect), and then woman (intuition). All are necessary for our proper functioning and growing to total oneness with the Father of All. And these are also stages in our own journey back to God.

To let go of the ideas that the Church has implanted in man's mind about the inferiority of women has not been easy, and we still have a long way to go. But little by little the understanding of the deeper esoteric truths of the Bible is surfacing, and in our New Age we will know what Paul was teaching.

Of course, the literal translation of the Bible would not allow such interpretation as I have given. The Church believed that Paul was guiding them to make women subservient to men. Perhaps this was necessary 2,000 years ago, when women were little more than chattel. But the Church must exist in the world and grow, change, expand, evolve with the times. This is what many men and women of today have come to realize and are working diligently to bring about. Women will lead, teach, write and inspire those who are on the spiritual path. Small groups meeting in homes, small churches, large religious groups, television ministry—all of these are organized by women and are successful. Intuition is finding its place with the intellect, and balance is being achieved.

How wonderful were the early Church Fathers! How many odds they had to overcome! How Paul suffered as he established the Christian teaching in the Western world! How grateful we are to them all! But we must move on to the teaching of Jesus. We can serve on an equal basis with men. Jesus meant it to be.

34

Mary, Mother of John Mark

(Acts 12:12-17, 13:13, 15:37-39)

A Mother's Spiritual Influence

She is mentioned so seldom that it would be easy to overlook her. But through the works of her son, John Mark, we know most about her. This is often true of mothers. She was called Mary of Jerusalem to distinguish her from the other Marys.

In Acts 12:12 we have Peter going to her home after he was miraculously released from prison. The followers of Jesus were meeting there. The maid, Rhoda, greeted him and then ran to the group to tell them that he had come. Herod had laid "violent hands on some who belonged to the Church." He had killed James, the brother of John, with the sword and then arrested Peter. So the small group could scarcely believe that Peter was at the door. He gave them a message and then departed.

This tells us that Mary's home was a meeting place for the early Church. Some believe that the Last Supper was held in her house, and that when Jesus appeared to the apostles after his resurrection, they were in her home. It is also suggested by some that the experience of Pentecost, after Jesus' ascension, occurred in her upper room. A meeting place for this group was of utmost importance and she, with great courage, allowed it. She was well off, had a large house in Jerusalem, had a maid, and was a loving hostess. She showed her love for Jesus and his followers by allowing them to meet there with her full consent.

John Mark, her son, gives us much more insight into her life and devotion to Jesus, for it was he who joined Paul on his missionary journeys, and he assisted Peter. Most importantly, he is said to have recorded the Gospel according to Mark.

John Mark grew up during the time of Jesus' mission and no doubt knew him well. He went with Paul and Barnabas on a missionary journey at a very early age, perhaps fourteen, but due to his youthfulness was irresponsible, and Paul and Barnabas separated over an argument about him. John Mark and Barnabas went their own way. Later he rejoined Paul and was with him for many of his missions. And so his mother lives on in his writing and service to the early Church.

As mothers, few of us realize the impact we have on our children. We take care of their physical needs, we teach them values which they unconsciously pick up, we rejoice with them in success, we grieve with them in their losses, and we finally free them to their own journey. And we live on through them.

It is supposed that Mary of Jerusalem was a widow. Perhaps she was an Essene and willingly shared all she had. Her son experienced all this and was affected by seeing Jesus, hearing about his miracles, listening to the conversations quietly, and then devoting his life to spreading the Word. His writing will be eternally a light to the feet of those who follow his words as they are rightly understood. Our responsibility as mothers is great. We cannot shirk it, for our children's lives reflect our devotion or lack of it. Fathers are, of course, important too, but because a woman carries this child next to her heart and is so closely attached to it in the first months of its life, there is a special psychic bond. Even the adopted child raised away from his or her natal mother feels this tug to know the real mother.

In this day of divorce, separation, and remarriage, mothers are having a particularly hard time keeping the channels clear between their children and themselves. There is much pain. But the joy of loving our children, teaching them our religious beliefs, and comforting and caring for them will balance the pain.

Religious training may or may not be your forte. So many mothers do not feel it important to take their children to church. And this freedom of choice is important. But the responsibility is heavier on the parents to give some kind of religious training. Talking about God, showing your dependence on God, expressing your faith in God, telling the stories of Jesus, reading to the children from the Bible or religious books, praying in their presence, teaching them how to meditate—all will influence them in a spiritual direction. They will eventually choose their own religious path and will never forget the time and attention you gave to their spiritual development.

Those parents who take their children to church are doing their part to impress on them the importance of worship. The children at some future time may reject the particular religious teaching that they were exposed to, but they will have a foundation on which to build their future belief.

Mary, the mother of John Mark, must have been upset when he left Paul and his work. But she knew that he would find the path best suited for him, and he did; he is remembered through the ages through his gospel. Often our rewards are slow in coming, but come they will as we wait with patience. "Train up a child in the way he should go, and when he is old he will not depart from it" (Prov. 22:6). Do not be disturbed if he seems to depart from it during his early years. The proverb says, "when he is old." It will come forth eventually.

Our homes are holy ground. Let us not allow things of the world to separate us from our holy task of giving, through love, this great gift of religious teaching—and start early!

Esoteric: LOVE, FAITH, AND SERVICE

The divine feminine is always necessary for the advancement of our spiritual consciousness. By providing a meeting place for the masculine teaching, we find the balance we need. Service, as Mary gave, is a feminine quality. And service will advance our horizons and our faith. They go together—service and faith.

As we open our consciousness (our home) to the love and teaching of Jesus, we attract more and more of the holy into our lives. And as our home or consciousness is blessed, so do we bless our thoughts, our emotions, our acts. And all of these reach out and bless others.

As women, it is easy for us to open to the movement of Spirit. It is easy for us to nurture and care for It. It is easy for us to follow. Let us be lights in this great world to lead others to the Truth.

Mary of Jerusalem (city of peace) left her mark (John Mark). Let us do likewise.

John means grace and mercy of the Lord. Mark means brilliant and shining. Mary symbolizes love. It is believed that Peter (faith) baptized John Mark. As love and faith become active in our consciousness and we are of service to others, we bring forth the beauty of God, which is our purpose. Mark always served and was not a great leader. We, too, who serve and wait are doing a great work.

The brilliance, grace, and mercy of John Mark are a true measure of the character of Mary, his mother. Within each of us is this ability. When placed in the service of God, we shine also.

35

Sapphira

(Acts 5:1-11)

SACRIFICES ON THE PATH

A man and wife, Ananias and Sapphira, were members of the early Church, of which Peter was apparently the head. As we have learned, all members of the Church had money and possessions in common. They often sold what they owned and gave the proceeds to the Church; then each member was given what he or she needed for a livelihood. They had a choice, however, of whether to sell or not. For Ananias and Sapphira, selling the property was all right. Their problem was pretending they were giving all proceeds to the Church. Lying to the head of the Church and the members was their sin.

When Ananias came to Peter to give him the proceeds from the sale, he withheld some for himself. He had his wife's full consent. They had discussed it. Now they were not poor or in want, else they would not have owned land. They were greedy. How human they were! When Ananias lied to Peter about the amount, Peter said, "You have not lied to men but to God." Then Ananias fell down and died. Others when hearing about the incident were filled with fear.

Then Sapphira came into the presence of the apostles. Peter asked her if they had sold the property for the amount Ananias had reported. She replied, "Yes." Peter asked how it was that she and her husband had agreed to tempt the Spirit of the Lord and then told her that her husband had died. She too died and was carried out. After this, great fear came upon the Church; many believers were added and many healings performed.

One wonders after thinking about this story if the organized Church has not continued to use fear to bring people into its ranks and to keep them devout members. Peter's action seemed less than Godlike in its apparent lack of forgiveness and the failure to grant Ananias and Sapphira a chance to make restitution. But it has a great teaching for each of us individually, whether in the Church or out.

When we commit our lives to the spiritual Path, to God, how sincere are we? How much are we willing to give up for our faith? What sacrifices in lifestyle, desires, attachments to friends and family, money and possessions will we make? Are we ready to use our wealth for the good of many? How honestly do we think, speak, act? Do we change our philosophy from *mine* to *Thine*? Do we realize what it means to confess our faith in God either verbally or silently? I doubt it.

When we turn from our old ways to the new, it is difficult to devote all to our confession of faith. But must we not? Is there any halfway measure? Thank God, we are forgiven when we fail, and we can start over with great intentions. Eventually, we grow to full faith and dependence on our Heavenly Father and do not withhold anything. We are open before all, for God knows All. Otherwise, we only delude ourselves.

As women, we are often faced with the choice of being totally honest or agreeing with something dishonest because our husband suggests it. We do not know whose idea it was for these two to be dishonest. Often women are more anxious about possessions and money than men are. Often they push their men to be dishonest to supply them with things to make them happy. But sometimes we as women have to choose between our husband and our conscience. Which shall it be?

I know all the arguments there are to go along with your husband, and so do you. It is so much easier to go along than to have a shouting match. And to keep a united front in society or in front of the children seems so important at the time. Unfortunately we do not see what we are bringing to death. It may take a while before we realize our mistake. But death will come when we are dishonest, and especially to our declared faith in God. Death comes in many guises.

Death to our integrity. Death to our good feelings about ourself. Death to our self-confidence. Death to our relationships. And most important, death to the trust others, including our children, have in us. Dishonesty—going against our own innate knowledge of what is honest—seems well hidden, but it waves its banner higher than we think. And death to our marriage may be in the offing.

A more important result is the tragedy of separating ourselves from Truth. Truth which is our Christ. Truth which is the only foundation of success and happiness. Truth which we often place on the scaffold and sacrifice for expediencey. Truth that will rise again.

Is "Truth on the scaffold" a part of your life? The old hymn with this line brought me to my knees literally and figuratively, and I was saved from death. Be sure your priorities are sound. Many of us women are so afraid that we will suffer scarcity in money or possessions that we sell our soul for a paltry dollar. If you are devoted to God, to growing in consciousness of your Divinity, a way will be prepared for you to survive materially while you give all to God. Remember Jesus' many admonitions along this line: "You cannot serve God and mammon" and "Do not be anxious about your life, what you shall eat or what you shall drink, nor about your body, what you shall put on. . . . Consider the lilies of the field, how they grow, they neither toil nor spin . . ." (Matt. 6: 24, 25, 28).

Sapphira. We will not be too hard on her. We understand. She made an individual choice and was responsible for the outcome. But we see her with love and realize that we have been there at some time in our life, or will be. It should not be *fear* of the Lord, however, but *love* of the Lord that keeps us honest. It is a must if we have made a commitment to being one with Him and following Jesus' example. Else we die! For Truth liberates. Truth frees. Truth is eternal!

Esoteric: TRUTH IS GOD

We have Peter (faith); Ananias, which means compassion of Jehovah; and Sapphira, meaning beauty, precious stone, sapphire. From these three we can derive a lesson that moves us on our journey.

The potential within these two, Ananias and Sapphira, was glorious, as it is with us. Compassion of Jehovah and the beautiful, the sapphire, together bring all the good into our lives. The sapphire stone is blue, and blue stands for Truth, according to some. God and Truth together: but they did not live up to their names. They functioned on the lower levels in their thoughts, words, actions.

And what are these lower levels called? For them, it was greed and deception. It may be something else for us.

Everything in our life starts with imaging and thought—that is, everything in the outer. Finally, through trial and error, we come to a higher level of intuition, gained through stilling the thoughts. But Ananias and Sapphira were not there. They were very much grounded in greed and deceit. They were afraid that they would not have enough. They were new members of the fellowship and not very far along on the Path.

Now how can we get rid of these negative propensities? Even at the beginning of the redemptive process we are all fairly materially minded. How do we let go of this? And this story answers: through Peter, who symbolizes faith. Through faith all is overcome. The lower nature dies or is overcome by faith. Faith is the foundation.

It is faith in God that brings our good to us! It is faith in His love for us! It is faith in our own Divinity! It is faith that lights when all seems dark. It is faith that will not let us go. We are made for faith. We cannot avoid it. And it will bring us up higher to Truth, to God.

Some of us get complete faith by one great leap, and it takes hold and lasts forever. Many of us build our faith step by step. It is individual! Faith is what we need to overcome fear. It is love and faith that help us relax and let go and let God. Faith said, "Satan has filled your heart to lie to the Holy Spirit"; and faith (Peter) put to rout all the deception and greed in their thoughts, words, and actions. The negative dies and is carried out and buried when faith is active in our life. Build your faith, for "Your faith has made you well," and "Whatever you ask in prayer, you will receive, if you have faith" (Matt. 21:22). Have faith and live. Have faith, and deception will die. Cast out fear with faith!

36

Tabitha

(Acts 9:36–43)

Too Much Good Works?

As we know, the accounts of healing and raising from the dead in our Bible have deeper meanings for us. Peter, who grew in consciousness from one who denied he knew Jesus to one who was enabled to perform the so-called miracles of Jesus, is also an example for us.

This account of Peter raising Dorcas, or Tabitha, from death is especially applicable to us, for it gives us a lesson in good works with faith. Later the Christian Church was divided over which was most important—faith or works. James said, "Faith without works is dead" (James 2:26). We could also turn this around and say, "Works without faith is dead."

The story goes that Tabitha, a disciple, was "full of good works and charity." She had been an adept seamstress and made clothes for the widows and probably the orphans. She was greatly loved and appreciated for her good works. She died and was washed and laid in an upper room. Peter, who had been doing miracles, was entreated to come to Joppa, where she lay. He immediately went. When he saw her body, he asked all the mourners to leave the room after they had showed him the tunics and garments she had made. Then, alone with Tabitha, he knelt and prayed and said, "Tabitha, rise." She opened her eyes, whereupon he gave her his hand and lifted her up. Then he presented her to the grieving saints and widows.

We of the Christian Church have a long history of charitable acts, missionary services to foreigners, Ladies Aid Societies to help the less fortunate, sewing circles to clothe the poor. Sometimes I wonder if this was encouraged by the Church fathers to keep women busy and less demanding for positions of leadership. Anyway, these groups were wonderful and needed in their way. The metaphysical churches do not follow this practice. Their teaching to each individual is to help oneself through faith in God with an expectation of prosperity, health, and happiness. They teach that our dependence should be on God and not on man or woman. Then each individual will help others as he or she has been helped.

I know many women outside the Church who are so caught up in good works that all of their energy is going in that direction. They belong to many clubs that have charitable projects, they give of their money to help others, they hold sales and sell magazines to raise money, and they are always busy. Not much time or energy is left for their own spiritual development. Indeed this is their spiritual service in their minds. But they are not at peace. They are always seeking.

There are wives and mothers who are doing the same in their homes. They are so busy! They give too much to their children and make them selfish. They do too much for their husband and make him dependent. They feel good and loving and giving and are encouraged by the teaching of the Church to give and expect nothing in return. Usually, however, these women reap the whirlwind, for to give too much to children and spouse is debilitating to the receivers and to the giver. Eventually resentment arises in the givers, and when no appreciation is forthcoming, they feel that all of their helping was for nothing. This is death.

When we balance good works with faith, we have life. It is only faith that can restore us. For primary in our life should be "to love thy God" and secondary "to love neighbor as self." Primary is devotion to our own spiritual consciousness development. Primary is listening to the inner Voice for direction as to what we should give and do for others. Primary is service to God!

Now it is true: we must act on our faith, or there is no faith. If we say we believe in Jesus' teachings and then do not make them a part of our life, we should question how much faith we have. But if we believe that all depends on us and our good works, then we should stop and examine our motives.

When Peter came, he cleared the room of those who were crying over losing Tabitha because she would not be there to supply them with more garments. They were focused on what she had done for them and not on her needs. These were negative influences. They were taking too much energy from the room, from the needs of Tabitha. So he dismissed them. Then he, Peter, symbolizing faith, appealed to God and through this channel raised her from the dead. Faith made her alive again.

Nothing more is said of her. Perhaps she learned from this experience to be more centered in using her energy to raise her own consciousness. Perhaps she responded to the importuning of the poor and continued to supply them with clothes. But I suspect that she was a very humble servant of God after that.

It is God that clothes and feeds us and everyone else. Even when it appears that the government is taking care of one's needs, it is the goodness of God that is behind it all. But this goodness can be ignored by those on welfare, and they become weaker and weaker as they depend on the government to supply their needs. They need to do good deeds for themselves and others. Then they will recognize that it is faith in God that raises them from their dependency on others to take care of their needs.

Kindness, goodness, love, compassion, perfection are all gifts of the Spirit, and we must let them flow through us as did Tabitha. But we must ever be aware of the Source, or we sleep. We need awakening.

We would hope that the saints and widows also learned something about faith. Peter remained in Joppa many days and taught, healed, preached. They learned the Truth from him.

Develop faith! Grow in faith! Depend on faith! Be alive to faith and it will lift you up and you shall live! And then go on to Knowing, where there is no doubt. That is the ultimate, and to *know* is to be at one with God. Then our faith changes to experiencing the ever-present God, and our works are rewarded.

Esoteric: DARK NIGHT OF THE SOUL

In our journey we may fall down and feel that we are dead to the inner Spirit. We go along fine for a while and then we have a time of depression, of unbelief, of not being able to touch our Christ Center in our meditation. All seems lost. The mystics all speak of this as the "dark night of the soul." It often happens when we seem at our highest point spiritually. But it too shall pass away, for our faith may lie dormant but is not dead.

Tabitha and *Dorcas* are Aramaic and Greek for *gazelle*. We think of a gazelle as being graceful, beautiful, the body and mind in perfect harmony. They are one with the Spirit, and this is the reality of each of us; but we go through many experiences before we are completely aware of this harmony.

As we are active and alive in producing this condition in our lives, we are happy. We move up the ladder of consciousness. We pass the tests of initiation. We clothe ourselves in the spiritual essence of Truth, and the saints (believers) and widows (mixed thoughts or half-truths) are clothed. But our Path is not complete. We need a challenge to bring us up higher. And so we go through this desert waste of "no water here."

Using the description of what happened to Tabitha symbolically, let us see whether within ourselves the beauty in harmony of mind and body is dead. Our first act should then be to wash, to cleanse, our outer circumstances of all that is soiling our bright and shining belief. Then we should go to the upper room or place ourself in our meditative position, get silent, and wait. The widows and saints may be crying and grieving. Our saintly thoughts as well as thoughts of half-truths try to invade our peaceful place. But we put them out. We stop our thoughts. And then we let Peter (faith) enter. We remain quiet and let faith do its work. And we kneel and pray.

Many of us have gotten away from kneeling when we pray. But there is something in the act that brings us closer to our Source. Maybe it is in our collective unconscious, for all of us have probably lived and worshiped where kneeling was a part of worship. And so we kneel, quiet our mind, center on the stillness and wait. And faith provides the answer and the solution. One may have to do this many times, however, before peace is restored. Few of us have the faith that Peter did.

Faith is natural to man and woman! Not faith in a church or faith in a person who represents God. But faith in a power greater than any man-made temple or organization. We are part of that faith, and although we may not be aware of it, we are a part of that God that our faith resides in. Faith will lift you up out of the Abyss.

Lydda, where Tabitha dwelt, means an exalted sense of beauty. She was in the right place for a resurrection. We too can experience a resurrection many times in our life as we turn from the outer works of intellect and turn within to the source of beauty. Peter grew from understanding to complete faith. We too can do the same. Peter helped others overcome illnesses and death. We too can do these good works as our faith becomes *I know*.

Ignorance of the Truth has been called deep sleep by some. Tabitha was in deep sleep, but Peter awakened her. Her ignorance was redeemed and she was awake. We too may be asleep, but faith awakens us to our goal of perfection.

Tabitha is the grace and beauty of the Spirit in full-flowing movement. We are grateful to her for teaching us that we can be awake to the beauty, peace, and joy of life and be fully *alive!*

37

Lydia

(Acts 16:13-15, 40)

THE CAREER WOMAN

Lydia, a facsimile of our modern-day businesswoman, lived in Philippi, a leading city of Macedonia. She was known by the people as a "seller of purple," which could have been purple cloth or dye. Purple was the color of royalty and power and much in demand. Lydia was a Gentile but she worshiped God, the Jewish God. She met with a small group of women each Sabbath on a river bank outside the walls of the city for prayer and ablutions.

Paul had received a vision that begged him to come to Macedonia, so he and Timothy and Silas had gone. They were in Europe for the first time. They went to the river to find a quiet place for contemplation and prayer and found the group of women led by Lydia. Paul taught them about Jesus Christ, and Lydia's heart was opened. She and her household were baptized, and she invited the men to come to her home to stay, which they did.

Lydia has a strong lesson to teach the woman of today who is deeply embroiled in the business world, where all the attention is focused on the outer, on profit, on materialism. Lydia did not give up all to her success in business. She gave heed to her spiritual needs also. She was a member of a prayer group and was eager to learn new information about God. She was open to change.

Now it took a great deal of courage, activity, energy, and desire in those days for a woman to be a successful businesswoman, even as it does today. In those days an independent woman was a rarity; now we have many. But often our businesswoman gets so caught up in her career that she forgets her spiritual needs. This will eventually bring "burnout" and disappointment. To give out continuously without infilling of the Spirit may bring sickness, depression, and restlessness. It does not satisfy the deepest level of our feminine needs to be successful in a so-called "man's world." We need something else.

Lydia belonged to a small Jewish prayer group who went to the river to perform Jewish ablutions. But when she heard New Thought, or New Truth, her heart responded and she opened up to the teaching and followed it. She chanced losing her business. She had no fear, for she was ready and recognized Truth when she heard it. She also offered her home as a gathering-place for followers of Paul's teaching, the Christian teaching, and the first church in Europe met in her home. She was not afraid to invite these new religious leaders to stay with her, and even after they had escaped from prison they knew they were welcome in her house. The Church grew there in Philippi, and later Paul wrote a letter to the Philippians, which we have in our Bible.

So many of our modern businesswomen are not satisfied with their equality with men in the marketplace. There is something missing. And it is the feminine factor of sensitivity, feelings, love, cooperation, and spiritual guidance. The competition of the marketplace tends to bring division and not cooperation. Analysis, not synthesis. And so we as businesswomen need spiritual infilling more than most to balance our masculine work.

Many women, and men, are disillusioned with traditional religion and are looking for something else. Many do not attend church or pray or read the Bible. This leaves a real vacuum in their lives, but there is such an upsurge of literature about the New Age belief, the metaphysical, that many are reading its literature and are feeling the Truth of it. The main theme is "Christ in you, your hope of glory." Meditation and listening to the inner Voice are leading many back to a spiritual center for their life. Small groups are forming to share ideas and intuitive knowing. And the metaphysical churches are growing and offering meeting places for such groups.

To turn within in prayer and meditation takes time and commitment. But at the first, only a few minutes a day will be most worthwhile. As the time is extended, the quiet and peace it brings will be very welcome, counterbalancing the chaos and distraction of the marketplace. If you need a meditation group at the start, there are many available.

Sometimes it takes courage to step out and do this. Paul was no doubt an inspiration to Lydia and her followers as he had been persecuted, beaten, and imprisoned for his teaching about Jesus. And Lydia showed her commitment as she had her entire household baptized and started a small church in her home. Courage comes from faith in God; so build your faith and be courageous too.

How glad we are that Paul brought Christianity to Europe, as the Christian Church in Europe carried the torch of the teaching of Jesus Christ and established it in a powerful position. It made many errors through the ages, but it did not allow the teaching of this great prophet to die. We of the New Thought want to take it further, and you, like Paul, may become a missionary of it.

Lydia had great power in the outer, but she needed power from the Inner. So do we!

Esoteric: THE PATH TO REDEMPTION

Let us interpret this teaching from Acts in terms of the names and places given. This should be an interesting venture.

Paul (representing the word of Truth) was in Troas (an "open" or "perforated" thought) and received a vision to go to Macedonia (symbolic of enthusiasm). He went with Silas (representative of understanding) and Timothy ("honor of God"). He met Lydia (the "travail" of the soul "giving birth" to spiritual ideas.) He met her by a river (current of vital force). He told her and her group about Jesus Christ (the I AM identity within each of us). In order to accept this teaching, we must put away negativity; then accept the teaching in faith; and then through understanding put the new concept to work in our thoughts, words, and actions.

When we put this all together we have the "recipe" for our own transformation, our own redemption.

At some time in our life we will be open to the word of Truth (Paul). In enthusiasm we accept this glimmering and follow it. Then as understanding (Silas) comes to us from what we have received, we try to make it a part of our life. But we are prevented by the world, by our work, by our aspiration for materialism, by our needs, by our fears. So we may have a period of travail (Lydia) before the soul can give birth to these spiritual ideas.

But Lydia (travail) listened to the word of Truth with an open heart (love). She brought the heart and the mind, love and intellect, together. She lived in Macedonia (a condition of enthusiasm) in the city of Philippi (symbolizes power). She was a seller of purple (also symbolizing power) in that city. So she was replete with power, was successful in business (prosperous), yet did not know the Source. There was enthusiasm and power in her environment. All she needed to do was focus it rightly. She was by the river (a current of vital force), which gave her energy to act.

She was baptized (cleansed of negative thought); she accepted the word of Truth in faith; she immediately spoke and acted on her new concept, having all her household (all the thoughts and ideas in her consciousness) baptized (cleansed). Then she invited into her house (consciousness) the word of Truth (Paul) as well as understanding (Silas) and possibly Timothy (inspired reason united with faith). She spoke, thought, acted from her conviction.

How beautiful is the Bible! How deep are its teachings! In this simple story we have, in a nutshell, the direction for our own redemption. The literal translation can never bring us this deep philosophy and Truth.

And so Lydia, the seller of purple, has given us our guidance. How appropriate for us modern-day women!

38

Priscilla and Aquilla

(Acts 18; Romans 16:3-5; I Corinthians 16:19; II Timothy 4:19)

UNEQUALLY YOKED COUPLES

Priscilla is usually mentioned with her husband, Aquilla, al-thought her name is given first in three of the five references. They were tentmakers who lived in Corinth, having come from Rome, where Jews were excluded. They were part of the early Church and great helpers of Paul, who spoke highly of them. They provided a meeting place in their home, worked with Paul in tentmaking, and taught and perhaps preached. Priscilla seemed to be a favorite of Paul's. He mentions her lovingly in his letter to the Romans, Chapter 16, and calls her Prisca. When Apollos, an eloquent man and well versed in the scriptures, came to Ephesus and was preaching the teaching of Jesus but practicing the baptism of John the Baptist (water baptism), which was for the remission of sins, Priscilla and Aquilla taught him the "way of God more accurately." After that Apollos accepted Jesus as the Christ and so taught the Jews.

Priscilla and Aquilla moved to Ephesus and worked in the church there, later returning to Rome. They could ply their trade anywhere and help support the Church as well as be leaders in it.

Because this man and wife are always mentioned together, I should like to discuss the necessity for the husband and wife to grow together in spiritual understanding and devotion to teaching the Way and serving others. When a couple are divided in religious understanding and practice, the result is real problems for the marriage.

Often in New Thought groups there are more women than men. Many of these women are more open to searching for and finding spiritual awareness than are men in general. Women are often leaders of heretical groups. They are inclined to find the answers to tribulation of earth by being religious. They are pliable, less set on the past, more open to future teachings. As a result, they are often far ahead of their husbands in accepting "new" Truth. And this can cause real trouble in a marriage.

So many women catch hold of the Truth for themselves and their children but are unable to inspire their husbands to follow the same. They then confront a dilemma. Many women feel that they must break the marriage and go off on their own because their devotion to God and the inner Guidance must be first in their life. And for some this is the only answer; we cannot force anyone to follow our own path. Each soul has its own path, and we should respect that. But for some, a better way is worked out.

Perhaps each of the partners may have to compromise for a season until one catches up with the other. A woman who has caught the Light and is focused on the Will of God may lead, but she cannot coerce. To continually speak of her belief, use the trite phrases that many New Thought people use, make a fetish of being positive about everything, be at church every time there is a class or service—all of this can be very annoying to her spouse. Perhaps she could slow down! Perhaps she could have friends who are receptive to this spontaneous affirmation of her belief, enabling her to express it with them. But continually to irritate her husband only makes him more resistant. It is often those who are most vocal about their faith, their Way, that are the least sure of It. Quiet devotion is often far more effective than outward speech. And quiet devotion has led many to curiosity and thus conviction. "Those serve best who serve and wait." Pushing, haranguing, arguing never convinces anyone.

The couple who are far apart in their religious convictions have a most difficult path. This is why so many couples who are divided on this issue have decided to leave religion and not include it in their daily living. A marriage is a very personal experience, and perhaps this way will serve them for years; but because our soul quietly clamors for attention from us, they inevitably will have to respond. And each may go a different way with the love and good wishes of the other. Marriages are the meeting ground and the trying out of diverse ways, and the religious dimension cannot be ignored forever if happiness and health are to be a part of that relationship.

How wonderful when the two are together, as were Priscilla and Aquilla! How musical their names as we say them in one breath!

Their names have been paired through the ages, serving as a wonderful example! They were one in marriage, one in the Lord, one in their vocation, one in friendship with Paul, one in service to the Church, one in God. This is the path of a truly happy marriage.

To be married in the same faith, to grow in awareness of God, to place the Will of God first in all decisions is bound to bring peace, prosperity, health, joy, and happiness to a family. And the children will be the greatest winners.

If you are unmarried and this consciousness development is primary in your life, and you feel you must marry, find a man who is on the same wavelength spiritually. I doubt if you will easily find one who is at exactly the same level as you, unless he is a twin-soul —but at least find one who is tolerant of all religious beliefs and especially yours. And then grow together in learning, in serving, and praising your Lord.

If you are married and feeling dishonest in the church or religious confession you are required to make because of the belief of your wife or husband, it behooves you to be led by the Spirit and follow your Truth as you see it. Any other route will bring death to your body or mind or emotions. Integrity in spiritual matters is *top priority*. Even breaking a marriage for this reason is better than losing your soul. However, kindness, love, faith, and tolerance can go a long way toward solving the problem. Priscilla and Aquilla are our example. They followed a great leader. They acted on their own and taught when it was necessary. They served in different locations. They were devoted to the work of spreading the gospel and healing the sick. And I am sure they grew spiritually as they did this work and helped the first Christian churches survive. What devotion! And we are grateful.

Esoteric: BUILDING THE SPIRITUAL BODY

Priscilla and Aquilla were tentmakers as was Paul. The tent is symbolic of the physical body, the temporal body, or a transitory state of mind. The tent in the wilderness was the Tabernacle for the Hebrews. It served as a temporary abode for their God. Later the Temple was built in Jerusalem by Solomon. This is symbolic of the spiritual—the etheric—body, that we will all build eventually, which is the home of the Spirit but without the physical dimension. Our physical bodies are sacred, too, housing the Christ Life during our journey.

Priscilla stands for the feminine force of nature repairing and rebuilding the body. Aquilla represents the eagle, the possibility of the body becoming like an eagle, able to fly, to move from place to place, at a great height, without interference. So we have the physical body and the ethereal. Both are together, with one becoming a part of the other.

As Priscilla and Aquilla served God, followed Paul, and taught Jesus Christ, they were transforming their bodies from the physical —the tent—to the spiritual. Within the physical is the Holy of Holies, the dwelling place of God, of the Christ. We are all high priests and can go to this Place any time, as I am sure they did in prayer and meditation.

These two symbolize the feminine and the masculine being taught by, and following, the word of Truth (Paul). Two thousand years ago this was the cutting edge of the (then) New Age, the Piscean Age: worship of an external Christ. Now we are on the cutting edge of the Aquarian Age, an intimate and inner awareness of the Christ. The teaching of New Thought is opening the way for the latter.

Both the physical and the spiritual bodies are important to us. The physical must be made healthy and well. The spiritual body can be built through devotion to God with meditation, living a moral life based on the teaching of Jesus, letting go of the unnecessary desires of our life that satisfy the physical, and conserving the divine energy within our physical to build the spiritual body. Jesus is again our prime example. He overcame death as can we when we truly follow his teaching on our own path and aspire to this perfection.

In I Corinthians 15 it seems to me that Paul is describing the changing of the physical body into the spiritual body and thus overcoming death. The building of the spiritual body I have spoken of many times. I should like, however, to speak of the "mystery" that Paul writes about in this scripture (vv. 51–53):

> Lo! I tell you a mystery. We shall not all sleep, but we shall all be changed, in a moment, in the twinkling of an eye, at the last trumpet. For the trumpet will sound, and the dead will be raised imperishable, and we shall be changed. For this

perishable nature must put on the imperishable, and this mortal nature must put on immortality.

The traditional Church interpretation of this scripture has been that when Jesus returns to earth, those who believe in him shall be transformed, and those who believed in him before death shall rise from the grave and be transformed, and all shall join Jesus in Heaven. However, to me this describes what I have been suggesting: the changing of the physical body into the spiritual. The dead —those who are asleep—are all of us, for in our material state we are not awake. But we shall put on the imperishable, and we shall be in an immortal state when this occurs. We shall then have a transfigured body and be able to serve on the physical as well as the spiritual plane. This is enlightenment or *samadhi* (an Eastern religious term). Our example is Jesus transfigured and witnessed by James, John, and Peter (Matt. 17:1–9). The second coming of Christ is our own recognition of the Christ within.

As tentmakers, like Aquilla and Priscilla, we must continue to weave our destiny in our physical body. It is to be blessed and cared for. It is through this physical body, the tent, that we gain the higher estate and can fly like the eagle and survey the material world from the highest level. The eagle symbolizes the spiritual principle in general. It is luminous in the sun just as our body has the potential of luminosity in God's Light.

The tentmakers served Paul well. As he brought the word of Truth to them they took it to others. The physical and the spiritual are in this great work. You and I, too, must take the word of Truth as we understand it to others in our teaching, preaching, writing, hospitality, generosity, and serving for the physical healing of others. Healing is one of our talents when we reach this level of Knowing. And so we preach repentance and forgiveness of sin in Jesus' name to all nations. "Go into all the world and preach the gospel to the whole creation," Jesus said in his last words before ascension (Mark 16:15).

Priscilla and Aquilla did their part in advancing the early Christian Church. Priscilla taught many as she continued to take care of the physical, and Aquilla, her counterpart, led many on to a higher spiritual level. We, too, are inspired by their devotion. Tentmaking, building the physical body or church, is first. Later, the building of the spiritual body is all-important.

39

Eunice and Lois

(Acts 16:1-3: Philippians 2:19-24; II Timothy 1:1-5;
3:14, 15)

THE INFLUENCE OF MOTHERS AND GRANDMOTHERS

Only once do we have these names mentioned in the New Testament. Only once is "grandmother" mentioned in the entire Bible. But the lesson to be learned from these two is for our enrichment and inspiration as parents.

Most of what we know of these two women comes from Paul's reference to Timothy, whose mother was Eunice and grandmother was Lois. Paul says, "I am reminded of your faith that dwelt first in your grandmother Lois and your mother Eunice and now, I am sure, dwells in you." In II Timothy 3:14, 15, Paul writes: "Continue in what you have learned and have firmly believed, knowing from whom you learned it and how from childhood you have been acquainted with the sacred writings which are able to instruct you for salvation through faith in Christ Jesus." Timothy was converted by Paul at age fifteen. His father was Greek and his mother a Jewess. Timothy became one of Paul's closest associates and was referred to as "my son" by Paul. He was the main preacher and teacher at the church in Ephesus. Eventually he met a martyr's death in Ephesus as he preached on the licentiousness of worshipers of Diana, the Greek goddess.

So often we have seen that the women spoken of in our Bible are closely related to their sons, husbands, fathers. We know that esoterically this is teaching the balance of the masculine and the feminine. Of course, women in those times had their identity through men. However, many of the women that Jesus touched stood alone—that is, from personal dependence upon the male— and the emphasis was on their association with Jesus. This indicates that the feminine element was more advanced spiritually. So with Eunice and Lois, we know about them through Timothy's accomplishments. They laid the foundation for those accomplishments.

How true for us as mothers and grandmothers today! Oh, yes, I know grandmothers do not seem to be much in evidence in the rearing of children today as in former times, but the effect that grandmother's rearing had on the mother's is still evident in the child's life.

Faith is again pointed out as the major characteristic of these two women and how it was passed on to Timothy. Also, acquaintance with the sacred writings from childhood is pointed out as a basis for Timothy's strength. He was given difficult duties while Paul was imprisoned in Rome, and the books of I and II Timothy are instructions to him.

We as mothers may try to put off our responsibility for teaching our children spiritual matters onto the Church, but the greatest teacher of children is the parent's example. If you want your children to grow up as musicians, you must appreciate music, expose the children to listening to good music, and if possible play an instrument or sing. If you want your son or daughter to appreciate the more cultural things in life—do not leave that instruction up to the school. If you want your child to grow up with faith in God, you will need to exemplify this faith. If you want your child to appreciate and revere God's word, so must you by your example.

I believe that each child should have some teaching about religion. It may be in a Sunday School, in the home, at grandmother's knee. But if the parents do not reflect a deep belief in the value of the religious ideas they teach, it will be an empty exercise for the child. The best training is the example of the parents in the home. That does not mean they have to be paragons of virtue, but the child learns best from example.

However, many children turn to religion as the sunflower to the sun no matter what their parents' belief or practice. Their soul is imprinted before birth, it would seem.

I wonder what Eunice and Lois thought when Timothy was converted by Paul at such an early age. Were they members of the church at Ephesus, or did Eunice follow her Jewish religious background? What part did his Greek (Gentile) father play in this? Did he object to Timothy's following Paul? How did his father feel when Timothy was circumcised by Paul? We do not know, but I have a feeling that if our fifteen-year-old son were converted by the leader of a suspected sect of religion and left home and followed the leader, we would be upset. What is our responsibility here?

Much "to-do" has been made over young people joining sects today and leaving their family and their early religious training. Families have hired men to kidnap these young persons and deprogram them to remove the influence of the religious sect from their minds. Most of these youths are over eighteen, though, and not fifteen. I wonder if we as parents have the right to control the religious leanings of our children to that extent. If Eunice and Lois had done this, the early Christian Church would have lost a faithful worker who helped get it started. How much authority should we exert over our children's spiritual growth after they have reached maturity? A good question to ponder.

Apparently Timothy had a leaning toward religious matters that was reinforced by the faith exemplified in these two women. This would lead us to suspect that he may have been born as a more advanced soul. We should be aware of this propensity in our own children and surround them with experiences that encourage it, remembering that each soul must find its own path.

As mothers, we have a tremendous effect on the future of our children. A trite statement! Fathers are equally important, but because fathers tend to focus on the outer, mothers have more effect on the inner life of the child. There are, of course, exceptions. The father in this case remains silent. He was Gentile, and so his leanings toward the Jewish religion may have been slight. It is the mother and grandmother that seem to have influenced this child to turn toward being a servant of God in the work of the early Church.

Rearing of children seems more difficult today than in former times, we are told. This is partly because the worship of authority figures, the Church, the government, the school, and even the parents has fallen. But the example of the parents is just as important as in days of yore. As a counselor of teenagers for twenty years, I have observed many families. The ones that seemed most successful in rearing children were those where faith and love were the cornerstones for the foundation of the family. Many children who are now rejecting the values of a spiritual life have had this example in their parents. The parents may panic and try to use force to make their teenagers conform to their orders and values, but the teenager runs away. Many times we find that the child has for years been given everything he wanted, from motives of what the parents considered love, and then when he carries the result, self-centeredness, into adolescence, the parents become frightened and punish severely. The young person then may run away or withdraw into himself and quit communicating. Love does not seem to be what the teenager is experiencing—at least in his own mind. The foundation laid earlier makes all the difference. Personal love comes in many guises, universal Love in only One. Remember, "Train up a child in the way he should go, and when he is *old* he will not depart from it" (Prov. 22: 6).

As with Eunice and Lois, our child-rearing should be based on faith, love, and instruction in spiritual matters. This should begin early. Prayer at meals, prayer before sleeping, discussion of God's Love and Will, openness to receiving guidance from intuition, and the practice of love will help all parents rear children who may be, as was Timothy, a "true child in faith" as Paul expressed it. "I am reminded of your sincere faith," he also wrote. What an accolade for any of God's children!

Esoteric: FREEDOM THROUGH GOD

Lois and Eunice symbolize faith, victory, freedom. Lois ("freed") and Eunice ("good victory"). The father of Timothy ("worship of God") was a Greek (representative of intellectual reasoning). We can see immediately that our own blending of intellectual reasoning and faith with love as a seasoner will bring us to worship of God as well as to the practice of His Presence in our own life.

The balance of male and female, as is so often observed, is a must for us in order to be at one with God. While we are achieving this, our worship is on the inner plane and not in the church, synagogue, or temple. Reason of the intellect is just as important as the feeling of love, for we need both in order to be effective in our life of devotion to things of the Spirit. The strong desire to be free (Lois) is the basis for our seeking this balance.

As a race, mankind has always sought freedom. Freedom from the pull of gravity, freedom from the physical body, freedom from restrictions and law, freedom from want, freedom from outer authority. Oh, yes, some of us do enjoy the authority of a religious figure or founder of a religion, but this need will finally be lost in the freedom of the authority of our inner Guide. For to me, the freedom of each individual to touch, to contact the best in his/her consciousness and be guided by It is true freedom. God has not restricted us. We have restricted our Self. To "Know thy Self" brings freedom. God is Freedom.

So Lois ("free") is that longing within that gives birth to faith in God, for who else can be depended upon? She gives birth to Eunice (faith and love blended), who in turn combines with intellectual reasoning (Greek) and brings forth worship of God (Timothy). And after this? Service, preaching, and teaching the Word through thought, word, and action. And being faithful is the basis of all: faith-full. That is the fire within that keeps us energized and protected and directed.

"Worship of God," "honored of God," "valued of God" will be our own name. This is Timothy. And Timothy will continue to express into infinity. And Eunice (love and victory) will be revered. The faith shown forth in the feminine will bring us victory.

40

The Woman of Proverbs and the Sun Woman of Revelation

(Proverbs 31:10–31; Revelation 12)

1. THE WOMAN OF PROVERBS 31
Caring for Physical Needs

In order to tie together the teachings of the *Women of the Bible,* I should like to draw your attention to the perfect woman as described in Proverbs 31 and the perfect woman of Revelation 12. There is a great deal of similarity and difference between the two, as one is a description of the women of the past with the potential of the future, and the other a description of the women of the future. When we read esoterically, we find many similarities, as we have found between women of the Old and New testaments and women of today.

I would encourage you to read both of these chapters before reading this one, for space does not permit the quotation of both.

In Proverbs 31 we have a very down-to-earth woman who is instructed in how to care for the needs of her husband, her children, the needy; she sells and makes money; her husband is well thought of; she dresses with dignity; she speaks wisdom; she always speaks kindly; she is not idle; she is blessed by her children and praised by her husband; she fears the Lord.

Verse 10 opens with "A good wife who can find?" and then gives the above description. I suspect that women through the ages have realized that to fulfill these verses is a well-nigh impossible task. Maybe the writer of Proverbs had his tongue in his cheek. I suspect further that many absolutist husbands have held this description over the heads of their hard-working wives. This is, of course, a description of the woman of those times. I doubt if many of those women lived up to it either. However, there are deeper meanings in each one of these verses, which I shall explore in the Esoteric section.

These verses do describe the lot of many women through the centuries. Even women today are trying to live up to it. The woman of Old Testament times had a heavy load. Perfection was expected of her; subservience to the male; production and raising of children to adulthood to go to war, work in the fields and tabernacles. In this way she drew praise and blessing from her family. All of these accomplishments were for the purpose of taking care of the physical needs of the family, to which may have been added the physical needs of the priests. And of course these women had no spare time, strength, or energy for anything else.

It is interesting that this chapter begins with, "The words of Lemuel, king of Massa, which his mother taught him." I wonder! Did she live up to this description of the perfect wife? And did he find such a wife?

In our discussion of women throughout this book we have said that the feminine aspect is being considered when woman is mentioned. I should like to suggest that it is the feminine aspect (wife) that is being discussed here and so has teaching value for each of us, man and woman. And I would agree that "She is far more precious than jewels."

I shall not repeat what I have said so often about the balancing that is taking place, except to point out that men are becoming more actively feminine now as demonstrated in length of hair; performance of female tasks, such as caring for children; wearing of jewelry; patronizing beauty salons; working under female supervision; learning more about loving relationships at various seminars; living alone; sharing in or assuming female responsibilities. Women are balancing with the masculine, as can be seen in participating in sports activities; wearing short hair; appropriating men's apparel; doing what has been considered men's work; becoming leaders and ministers in churches; acquiring more education; assuming the role of breadwinner in many families; leading in politics; living alone and rearing children. Both men and women are flocking to the New Thought churches, where there is greater balance between the sexes. These are signs of the times.

Men who continue to expect their wives to fulfill the role of woman as described in Proverbs 31 will find that they are "left at the gate," especially in America. Not all cultures and countries have given the freedom to women that America has. But they will as we lead the way.

As a female, I can choose out of this long list of perfect women those that I feel I can and should fulfill. But I shall not feel guilty if I do not meet all the tests. The one I do want to choose is "A woman who fears [is in awe of] the Lord is to be praised." That will be valuable for all generations of women.

Taking care of our physical needs and the needs of others is most important. Our bodies are to be cared for with reverence, for they are the "temple of the living God." But we have learned that in order to reach the height of the Sun Woman, spoken of in Revelation 12, we need balance in the physical, mental, emotional, and spiritual. Women can take care of the physical needs of their families now with much less effort than in the past. However, if they are the provider of funds as well as head of the household, they may not fit this description of excellence. Many married women who are now attempting the impossible, being wife, mother, nurse, housekeeper, career woman, nurturer of children, and an understanding wife to her husband may find this description appropriate. Our "modern woman" is finding it difficult to fill all of these roles, however. Perhaps she should take another look at her priorities and set them straight. Most women need a strong spiritual base and lots of help from children and husband to fulfill this multitude of roles. And there is not much time left for spiritual development, which is basic.

Our freedom from subservience to the male may demand a very high price. However, if our spiritual needs are given priority, the other needs will fall in line. Again we are back to *First things first,* and I happen to believe that God is first. (Are you surprised?)

So much for the literal interpretation. Now let us go to the real meaning, the secret teaching.

Esoteric: WISDOM: SHE CARRIES THE LIGHT

Proverbs is said by the esotericist to be for those who are on the Mystical Path. It has many secret meanings that will not become apparent until a certain degree of Wisdom has been reached. It gives help on the Way of Light and the quest for perfection. Its main focus is on the marriage of Wisdom (feminine principle) and Understanding (masculine principle). The last chapter of Proverbs—the thirty-first—describes the result, the fruit, which is riches and honor in the Kingdom of Heaven.

All of the verses have a deep meaning. I shall choose only a few. Let your creative imagination roam and interpret the others for yourself.

Wisdom is the object of the Great Work. It is lifting up the feminine pole and marrying it to Understanding. When we look at the message of this chapter as being to Lemuel ("consecrated to God") from his mother (the great feminine aspect of God), we can see its importance. It is the feminine aspect of God that is giving this advice, this description of one who is consecrated to God and needs some guideposts. The entire book of Proverbs has such teaching along this line. The verses we are dealing with here describe the divine feminine in the New Race as it has been lifted up to an upright position.

[*Please have your Bible at hand when you study the following section.*]

As a preliminary, remember that one of our basic teachings in this book has been the changing of our physical, emotional, and mental components from the material consciousness to the spiritual—to complete oneness with Spirit.

Verses 10–11 point out the value of a good wife to a husband. All the way through this, let us translate *wife* into *feminine principle,* which is Wisdom. Wisdom has been considered feminine through the ages. The Greeks called her Sophia; the Egyptians, Isis. The husband is Understanding. So in these verses there is pointed out how Wisdom—God, the Intuitive Knowledge of God —and Understanding (of the intellect and logic) are both necessary.

"A good wife [Wisdom] who can find? She is far more precious than jewels [logic]" (v. 10). "The heart of her husband [Understanding] trusts in her, and he will have no lack of gain" (v. 11). The King James Version says "more precious than rubies." The alchemist relates the ruby to the head, where the reasoning, logical mind has been placed. And Understanding will gain when Wisdom is active.

Verses 12-13: Wisdom (the feminine, the Kundalini power) provides for the ethereal body and brings energy (food) to it.

Verse 18: "Her lamp does not go out at night." The lamp is held high by those who go through the dark when helping, serving others. Wisdom carries the Light, the Truth, into the darkest recesses of the human condition. We keep our lamp lighted in our own life also, as we experience God through meditation and love the Lord.

Verse 20 shows how we, as balanced souls, serve those who are in need. Our service at this point, however, is to their spiritual needs, not the material. When the spiritual needs are fulfilled, the material will follow.

Verse 21: "She is not afraid of snow for her household, for all her household is clad in scarlet." Snow or white is descriptive of the head. Scarlet is symbolic of heart. So Wisdom knows that thoughts are not to be feared, as love (the heart) is there to protect it.

Verse 22: We ourselves made our spiritual body by balancing spirit and thought. It is the natural covering, linen (light), that causes it to develop. And it is royal (purple). We shall see that the Sun Woman wears a crown, symbol of royalty.

Verse 23: "Her husband is known at the gates, when he sits among the elders of the land." When Wisdom is active, Understanding is honored, for our thoughts will lead others to the Way. The gates also refer to the inner plane, where we experience the guidance of those exalted Wise Ones who are actively working on the spiritual and physical planes for our Understanding. Jesus Christ is such an exalted being. The "elders" are these Wise Ones.

Verse 25: Strength and dignity surround Wisdom, and *now* is the only time there is. Wisdom laughs at the future, for there is only *now*. We have arrived!

Verse 28: "Her children rise up and call her blessed; her husband also, and he praises her." Children are born of thought and love.

Understanding and Love (Wisdom) bring forth thoughts that bless us. And Understanding praises Wisdom.

Verse 29: "Many women have done excellently, but you surpass them all." Wisdom surpasses all other feminine characteristics, for it is God, and God contains all there is, or all is contained in God.

Verse 30: Wisdom is in awe of the Lord. Wisdom is the Lord. The feminine principle within each of us loves the Lord, for God is Love, Wisdom, Beauty, etc.

Verse 31: "Fruit of hands" is the result of years and lifetimes of evolving upward to oneness with God: the results of reaching the Kingdom of Heaven, of reentering the Garden that Adam and Eve had to leave because of the belief in the duality of Good and Evil. God is All! In our perfection we *know* this!

At the mystical level of consciousness we are being monitored by those at the gates of the Kingdom of Heaven. The Kingdom of Heaven, let us realize, is "at hand" as Jesus taught. It can be yours here and now. Our inner plane of awareness of Christ is also the gate. The work of Wisdom, the feminine, is praised on the inner plane.

The literal and esoteric meaning of Proverbs 31 is important to us as women, for it describes the outer and the inner paths to our goal. It makes a balance of the human and the Divine. Eventually the Divine will outbalance, will transform, the human, and our path will become easier and less beset by blocks of material desires.

Consecration to God and the great feminine principle of God has defined our path and our reward. The Sun Woman of Revelation is the capstone of our seeking. Let us go to her now.

2. The Sun Woman of Revelation 12
Divinity Achieved: Generation to Regeneration

It is said by some that this chapter contains all that is implied in the Bible, especially the New Testament. It portrays mankind at its highest as well as the temptation of the negative in the life of mankind. It is a picture of the human and Divine as one. It is the foundation of what we have taught in this book, I believe.

We have been speaking of the ascension of the feminine principle in humankind's consciousness. We have pointed out many times the potential attackers of this ascension. We have showed the necessity for the physical body to become pure Light. We have discussed the birth of the awareness of our Divinity. And we have spoken of the odds against all of this. Chapter 12 of Revelation contains these teachings also.

In Genesis we studied Eve, who was betrayed by her need for children, for companionship. In the Sun Woman we see the woman of the future afire with the Light of God (the sun) and with the moon (generation) under her control (her feet). (Her being clothed with sun and standing on the moon is a mythological symbol for her androgynous state.) She, the feminine, is one with the masculine. She is liberated and is with God. She has ascended to her divine awareness of Oneness. She is no longer hungry for companionship—note that she did not try to get her baby back—but was protected by the nurturing power of the earth (feminine) and eventually was given great wings of the eagle (Divinity), and so she escaped the negative forces.

Now to understand what was pursuing her, called the Devil and Satan, we must do some self-analysis. For that which prevents each of us from having the full Wisdom (divine feminine) of God active in our lives is individual. To say, "Oh, that was the power of the Devil that made me do it" is to be pursued, and overcome, by this belief. The Sun Woman would not have escaped if she had given in to that belief. She is surrounded by, impregnated with, the completely spiritual, and so she is all Good. That is all there is as power—Good. For Good is God and is all there is. "There is only one Presence and one Power in my Life and in the Universe, God the Good Omnipotent." This is a basic Truth of the New Age Thought. If you believe this—and there is manifold evidence for it —then you cannot blame the Devil.

That which lies within our consciousness is what determines our future. If we have brought God or Good into our daily prayer and meditation; if we have pledged our life to God consciousness; if we have cleansed our life, our thoughts, our words, our actions of all negativities, then we will be protected by the all-pervasive Spirit of God. His grace is over all.

The Sun Woman, the cosmic feminine principle, gives birth to a male child, the Christ within our consciousness (v. 5). This Christ, born of high consciousness of the feminine pole, is taken to God, becomes one with God. This male child "is to rule the nations with a rod of iron." This is the Christ Spirit within each of us, and it is now ruling the nations although they are unaware of its power. This Spirit dwelling within each of us is the ruler of the earthly kingdom and will become one with God when we are clothed with the Sun and the Moon under our feet.

It will be up to the feminine principle in man and woman to put generation (the moon) under their feet and to accept "the two wings (intellect and intuition) of the great eagle that they may escape the desires of the earth plane, called desires of the flesh by Paul (v. 14). The wilderness she fled to is the primitive condition, "in the Beginning," before man was created. It will be the feminine principle that leads. It will be womankind. And regeneration will follow.

The Sun Woman is womankind. The Sun Woman (intuition, creativity, love) gives birth to our Christ awareness. It is the Sun Woman, "clothed with the Sun," who is pure Love. It is Universal Love, God the Mother, that will save all of humankind, and as woman ceases to depend on the intellect (on man) to save her, but is equal with it, she will lead humankind to that enlightenment which is the goal taught by all the major religions of the world. Man, expressing his feminine principle, will be by her side.

We cannot escape our responsibility. It is the coming together in our consciousness of the male principle of God (as taught for generations) and the female principle of God that will save us. The wings of the eagle saved this Great Mother. We are all a part of her; we only need to realize it.

But the duality of earth, Good and evil, must be overcome. And the power of evil resides in the mind of humans. Through the grace of God we can overcome that. We are also saved by the goodness in our own subconscious mind (the water of the earth) (v. 16). Within it resides the Spirit, the Christ. Our whole journey is about making this conscious (= consciousness).

The Sun Woman wears a crown of twelve stars (v. 1). Twelve is the number of spiritual completion. The halo around her head indicates her high spiritual state and is often depicted, in art forms, surrounding the heads of saints. Her divine energy has lifted her to completion. She wears a "Crown of Glory." She is Love. For more about the Sun Woman, see Chapter 12 of my *Revelation: For a New Age.*

What more can I say in ending this revelation of the wonderful teachings of the women of the Bible? Such a vast topic, such rich analogy, such beautiful souls as these women exemplified! We women of earth are writing the next Bible in our very lives. We, no less than the women of the Bible, have our part to play in the evolution of humankind. We too can put the moon (generation) under our feet and express our divine energy in regeneration. We too can be the Sun Woman fully enlightened, clothed with the sun (Light), and we too can be that Eve who worked her way out of delusion through all the steps portrayed by the women of the Bible, and become the Sun Woman. That is our destiny, yours and mine. Whatever you want, you can have. It is up to you. The woman of Proverbs 31 and the Sun Woman have come together, and we can choose to follow or not.

Be with God and serve, for that is all the joy there is. Love is the answer. We, as the cosmic divine principle, "keep the commandments of God and bear testimony of Jesus." And "a woman who is in awe of the Lord is to be praised."

I thank Mother/Father God for these inspirations. This Presence "waves its banner" over me. Amen.

Glossary

ANDROGYNY—A state of perfect balance between the masculine and feminine elements in our psyche. An innate sense of cosmic unity; Oneness; Wholeness.

ANIMA—The feminine element within a man's psyche. (See Jung's psychology.)

ANIMUS—The inner contrasexual, masculine, element within a woman's psyche. (See Jung's psychology.)

ARCHETYPE—Original idea, model, or type. Archaic psychic components in the individual psyche on an unconscious level, from the collective unconscious. (See Jung's psychology.)

BAAL—The god of nature worship in Canaan. A god of fertility.

CHAKRAS—Centers or whirls of energy at certain locations in the ethereal (energy or auric) body or spirit body. They are connected to the physical body at the location of the endocrine glands.

CHRIST—The spark of Divinity within each consciousness. The inner Voice; the Counselor, Mighty God, Everlasting Father, Prince of Peace (Isaiah 9:6). Jesus called It the Father.

CONSCIOUSNESS—An awareness, a knowing of the Divine, of the Christ, of God. The sum total of all ideas accumulated and affecting the person.

EGO—The controlling element in personality based on the limited belief in our own power. The small self that believes it is responsible for all good in the individual life.

ESOTERIC—Secret teaching as given to the initiates of a philosophy or religion. Private teaching for disciples or initiates.

FEMININE PRINCIPLE—Christ consciousness; feelings; love; intuition; imagination; wisdom; creativity. Gives birth to the awareness of the Spirit.

GENERATE—To procreate; to beget; to reproduce.

INTUITION—Immediate knowing of spiritual Truth, above and beyond the intellect. Wisdom; God in man revealing the realization of Spirit.

KARMA—The result of the law of cause and effect.

KINGDOM OF HEAVEN—Christ consciousness. Oneness with God. A state of perfect harmony and peace. (See Jesus' many definitions.)

KUNDALINI—An Eastern word for divine energy. The serpent fire of regeneration located at the base of the spine. (The spine is the path up which it travels to regenerate the physical body, to change the physical to Light or spiritual essence.)

LAW OF CAUSE AND EFFECT—Thoughts, words, and deeds that have ethical consequences for the future. These consequences are self-generated and are overcome by forgiveness and centeredness in God's Will. "As you sow so shall you reap"; "Do unto others as you would have others do unto you."

MASCULINE PRINCIPLE—Understanding; reason; logic; aggression; strength. The assertive principle of Being.

MEDITATION—A stopping of the thoughts by focusing on one thought, one thing, on the breath, on a mantra. A touching of the inner Divinity in the Silence.

METAPHYSICAL—That knowledge which is beyond, which transcends, the physical. A study of the science of Being. Beyond the laws of physics.

MYSTIC—One who centers his/her life on knowledge and activity of the Spirit. The mystic follows the invisible Presence that lies within and that forms the outer experiences.

Mysticism—Soul consciousness; the practice of the Presence of God in thought, word, and deed.

New Age—A new spiritual understanding based on inner guidance from the Spirit that resides in the consciousness of each. It is also called the Aquarian Age. It has ushered in new discoveries in science, business, communications, outer space, etc.

Occult—Using the intellect to control events and to go beyond three-dimensional understanding. Used in this work to denote the combination of knowledge and certain related practices.

Race Consciousness—The totality of beliefs, thoughts, memories, feelings, and experiences of the human race; more specifically, the beliefs and actions of that society in which we live that affect our own choices.

Regenerate—To change the body from the physical to the spiritual. (This spiritual body is called the "body celestial" by Paul; it is manifested by spiritual thought, spiritual emotion, and spiritual action.) The act of uniting body, mind, and spirit into Oneness.

Reincarnation—The soul rebirthing in a physical body in order to continue expanding the conscious awareness of the totality of the Spirit.

SELF—Christ; the divine Idea; the true Self of every person; the Spirit within.

Self—The human self, fearful and often egotistical, resulting from belief in self-will.

Bibliography

Books

Braden, Charles. *Spirits in Rebellion: The Rise and Development of New Thought*. Dallas: Southern Methodist University Press, 1963.

Buscaglia, Leo. *Loving Each Other*. Thorofare, N.J.: Slack Inc., 1984. (Distributed by Holt, Rinehart, and Winston, New York.)

Deen, Edith. *All of the Women of the Bible*. New York: Harper and Bros., 1955.

Davies, A. Power. *Dead Sea Scrolls*. New York: New American Library, 1956.

Elder, Dorothy. *Revelation: For a New Age* (The Book of Revelation). Marina del Rey, Calif.: DeVorss & Company, 1981.

Fillmore, Charles. *Atom-Smashing Power of Mind*. Unity Village, Mo.: Unity School of Christianity, 1949.

Fillmore, Charles. *Metaphysical Bible Dictionary*. Unity Village, Mo.: Unity School of Christianity, 1931.

Fillmore, Charles. *Twelve Powers of Man*. Unity Village, Mo.: Unity School of Christianity, 1934.

Hall, Manly. *Healing, the Divine Art*. Los Angeles: Philosophical Research Society, 1972.

Hall, Manly. *The Mystical Christ*. Los Angeles. Philosophical Research Society, 1951.

Heline, Corinne. *New Age Bible Interpretation*. 7 vols. Los Angeles: New Age Press, 1935-1954. (Distributed by New Age Bible and Philosophy Center, Santa Monica, Calif.)

Jung, Carl. *Psychology and Religion, West and East*. Princeton: Princeton University Press, 1969. Bollingen Series XX.

Krishna, Gopi. *Kundalini: The Evolutionary Energy.* Boston: Shambhala, 1970.

Pagels, Elaine. *The Gnostic Gospels.* New York: Vintage Books, 1981.

Read, Anne. *Edgar Cayce on Jesus and His Church.* New York: Coronet Communications, 1970.

Robinson, James (ed.). *The Nag Hammadi Library.* New York: Harper & Row, 1981.

Singer, June. *Boundaries of the Soul.* New York: Anchor Books, 1973.

Troward, Thomas. *The Law and the Word.* New York: Dodd, Mead & Co., 1917.

Underhill, Evelyn. *Mysticism.* Cleveland: World Publishing Co., 1967.

. . . .

Bibles

Good News Bible

King James Version

Living New Testament

New Jerusalem Bible

Revised Standard Version